Simply
C.S. Lewis

Simply
C.S. Lewis

A BEGINNER'S GUIDE
TO THE
LIFE AND WORKS OF C.S. LEWIS

Thomas C. Peters

CROSSWAY BOOKS • WHEATON, ILLINOIS
A DIVISION OF GOOD NEWS PUBLISHERS

Simply C. S. Lewis.

Copyright © 1997 by Thomas C. Peters

Published by Crossway Books
     a division of Good News Publishers
     1300 Crescent Street
     Wheaton, Illinois 60187.

Editing: Leonard G. Goss and Ted Griffin

Cover design: Christopher Tobias

Cover photo: Arthur Strong

Printed in the United States of America

Library of Congress Cataloging-in-Publication Data
Peters, Thomas C., 1948-
   Simply C. S. Lewis: a beginner's guide to the life and works of
C.S. Lewis / Thomas C. Peters.
      p.   cm.
   Includes bibliographical references (p.   ) and index.
   ISBN 0-89107-948-3
    1. Lewis, C. S. (Clive Staples), 1898-1963. 2. Christian
literature, English—History and criticism. 3. Fantastic fiction,
English—History and criticism. 4. Authors, English—20th century—
Biography. 5. Church of England—England—Biography. 6. Christian
biography—England. I. Title.
PR6023.E926Z835   1997
823'.912—dc21   97-8203

07	06	05	04	03	02	01	00	99	98
15	14	13	12	11	10	9	8	7	6	5	4	3	2

To my greatest joy,
Barbara Lynn Peters

CONTENTS

PREFACE

12-11-06

It is entirely fitting that we should be preparing to celebrate the centennial year of C.S. Lewis's birth at the same time as we look forward to the beginning of the third millennium of the Christian era. For the century that is now coming to its conclusion has been a pivotal one, to say the least, in accentuating the challenges that the dominant social, economic, and intellectual forces have thrust upon the Christian church in the world.

If the nineteenth century witnessed the rise of urban-industrial phenomena that transformed the very foundations of modern human existence, the twentieth century witnessed the consistent consequences of the new materialist and relativist ideologies that developed in their wake. Thus, while the "developed" countries have enjoyed the labor-saving and capital-generating fruit of scientific discovery and technological invention, they have also suffered a plethora of effects including personal alienation, widespread human exploitation, fear of nuclear holocaust, environmental pollution, rising crime rates, runaway public debts, and even attempts at racial extermination.

The optimistic view in the nineteenth century was that there was no problem science could not solve. Yes, it was conceded, the Industrial Revolution has produced various ill effects such as high unemployment and the displacement of the poor; but the dominant ideology was that science would come to solve these problems as well. The popular notion was that modern men and women were qualitatively different from their ancestors and that humanity then stood on the threshold of taking its destiny into its own hands.

Such progressive optimism was tested sorely by the follies of the First World War and then stretched to near breaking point by the Nazi horrors in the Second World War. By mid-century the Cold War and its terrifying threat of worldwide nuclear annihilation had convinced all but a stubborn few that science, technology, and progressive thinking were not sufficient to ensure human happiness or even survival.

At the same time that the brave new ideologies of technology and progress were proliferating among the intelligentsia of the industrialized nations, the traditional doctrines of the Christian church were increasingly abandoned as outmoded, outgrown, even refuted in view of modern developments. Even churches acquiesced as modernist clergy and liberal theologians accepted the thesis that Christian beliefs were in need of alignment with the latest pronouncements from the human sciences.

Perhaps more importantly, the great masses of people in the urban-industrial societies turned away from traditional beliefs and espoused instead the materialist view, the free-floating relativism, and the vague, progressive, evolutionary optimism that was disseminated in the popular media and on most university campuses. Indeed, by the end of the twentieth century the United States has become a nation in which relatively few highly educated people are willing to admit publicly that they believe anything at all—and particularly that they believe in the non-material, the non-empirical, the spiritual, and especially the traditional doctrines of a 2,000-year-old church.

It has apparently occurred to very few of our famous public thinkers and social analysts that there may be a causal connection between the dominant values of our urban-industrial societies and the extant personal and social problems we are experiencing at an increasing rate. Yes, we Americans hear a certain amount of rhetoric along these lines every four years during elections, and there are a number of stalwarts among the clergy who continue to remind us of the connection. But for the most part the public debate rejects the idea that what we believe has a great impact upon the quality of our collective lives.

But now as we approach a new decade, a new century, and a new millennium, we hear a growing chorus of voices no longer singing the praises of modern society, but asking painful questions: "Why didn't things turn out the way we planned? Why are we suffering these problems and pains? Where did we go wrong? Where should we go from here?"

We are beginning to see a rebirth of interest in some of our cultural underpinnings and our traditional beliefs and values. People are rediscovering that there are sensible answers, viable solutions, and reasons for hope in the writings of such thinkers as John Newman, Thomas Merton, G.K. Chesterton, Dorothy Sayers, and C.S. Lewis. People are finding that we were warned and that many of the warnings have turned out to be painfully accurate. People are coming to see that the way out of our mess depends very directly upon what we believe about God and about ourselves.

It is again fitting that at the dawn of the new millennium we should pause to salute the one hundredth year of C.S. Lewis's birth, because the works of C.S. Lewis stand like homing beacons in a world adrift and foundering. Like G.K. Chesterton before him, Lewis saw clearly the shoals hidden under the waves of popular thought, and he wrote indefatigably in his attempts to reverse the drift of modern men and women toward their own destruction.

In this introductory collection of reviews we shall look at Lewis's writings in the context of our modern dilemmas, and we shall find that C.S. Lewis remains as fully relevant and now even more urgent than when he lived and wrote in the first half of the twentieth century. The spiritual and moral problems have not gone away; they have grown and multiplied. Lewis's insights have not been outgrown or refuted; they have been largely ignored. If we are wise, we have come to the point where we realize that we can afford to ignore them no longer.

This book is intended to be used in two ways. One method would be simply to read it through from cover to cover as an introductory overview of the life and works of C.S. Lewis. The other method would be to use it as an introduction when preparing to read a particular book by C.S. Lewis. In the latter case the appropriate review will be helpful in alerting the reader to the issues at hand. Consistent with this latter use, I have avoided wherever possible saying too much about the plots in the fictional writings so as not to spoil the surprise for the reader of the original work.

Though C.S. Lewis is a highly popular author and many of his books have been international bestsellers, a surprising number of people have never really read much of Lewis. Again and again I have heard comments such as, "I tried to read *Till We Have Faces*, but I couldn't follow what was going on. I guess I don't understand Lewis." It seems that many have read his Narnia stories, fewer his science fiction, still fewer his apologetics, and even fewer his scholarly books.

The problem is, I think, remediable. C.S. Lewis was a man of great intellect and many interests. His books reveal an astonishing array of purposes, styles, and intended audiences. The Lewis who wrote *The Horse and His Boy* is the same Lewis who wrote *English Literature in the Sixteenth Century—Excluding Drama*, and he does, in fact, adjust his language to his various readers remarkably well. This ability to make himself understood I consider a great part of his special genius.

But we should not be surprised at the number of disastrous beginnings into the world of C.S. Lewis. With an author of Lewis's incredible diversity, a merely random beginning is not a good idea. Different readers, of course, have differing interests, and we all find ourselves at various points in our respective intellectual and spiritual journeys. The reader needs to enter the world of C.S. Lewis through the most appropriate door. That is why I have written this book: to give the C.S. Lewis beginner a broad view of the field, as well as some basic helps in understanding certain of Lewis's books.

I have not here included all of C.S. Lewis's works. In choosing what I consider to be the most representative samples for the various categories, I have admittedly neglected the poetry altogether, and I have omitted many fine volumes of short essays and addresses. The reader is certainly encouraged to explore these other volumes as well. The purpose here is introduction, and it is my intention and hope that the reader of this book will go on to enjoy many hours of delight and discovery among the pages of C.S. Lewis's original works.

T.C.P.

I

A SNEAK PREVIEW

The year A.D. 1998 marks the centennial year after the birth of C.S. Lewis, a remarkable man by any standard. Lewis was a gem of numerous aspects—a first-rate scholar, a romantic poet, a popular essayist, a formidable debater, an imaginative novelist, a writer of children's stories, a university professor, a science fiction enthusiast, a personal counselor, and a Christian apologist. He was a man whose stories could delight the smallest of children, and yet whose polemics could confound the greatest of intellectuals. In his letters he might nurture the needy spirit, or he might castigate a student for faulty logic. There are so many sides to C.S. Lewis that some people do not know what to make of him.

In this book we will explore the man C.S. Lewis—his context, his life, and many of his writings. However, in this opening chapter our task is an easier one: to sit back and enjoy a narrative sneak preview of the many sides of C.S. Lewis. Here in a series of short entries we shall sample the breadth and depth of Lewis's mind and begin our appreciation of the marvelous variety of his interests and work.

C.S. Lewis's Sense of Play

A very important side of C.S. Lewis—and one that contributes greatly to our enjoyment of his fiction and nonfiction alike—is his wonderful sense of play. We find everywhere not only his wordplay and his toying with ideas, but also woven through his work is his profound sense of play as an essential element in the divine purpose of life. For Lewis, play is not a frivolous interlude; it is an important part of the very essence of the Creator's being and activity. In Lewis's reckoning, to seek enjoyment and play is our incumbent duty as creatures made in the image of the joyful Creator. Conversely, a deliberate choice to make oneself unhappy amounts to ingratitude and sin.

In the Chronicles of Narnia the great lion Aslan becomes Lewis's vehicle for showing the instinctive mirth of God. In Aslan's first appearance after his sacrifice on the Stone Table, the lion frolics happily with Lucy and Susan before getting down to the business of the battle ahead. Similarly, in *Prince Caspian* we find that even as our mortal friends are engaged in a losing battle to save their own lives and the kingdom, the great lion is busy organizing a grand parade and party:

> Everyone was awake, everyone was laughing, flutes were playing, cymbals clashing. Animals, not Talking Animals, were crowding in upon them from every direction.
>
> "What is it, Aslan?" said Lucy, her eyes dancing and her feet wanting to dance.
>
> "Come, children," said he. "Ride on my back again to-day."
>
> "Oh lovely!" cried Lucy, and both girls climbed on to the warm golden back as they had done no-one knew how many years before. Then the whole party moved off—Aslan leading, Bacchus and his Maenads leaping, rushing, and turning somersaults, the beasts frisking round them, and Silenus and his donkey bringing up the rear.[1]

There are many celebrations in C.S. Lewis's stories, for the author knew that celebration is an important part of the meaning of life.

C.S. Lewis the Teacher

As a university professor, C.S. Lewis taught many courses in literature and philosophy. What distinguished Lewis from far too many of his colleagues in this regard was his genuine concern that his students learn how to do scholarship as he did. In other words, it was not enough simply to lay out the facts in lectures and then test the students to see if they understood. Lewis took great pains—in his lectures and in his scholarly writing—to model the kind of approach that would gain the desired knowledge. For example, here is a bit of extemporaneous instruction on how not to read a sonnet:

> The first thing to grasp about a sonnet sequence is that it is not a way of telling a story. It is a form which exists for the sake of prolonged lyrical meditation, chiefly on love but relieved from time to time by excursions into public affairs, literary criticism, compliment, or what you will. External events—a quarrel, a parting, an illness, a stolen kiss—are every now and then mentioned to provide themes for the meditation. Thus you get an island . . . of narrative in a lyrical sea. It is not there to interest you in the history of a love affair, after the manner of a novelist. To concentrate on these islands, and to regard the intervening pieces as mere links between them, is as if you valued Mozartian opera chiefly for the plot. You are already turning away from the work of art which has been offered you.[2]

From such instruction the student gains a skill—a method for reading sonnets as they were meant to be read.

C.S. Lewis's Sense of Humility

A characteristic aspect of Lewis that further endears so many readers to his work is his humble, even rather critical opinions of his own writings. Though Lewis himself was surely an intellectual and scholar of the first order, his avoidance of the standard erudite pretension won him the admiration of readers from broadly differing backgrounds. We find sprinkled through much of his nonfiction work a sincere humility that we cannot help but appreciate.

A good example is found in the final paragraph of the preface in his autobiography *Surprised by Joy*:

> The story is, I fear, suffocatingly subjective; the kind of thing I have never written before and shall probably never write again. I have tried so to write the first chapter that those who can't bear such a story will see at once what they are in for and close the book with the least waste of time.[3]

Surely, these are not the words of a man full of his own importance.

C.S. Lewis's Pet Peeves

One of the many pleasures in knowing C.S. Lewis comes from witnessing his occasional diatribes concerning his pet peeves. These rather heated asides appear here and there throughout his writings, and they serve to remind us that Lewis was, after all, an irritable human like the rest of us, and at times rather passionate in his peevishness.

As an example, here is a note that appears in the middle of one of Lewis's lengthy discussions of the English language and literature. Regarding the grammatical rule that a sentence should not end in a preposition, Lewis writes:

> No one can pretend that this curious taboo was inherent in the genius of the language and would have developed even without the action of Dryden and his fellow Gallicists. On the contrary, it is so alien from the language that it has never penetrated into the conversation of even the worst prigs, and serves no purpose but to increase those little bunches of unemphatic monosyllables that English was already prone to. On the other hand, it has so established itself in our formal

style that thousands obey it unconsciously. It is, very precisely, a thing that prompts us to write in a certain way; even I, who detest it for a frenchified schoolroom superstition, often feel it plucking at my elbow.[4]

One can only smile and reflect that there is certainly no question as to where Lewis stands on the issue of sentences ending in prepositions.

C.S. Lewis on Animals

Biographers tell us that C.S. Lewis was always particularly fond of animals. Even if we were not told this fact, we would have known it from his writings, both nonfiction and fiction. Especially in the Narnia stories where his animal characters interact and speak with humans, one can feel the delight that Lewis felt in the various animals and their unique characteristics.

Once having met them, who can forget the beavers in *The Lion, the Witch and the Wardrobe*, or the horses in *The Horse and His Boy*, or the ape and the donkey in *The Last Battle*? It is in the latter that we find a good example of Lewis's artistry in putting animal characteristics to good use in his story. The situation here is that a poor, unintelligent, old donkey named Puzzle has unfortunately befriended a clever ape named Shift. Using his superior mental capacities, the ape is forever exploiting the donkey by inducing him to do objectionable tasks. Here is an example where Shift is trying to make Puzzle plunge into the icy water to retrieve a floating object:

> "Hop into the Pool?" said Puzzle, twitching his long ears.
> "Well how are we to get it if you don't?" said the Ape.
> "But—but," said Puzzle, "wouldn't it be better if you went in? Because, you see it's you who want to know what it is, and I don't much. And you've got hands, you see. You're as good as a Man or a Dwarf when it comes to catching hold of things. I've only got hoofs."

"Really, Puzzle," said Shift. "I didn't think you'd ever say anything like that. I didn't think it of you, really."

"Why, what have I said wrong?" said the Ass, speaking in a rather humbled voice, for he saw that Shift was very deeply offended. "All I meant was—"

"Wanting me to go into the water," said the Ape. "As if you didn't know perfectly well what weak chests Apes always have and how easily they catch cold! Very well. I will go in. I'm feeling cold enough already in this cruel wind. But I'll go in. I shall probably die. Then you'll be sorry."[5]

Of course, the simple Puzzle is eventually shamed into doing the onerous task—the first among many that Shift contrives for him throughout the story. As the story unfolds, we can see how aptly Lewis has chosen these animals for their parts.

That C.S. Lewis Sarcasm

One can never be too sure when C.S. Lewis might launch into one of his many episodes of sarcastic wit, for he is liable to engage any passing topic in any context without the slightest warning. For example, we are engaged in reading the letters of Screwtape, a senior devil, to his nephew and apprentice Wormwood when suddenly Lewis brings us into the center of an academic controversy concerning literary criticism. Screwtape writes:

Only the learned read old books, and we have now so dealt with the learned that they are of all men the least likely to acquire wisdom by doing so. We have done this by inculcating the Historical Point of View. The Historical Point of View, put briefly, means that when a learned man is presented with any statement in an ancient author, the one question he never asks is whether it is true. He asks who influenced the ancient writer, and how far the statement is consistent with what he said in other books, and what phase in the writer's development, or in the general history of thought, it illustrates, and how it affected later writers, and how often it has been misunderstood (specially by the learned man's own colleagues), and what the general course of criticism has been on it for the last ten years, and what is the "present state of the question." To regard the ancient writer as a possible source of knowledge—to anticipate that what he said could possibly modify your thoughts or your behaviour—this would be rejected as unutterably simple-minded. And since we cannot deceive the whole human race all the time, it is most important thus to cut every generation off from all others. . . .[6]

What makes C.S. Lewis's sarcasm about intellectuals so effective is the fact that he was one, and he most certainly knew what he was talking about. In this example Lewis points to a very widespread and short-sighted intellectual habit of pretending that today's intelligence is necessarily more insightful and free of error than ancient intelligence.

Lewis's Tongue-in-Cheek

While Lewis was perfectly capable of the most serious discussions of the gravest of matters—he wrote an entire book about pain—he was at ease with occasional frivolity. For example, on the uneasy relations between the soul and the body, Lewis writes:

> 'You are always dragging me down,' said I to my Body.
>
> 'Dragging you down!' replied my Body.
>
> 'Well I like that! Who taught me to like tobacco and alcohol? You, of course, with your idiotic adolescent idea of being "grown-up." My palate loathed both at first: but you would have your way. Who put an end to all those angry and revengeful thoughts last night? Me, of course, by insisting on going to sleep. Who does his best to keep you from talking too much and eating too much by giving you dry throats and headaches and indigestion? Eh?'
>
> 'And what about sex?' said I.
>
> 'Yes, what about it?' retorted the Body. 'If you and your

wretched imagination would leave me alone I'd give you no trouble. That's Soul all over; you give me orders and then blame me for carrying them out.'[7]

One of Lewis's many talents was the use of humor to make an important point.

C.S. LEWIS AND FREE WILL

C.S. Lewis never tired of refuting the popular determinisms that sought to take human will and responsibility out of human hands. Whether the opponent was a classical evolutionist, a Shavian, a Marxist, a capitalist, or an advocate of psychoanalysis, Lewis's argument was always the same: people do make choices for which they are responsible and by which history is indeed formed. Lewis put it this way:

> We know that we can act and that our actions produce results. Everyone who believes in God must therefore admit ... that God has not chosen to write the whole of history with His own hand. Most of the events that go on in the universe are indeed out of our control, but not all. It is like a play in which the scene and the general outline of the story is fixed by the author, but certain minor details are left for the actors to improvise.[8]

Even theistic determinism is rejected by Lewis. While he sees God as the author of history, he also sees individual humans as free to influence specific events in one way or another.

C.S. LEWIS ON HUMAN FOIBLES

In most of his writing, both fiction and nonfiction, Lewis is apt to give examples and analogies that have a way of hitting the mark precisely. On reading such an illustration, we find ourselves more times than not saying, "Yes, I know someone exactly like that!" For example, in *The Four Loves* Lewis describes an imaginary—but all too familiar—Mrs. Fidget:

> I am thinking of Mrs. Fidget, who died a few months ago. It is really astonishing how her family have brightened up. . . . Mrs. Fidget very often said that she lived for her family. And it was not untrue. Everyone in the neighborhood knew it. "She lives for her family," they said; "what a wife and mother!" She did all the washing; true, she did it badly, and they could have afforded to send it out to a laundry, and they frequently begged her not to do it. But she did. There was always a hot lunch for anyone who was at home and always a hot meal at night (even in midsummer). They implored her not to provide this. They protested almost with tears in their eyes (and with truth) that they liked cold meals. It made no difference. She was living for her family. . . . For Mrs. Fidget, as she so often said, would "work her fingers to the bone" for her family. They couldn't stop her. Nor could they—being decent people—quite sit still and watch her do it. They had to help. Indeed they were always having to help. That is, they did things for her to help her to do things for them which they didn't want done. . . .[9]

One realizes that C.S. Lewis possesses extraordinary insight into the subterfuges of his fellow mortals.

LEWIS'S LINGUISTICS

In response to criticisms that Christians tend to use anthropomorphic metaphors concerning God—such as that of the Son "coming down from heaven" and now "sitting at the right hand of the Father"—Lewis offers the following linguistic analysis:

> . . . any language we attempt to substitute for it would involve imagery that is open to all the same objections. To say that

God "enters" the natural order involves just as much spatial imagery as to say that He "comes down"; one has simply substituted horizontal (or undefined) for vertical movement. . . . All language, except about objects of sense, is metaphorical through and through. To call God a "force" (that is, something like a wind or a dynamo) is as metaphorical as to call Him a Father or a King. On such matters we can make our language more polysyllabic and duller: we cannot make it more literal.[10]

Those who are embarrassed by the metaphor of God the Father in heaven are hard pressed to provide a description of God that is not metaphorical. If God is not merely an object of our senses, then we have no way of describing God literally.

C.S. Lewis's Use of Imagery

The use of imagery in literature is perhaps the most effective way to appeal to the feelings of the reader. To awaken the reader's senses of seeing, hearing, smelling, tasting, and touching in one's descriptions is to invite the reader to experience something rather than simply to read about it. Lewis's mastery of the art of imagery is well illustrated in this paragraph from his science fiction story *Perelandra*:

At long last he reached the wooded part. There was an undergrowth of feathery vegetation, about the height of gooseberry bushes, coloured like sea anemones. Above this were taller growths—strange trees with tube-like trunks of grey and purple spreading rich canopies above his head, in which orange, silver, and blue were the predominant colours. Here, with the aid of the tree trunks, he could keep his feet more easily. The smells in the forest were beyond all that he had ever conceived. To say that they made him feel hungry and thirsty would be misleading; almost, they created a new kind of hunger and thirst, a longing that seemed to flow over from the body into the soul and which was a heaven to feel.[11]

If the reader is responsive, Lewis's imagery serves as a transport to the surface of Venus, and not simply a flat description printed on a page.

LEWIS THE SELF-CRITICAL SCHOLAR

C.S. Lewis was indeed a first-rate scholar, serving on the faculties of both Oxford and Cambridge Universities. As such he was aware of the many follies and shortcomings of higher education and the men who were its principal participants. Though he truly loved the scholarly life, Lewis was not adverse to critiquing his own kind:

> I have heard the scholar defined as one who has a propensity to collect useless information, and in this sense Martianus is the very type of the scholar. The philosophies of others, the religions of others—back even to the twilight of pre-republican Rome—have all gone into the curiosity shop of his mind. It is not his business to believe or disbelieve them; the wicked old pedant knows a trick worth two of that. He piles them up all around him till there is hardly room for him to sit among them in the middle darkness of the shop; and there he gloats and catalogues, but never dusts them, for even their dust is precious in his eyes.[12]

One takes the impression that it is not so much the piles of useless information that Lewis finds irritating, but the bloodless scholarly habit of refraining from belief in anything.

LEWIS'S DIVINE IMAGINATION

Though Lewis is widely known for his diabolical imaginings in *The Screwtape Letters*, an even greater amount of his work concerns his dreams and images of heaven. The Narnia stories contain ample images of the divine landscape, and one runs into numerous speculations on heaven while reading Lewis's essays. Possibly his most extensive speculations on heaven, though, are found in *The Great*

Divorce. Here Lewis gives us many marvelous images, including the following description of a former mortal who had been especially kind and generous during her life on Earth:

> Then, on the left and right, at each side of the forest avenue, came youthful shapes, boys upon one hand, and girls upon the other. If I could remember their singing and write down the notes, no man who read that score would ever grow sick or old. Between them went musicians: and after these a lady in whose honour all this was being done.
>
> I cannot now remember whether she was naked or clothed. If she were naked, then it must have been the almost visible penumbra of her courtesy and joy which produces in my memory the illusion of a great and shining train that followed her across the happy grass.[13]

Of course, this picture is all imagined—as C.S. Lewis is careful to admit—but such vivid imaginings cannot but contribute to our beatific visions and hopes of things to come.

Lewis the Defender of the Faith

In Lewis's time, as in ours today, one often heard Christianity attacked on the grounds that stories and images from older pagan myths seem to have been incorporated into Christian doctrine. These myths have been a stumbling-block for many a college sophomore through the years, but Lewis meets this challenge head-on:

> We must not be ashamed of the mythical radiance resting on our theology. We must not be nervous about "parallels" and "Pagan Christs": they ought to be there—it would be a stumbling block if they weren't. We must not, in false spirituality, withhold our imaginative welcome. . . . For this is the marriage of heaven and earth: Perfect Myth and Perfect Fact: claiming not only our love and our obedience, but also our wonder and delight, addressed to the savage, the child, and

the poet in each one of us no less than to the moralist, the scholar, and the philosopher.[14]

Truth, in other words, has broken through the veil of myth and history many times before—sometimes incompletely, sometimes inaccurately, but always anticipating the moment when Truth would come incarnate and declare itself in history.

Lewis's Sense of Practical Psychology

One of the very things that gives such power to C.S. Lewis's writing is his remarkable understanding of human interactions. In reading his fiction, his apologetics, and especially his popular nonfiction, we often find penetrating and useful insights revealing a man who paid very close attention to the ways of the people around him. The examples are legion, but here we will look at a good one from *The Four Loves*, where Lewis discusses the curious habit of demanding affection from others:

> The most unlovable parent (or child) may be full of such ravenous love. But it works to their own misery and everyone else's. The situation becomes suffocating. If people are already unlovable a continual demand on their part (as of right) to be loved—their manifest sense of injury, their reproaches, whether loud and clamorous or merely implicit in every look and gesture of resentful self-pity—produce in us a sense of guilt (they are intended to do so) for a fault we could not have avoided and cannot cease to commit. They seal up the very fountain for which they are thirsty. If ever, at some favoured moment, any germ of Affection for them stirs in us, their demand for more and still more petrifies us again.[15]

Such insights as this abound in Lewis's writing, and they are no doubt the cause of Lewis's popularity as a personal counselor by correspondence through the mail.

LEWIS THE ANTAGONIST

C.S. Lewis was to some a surprisingly aggressive man in argumentation. It is true that he loved to argue, and his method of argument was seldom simply to put up a mild defense of his positions. Instead, Lewis was one to go out into the opponent's territory and to attack with the same vigor with which the opponent was attacking him. An example is Lewis's response to the materialists' attacks on the very idea of miracles:

> Hence, whether miracles have really ceased or not, they would certainly appear to cease in Western Europe as materialism became the popular creed. For let us make no mistake. If the end of the world appeared in all the literal trappings of the Apocalypse, if the modern materialist saw with his own eyes the heavens rolled up and the great white throne appearing, if he had the sensation of being himself hurled into the Lake of Fire, he would continue forever, in that lake itself, to regard his experience as an illusion and to find the explanation of it in psycho-analysis, or cerebral pathology.[16]

Having been called a closed-minded dogmatist, Lewis responds by pointing out the unquestioned dogma of the materialist.

C.S. LEWIS'S SENSE OF CHARACTER

Character development is one of the subtlest and yet most important skills of the writer's art. One of the remarkable things about Lewis's fiction and fantasy writing is his ability to portray character in very short order. This particular genius is especially apparent in the children's stories, as Lewis seems to go right to the heart of a character in only a few lines.

For example, in the story *The Voyage of the "Dawn Treader,"* the character of Eustace Scrubb is revealed in the boy's own words as written in his journal. Scrubb has been miraculously transported—along with his cousins Lucy and Edmund—into another time and place, where he finds himself aboard the *Dawn Treader* under the leadership of King Caspian. But here is what Eustace writes in his journal:

> It's madness to come out into the sea in a rotten little thing like this. Not much bigger than a life boat. And, of course, absolutely primitive indoors. No proper saloon, no radio, no bathrooms, no deck-chairs. I was dragged all over it yesterday evening and it would make anyone sick to hear Caspian show off his funny little toy boat as if it was the Queen Mary. I tried to tell him what real ships are like, but he's too dense. . . . Needless to say, I've been put in the worst cabin of the boat, a perfect dungeon, and Lucy has been given a whole room on deck to herself, almost a nice room compared to the rest of this place.[17]

Thus, it doesn't take us long to know Eustace Scrubb as a self-centered, petty, complaining boy, as Lewis masterfully weaves these characteristics into Scrubb's own words.

LEWIS THE COSMOLOGIST

The study of the cosmos, the universe, and all that is in it was not a subject from which C.S. Lewis retreated. Lewis was never one to denigrate scientific discoveries per se, but neither was he one to cower in the face of pseudo-science, the tendency of many to make "scientific" claims that were beyond the scope of science. And taking a step farther, Lewis was not shy about offering his own theories to explain the observable events. On the very workings of nature, Lewis wrote:

> Either the stream of events had a beginning or it had not. If it had, then we are faced with something like creation. If it had not (a supposition, by the way, which some physicists find difficult), then we are faced with an everlasting impulse which, by its very nature, is opaque to scientific thought. Science, when it becomes perfect, will have explained the connection between each link in the chain and the link before it. But the

actual existence of the chain will remain wholly unaccount-
able. We learn more and more about the pattern. We learn
nothing about that which 'feeds' real events into the pattern.[18]

Here Lewis reminds us of the limitations of empirical science, and
he offers his own logic as to why the ultimate cause cannot be found
by the scientific method.

LEWIS'S SENSE OF IRONY

The fiction and fantasy writings of Lewis are enriched throughout
by the author's keen sense of irony. The appreciation of ironic situations is, in fact, one of the great joys to be found in reading Lewis
and one of the important keys to understanding his meanings.
Many of Lewis's ironies result from the inherent ironies in
Christianity itself. A good example appears in *The Great Divorce*,
where the Teacher explains:

> There are only two kinds of people in the end: those who say
> to God, 'Thy will be done,' and those to whom God says, in
> the end, 'Thy will be done.' All that are in Hell, choose it.
> Without that self-choice there could be no Hell. No soul that
> seriously and constantly desires joy will ever miss it. Those
> who seek find. To those who knock it is opened.[19]

There is, after all, great irony in the divine fact that we get what we
really seek. For much of what humanity considers seeking joy actually amounts to seeking self-destruction and misery. Of course, the
Christian knows that the wisdom behind the irony is that seeking
God is the same thing as seeking joy.

C.S. LEWIS ON INTELLECTUAL ELITISM

Lewis had a way of making himself quite unpopular in academic circles by his disregard for the pretensions of his fellow intellectuals.

For example, the celebrated modern poet T.S. Eliot is quoted as having said that only poets are qualified to judge the quality of a poem. To this idea Lewis replied:

> We may therefore allow poets to tell us (at least if they are experienced in the same kind of composition) whether it is easy or difficult to write like Milton, but not whether the reading of Milton is a valuable experience. For who can endure a doctrine which would allow only dentists to say whether our teeth were aching, only cobblers to say whether our shoes hurt us, and only governments to tell us whether we were being well governed?[20]

Eliot's idea perhaps seems reasonable enough, until Lewis's analogies put it in a different light.

LEWIS'S EPIC IMAGINATION

In his scholarly works on literature, Lewis's love for epic poetry is obvious. The epic, as he explains, is concerned with great events placed on sweeping panoramas of time and place. Well-known examples of epic poetry are Dante's *Inferno* and Milton's *Paradise Lost*. Lewis himself indulges the epic urge in his space trilogy and especially in the Narnia stories. Here is an exemplary epic scene from *The Last Battle*, where the Narnian world is coming to an end:

> The spreading blackness was not a cloud at all: it was simply emptiness. The black part of the sky was the part in which there were no stars left. All the stars were falling: Aslan had called them home. . . . The last few seconds before the rain of stars had quite ended were very exciting. Stars began falling all round them. But stars in that world are not the great flaming globes they are in ours. They are people (Edmund and Lucy had once met one). So now they found showers of glittering people, all with long hair like burning silver and spears like white-hot metal, rushing down to them

out of the black air, swifter than falling stones. They made a hissing noise as they landed and burnt the grass.[21]

A great deal more of Lewis's epic imagination is to be found in the other Narnia stories as well.

In the pages that follow are reviews of many of C.S. Lewis's fiction and nonfiction works. The very fact of his remarkable breadth of interests and diversity of styles actually increases the chances that your first reading of C.S. Lewis might turn out to be unsatisfactory. There are, in fact, many readers who thoroughly enjoy one kind of C.S. Lewis book and yet dislike another. The trick in becoming acquainted with C.S. Lewis is to determine which genre you most enjoy, and to begin with that.

Though Lewis's books range from fairy tales to scholarly expositions, there is a consistent thread running through them all and holding them together. It is a thread that can be roughly characterized as Romantic and Christian and perhaps—in a very special sense defined by Lewis himself—Medieval. It is a thread that calls for a certain way of looking at humanity and history, and from thence a certain way of approaching the arts and sciences. And so, no matter which door you choose for entry into the world of C.S. Lewis, you will very soon begin to see that thread of meaning that defines and connects all of his writings.

So, where do you begin? Finding the answer to that question is as simple as answering another question: What do you like best to read? Do you enjoy classical scholarship? Do you like science fiction? Do you prefer logical apologetics? Are you partial to allegory? Do you relish imaginative fantasy? Do you like children's stories? What about discussions of important issues such as pain, love, or miracles? Maybe mythology is more to your taste. Or perhaps you are simply not sure.

The remainder of this book is designed to introduce the reader to the works of C.S. Lewis. You will find in each section a representative sampling of Lewis's major works. There will be a brief review, followed by a few words of guidance toward important things to look for while reading. My intention is that you will use these reviews as an introduction to—and not as a substitute for—Lewis's original work. My hope is that you will go on from here to many happy years of reading and enjoying this remarkable author, C.S. Lewis.

2

THE STAGE IS SET

Arguments are not easily understood when joined at midpoint. To appreciate the significance of the life and work of C.S. Lewis, it is important to know his historical and intellectual contexts. As Lewis was born in Great Britain at the dawning of the twentieth century, the stage onto which he strode had already been set and furnished by the ideas and controversies of the previous century. It is therefore to the popular ideas of nineteenth-century Europe that we must turn if we are to understand why C.S. Lewis believed what he believed, argued what he argued, and wrote what he wrote.

By the early decades of the nineteenth century, the dominant strands of western European intellectual thought gave their attention to issues of history, society, humanity, nature, and God. During the previous era, the Age of Enlightenment, the ideas of Montesquieu, Hobbes, Locke, Rousseau, and others tumbled through the American and French Revolutions and into many an argument and discussion in the boardrooms, classrooms, and living rooms of Europe and America.

There may have been a relative consensus on these great issues in earlier times, but the nineteenth century marked a shattering of any illusions of a unified view thereafter. By mid-century there were at least three major streams of thought competing for dominance in western Europe. One was a continuation and revision of the earlier Enlightenment ideas. The second was a Romantic reaction against many of the Enlightenment ideas. The third was a stubbornly resilient Christian tradition, both Roman Catholic and Protestant, that simply refused to die in spite of the widespread attacks against it.

THE NEW ENLIGHTENMENT STREAM

While the traditional Enlightenment thinkers had extolled the virtues of reason as the way to humanity's salvation and progress, the advocates of the New Enlightenment thinking in the nineteenth century emphasized the rational-empirical methods of science. Until his death in 1857 French sociologist Auguste Comte vigorously promoted the cause of science in all aspects of human life. Indeed, throughout the nineteenth century scientific methods were advocated with missionary zeal by Comte and others, as illustrated in Comte's "social physics," Renan's science of religion, Marx's scientific socialism, John Stuart Mill's science of human nature, and even Zola's scientific novels.

This widespread enthusiasm for science is certainly understandable in view of the amazing discoveries and inventions that were at that time taking place. As early as 1831 Michael Faraday invented an electric dynamo. By mid-century John Dalton had presented atomic theory, Samuel Morse had invented the telegraph, and the physical scientists had declared the first law of thermodynamics.

During the second half of the century, science brought great advances in the field of health and medicine. Among these amazing discoveries were Pasteur's substantiation of germ theory and his subsequent development of vaccines for anthrax and rabies, as well as Wilhelm Roentgen's demonstration of X-rays for medicinal use.

In 1870 the Russian chemist Mendelyev developed the periodic table of chemical elements. Thomas Edison, Alexander Bell, and Guglielmo Marconi revolutionized communications with the duplex telegraph, the telephone, and the wireless radio. Finally, Europeans in the 1880s saw the inventions of the steam turbine, the internal combustion gasoline engine, and Rudolf Diesel's heavy petroleum engine.

Perhaps it is no wonder that many people came to believe science could and would solve all possible human problems. In time the older Enlightenment idea that humanity could conquer nature through reason was modified somewhat to claim empirical science as the new road to human perfection. This message was clearly advocated in the positivism of Auguste Comte, but it subsequently gained acceptance among a wide array of nineteenth-century thinkers, including the French sociologist Emile Durkheim, the socialists Karl Marx and Friedrich Engels, many of the new Hegelians, and later the scientist Thomas Huxley.

But it is important at this point to digress to some of the philosophical roots of this updated Enlightenment thinking before we launch into the greater modifications that would soon follow. Returning to the basic questions on the nature of humanity and of God, the essential Enlightenment position was that humans are rational beings, and as such they are perfectly capable of controlling their environment and therefore their destiny. In this sense humans are their own gods. The Christian God or any other transcendent being was rejected as unnecessary and, in fact, a mythical holdover from a previous, unenlightened era.

In the hands of Comte and others, however, these Enlightenment ideas took a turn toward scientific positivism. Briefly, the central positivist tenets are (1) a complete rejection of anything metaphysical, (2) a consequent rejection of all religious beliefs, (3) a belief that the rational-empirical methods of the natural sciences are the only way to discern the truth, and (4) a residual optimism about humanity's propensity to use science to master nature and control the future.

That the rational-empirical method was serving extremely well in the natural sciences seemed beyond question. Because of this obvious success and through the enthusiastic efforts of popularizers including Bacon, Comte, Mill, and Huxley, scientific positivism came to take on the character of a cult. As historian Franklin Baumer described the situation:

> Science in this sense was now widely assumed to provide the only truly reliable knowledge. The "moral sciences," as theology, politics, psychology, history and the like were still widely known, could carry credibility only insofar as they succeeded in assimilating, or at least approximating, the methods and aims of the physical sciences.[1]

While the influence of this "cult of science" probably reached its apex in the period from 1860 to 1914, many of its assumptions remained widely popular through the entire twentieth century. As time passed, the universities of western Europe and America witnessed one academic field after another clamoring for recognition as being adequately "scientific" to be taken seriously, and even today there remains a habit among intellectuals of legitimizing their ideas with the incantation, "Scientific studies have shown. . . ."

But in mid-nineteenth century the New Enlightenment school began to take yet another turn toward evolutionary theory. Even before Charles Darwin published his famous *Origin of Species* in 1859, evolutionary ideas had appeared in the works of Laplace, Lamarck, Lyell, and more recently Herbert Spencer. But it was Darwin's work that catapulted evolutionism into dominance in European intellectual circles. Echoing the rapid diffusion of science into the various intellectual fields, the evolutionary model soon spread from biology into the social sciences and even into the arts, literature, and theology. With remarkable speed the notion was accepted that in order to be valid or square with the facts, all other ideas needed to be reconciled with the evolutionary paradigm.

Now this newly dominant theory of humanity stated that human beings were simply another adaptation in a long chain of animals adapting to their environments. The theory took a necessarily materialist view of humanity, rejecting all ideas of a soul or a spirit or any other metaphysical qualities. It was a deterministic theory in the sense that the laws of natural selection were said to determine which species were most fit to survive. Predictably and inevitably, it was antagonistic to the Christian idea that humans were specially created in the image of their Creator.

In 1871 Darwin published his *Descent of Man*, in which the author proposed that humans descended from monkeys. Later Thomas Huxley, the great apologist of the scientific worldview in such titles as *Science and Morals* and *Evolution and Ethics*, continued his attacks against religious beliefs and his advocacy of a new moral order based on scientific principles. Huxley maintained that skepticism was the highest human calling and that "blind faith" was the greatest roadblock to human progress.

By the end of the nineteenth century the theory of evolution had been assimilated into the political-social spheres under the banner of social Darwinism. Here Herbert Spencer's phrase "survival of the fittest" took on new meanings in connection with the rapid growth of industry and capitalist enterprises. There was the now-famous incident when railroad tycoon James J. Hill justified his rapacious business practices by use of evolutionary terms. There also developed a dubious ethical basis for the popular racial theories widely used to justify imperialist expansion, nationalist doctrines, the exploitation of labor, and even the booming slave trade.

The essence of social Darwinism was the idea that the history of societies was simply one more manifestation of the natural laws of evolution. As such, cultures evolve through successive stages from savagery through barbarism to civilization; and even in civilized cultures there is a continuous struggle for dominance between societies and within societies. Those peoples or groups or individuals who fall behind in the struggle, then, are obviously not the most fit to survive.

This paradigm of the natural struggle for survival in turn had many social implications. To Herbert Spencer the notion implied the laissez-faire doctrine that one should keep one's hands off the natural workings of the economy and its consequent social arrangements. To Karl Marx and other socialists it implied an inevitable dialectic moving toward a classless society and justice for all. To industrialists such as James J. Hill and John D. Rockefeller it implied a naturally legitimized right to acquire and accumulate wealth and power.

Herbert Spencer developed an evolutionary theory of society as an organism, in which each organ performed a specialized function. Spencer's organismic analogy was popularized in America by Lester Ward and William Graham Sumner, who carried the notion further by defining exactly which bodily organs corresponded to which social institutions. Though these evolutionary social theories were presented as objective explanations of social phenomena, they hid within them a rather strong bias in favor of going along with the system and against any tinkering with the relations between, for example, management and labor.

Another idea that proved to be a most motivating force in the New Enlightenment camp was the notion of "progress." The idea of progress is, of course, terribly vague, and as such it can be an effective tool in the hand of anyone who will take it up. The biological Darwinists, for example, measured progress as movement toward more complex and efficient forms of life. The capitalists considered progress to be greater profits gained and capital accumulated. The socialists, on the other hand, thought of progress as placing ownership of the means of production into the hands of the workers. But strictly speaking, progress means nothing more than movement toward a goal.

Nevertheless "progress" became the rallying cry, the dominant motivating creed of the nineteenth century. Certainly no one wanted to be accused of being against progress, and progressive sentiments soon became the litmus test of sophistication and intellectualism in western Europe and America. Progress also rather quickly became the handy and irrefutable slogan to justify everything from the displacement of the agricultural poor into urban slums to filling the skies with unsightly and poisonous residues from the factories.

Considered in context the notion of progress contained the Enlightenment idea that humanity was on the move, conquering its environment and taking control of its future. Since the scientific method and industrial growth were the grand vehicles of this campaign into the future, progress came to mean whatever might aid and abet the advances of science and industry. Thus, the progressive sentiment merely added an aura of inevitability and natural sanction to the urban-industrial developments that were taking place.

There were dissenters, however, such as George Bernard Shaw and G.K. Chesterton in England, who pointed out that progressivism as an unquestioned creed merely begs the question as to whether things are actually improving. There is a residual assumption that what is newer is therefore better, though this highly arguable notion is often hidden under such truisms as, "the only constant is change" and "you can't turn back the clock" and the fear of falling "behind the times." Nevertheless, the progressive assumptions came to dominate nineteenth-century popular thought and continued to wield a great influence through the twentieth century as well.

Any impression that the New Enlightenment forces consisted of a unified front would be a false one. Even among the scientists there were many controversies and conflicts. For example, many physical scientists objected strongly to the teleological aspect of "Nature's hand" in evolutionary theory. And there were many among the more traditional Enlightenment camp, such as the Hegelians, who objected to the narrow positivism that had come to dominate scientific thinking.

Also, as the nineteenth century came to a close, the fact was becoming increasingly and painfully clear that science was not solving the problems of environmental pollution, widespread unemployment, and wretched slum conditions resulting from the rapid urban-industrial growth. Sociologist Emile Durkheim had for some time warned of the dysfunctions of modern industrial life—particularly of the *anomie*, or normlessness, of the urban-dwellers. Similarly, Karl Marx had lamented the alienation of the workers and their exploitation by the captains of industry.

In the 1890s Vienna psychologist Sigmund Freud began using

his new psychoanalytic theory to suggest the dark side of the human psyche. Freud's message was that the human mind was not nearly as rational as Enlightenment thinking had assumed, and in fact that the real foundation of human behavior was subconscious sexual urges. To the many intellectuals worldwide who took Freud's ideas seriously, this news was alarming indeed. The Enlightenment camp had begun the century with high optimism about the nature of humanity and the hope of a rationally controlled future. But at the close of the century they found themselves having to choose between claims that humans were either (1) highly developed apes whose fate would be determined by the natural laws of evolution or (2) basically irrational beings whose actions and fate would be shaped by their subconscious sexual drives.

But before we can bring C.S. Lewis into the story, we need to consider the other two major intellectual streams that competed against this New Enlightenment thinking in the nineteenth century. Despite the overwhelming popularity of science and the phenomenal growth of technology and industry, there were those who had dissented and protested these New Enlightenment trends from the beginning. It is to this Romantic reaction that we now briefly turn our attention.

THE ROMANTIC STREAM

The Romantic counter-movement to the Enlightenment had been well underway by the dawn of the nineteenth century, as the rather stark and rigid views of rational humanity had drawn protests particularly from among certain philosophers and practitioners of literature and the arts. There had been, of course, the tradition of Jean Jacques Rousseau, whose *Social Contract* (1762) and other writings had emphasized nature as the source of wisdom and who popularized the notion of the "noble savage" in contrast to the corrupted people of modern urban society.

As the nineteenth century dawned, there came a new breed of Romantics to assert vigorously that the Enlightenment picture of material-rational humanity was an egregious error that would bring dire consequences. As a recent historian has written:

> The appeal to reason, it appeared, was insufficient to create a new society or to defend an old one. Disillusioned with the supposed rationality of man, the Romanticists exalted instinct and emotion.[2]

The Romantic stream of the nineteenth century grew as a reaction against the materialist, rational-empirical, and positivist views promoted by the cult of science.

The Romantic reaction can be defined generally as an appeal to humanity's instincts and emotions. The Romantics pointed out that the human being is a creature of feeling no less than of thought. They asserted that individuals can and do act independently, sometimes nonrationally and even irrationally, and that each has a right to self-determination as far as possible. In their stories and arts the Romantics preferred the natural, wild, and unpredictable aspects of life. They tended to embrace the transcendent and long for the ultimate.

Some of the literary names to be mentioned in connection with the early-nineteenth-century Romantic stream are Schiller, Goethe, Hugo, and Scott. The Germans Schiller and Goethe were both passionate individualists and defenders of liberty. In 1808 Goethe published the first part of *Faust*, in which a supernatural theme was used to illustrate the irrationality of humanity. Similarly the French author Victor Hugo emphasized individual heroism, casting a Romantic hue across the national history of France. And what Hugo did for France, Sir Walter Scott did for Great Britain. Scott's *Ivanhoe* in 1819 told a tale of individual heroism in a Romantic telling of England's national past.

Other notable British Romantics were William Wordsworth and Samuel Taylor Coleridge. Wordsworth was an unabashed transcendentalist whose poetry lauded the intuitive beauty of nature and who defined poetry as an "overflow of powerful feelings." Coleridge also emphasized the nonrational, spicing his works with fantasy, symbol, and the supernatural, as illustrated in his *The Rime of the Ancient Mariner*.

Recall as well the Romantic elements in the writings of Lord Byron, whose Don Juan illustrated a rebellion against the constraints of society; and of Percy Bysshe Shelley, whose *Prometheus Unbound* celebrated individualism and human liberty. Another noted contemporary, John Keats, filled his works with beautiful and sensuous imagery, reflecting the "estheticism" that worshiped beauty as the highest good. A defining line from Keats's *Ode to a Grecian Urn* says:

> *Beauty is truth, truth beauty—that is all*
> *Ye know on earth, and all ye need to know.*

It is easy to see how such Romantic ideas as these would be abhorrent to the scientific positivists and others of the New Enlightenment stream of thought.

At about mid-nineteenth century the poet-essayist Matthew Arnold wrote prolifically about the troubling aspects of the emerging urban-industrial society—the disintegration of the social fabric, the retreat of men into their self-seeking schemes, and the loss of what was best in humanistic culture. The materialism and shoddy commercialism of the day were nothing less than "diseased," according to Arnold, and he warned of an impending catastrophe if the modern western societies did not return to the classical values of the past.

Another very important figure in the intellectual debates of nineteenth-century western Europe was the Scottish historian Thomas Carlyle. Like Arnold, Carlyle railed against the swindling and lying and exploitation that had become the norm in urban-industrial life. But Carlyle went further in claiming that material relations result from spiritual relations. In other words, the cause of modern society's sickness was ultimately an underlying sickness of spirit.

The fact that Carlyle's brand of Romantic historicism is today widely rejected does not alter the arguability of his thesis. In direct opposition to the various historical determinisms—such as Spencerian laws of evolution or Marxist economic determinism or the widely heralded hand of "progress"—Carlyle asserted that the human will was still the driving force behind history. Carlyle's histories made much of courageous action and heroic people and strongly denied that nonhuman forces determine human action. While the New Enlightenment thought promoted an environmentalism featuring grand epochs and irresistible forces, Carlyle's Romantic historicism featured great heroes acting decisively to turn the tides of human events.

The growing revolt against the cult of scientific positivism was not carried entirely by the literary Romantics. In fact, by the end of the nineteenth century there had grown a rather impressive roster of opponents, including many scientists, philosophers, sociologists, psychologists, and historians whom we cannot properly call Romantics at all. However, these will be discussed here as comprising a very important force in the growing reaction to the New Enlightenment stream of thought.

For example, English psychologist James Ward protested the encroachment of the scientific method beyond its purview. Likewise, T.H. Green objected to the evolutionists' grounding of ethics in biological processes. But it was the German philosopher Wilhelm Dilthey who most effectively argued against positivism for the study of history in particular and the understanding of the human being in general.

In 1883 Dilthey asserted forcefully that the natural science model could not be applied effectively and accurately to the study of human history. The subject of the human studies, Dilthey pointed out, is humanity and the human mind—complete with individual values, beliefs, feelings, and motives. Therefore he argued that history can never be reduced to a mere search for types and cause-effect propositions.

Philosopher Wilhelm Windelband clarified Dilthey's argument by distinguishing "nomothetic" from "idiographic" methods of

study. The nomothetic method—basically the naming and classify-
ing of phenomena and the discovering of general laws—was
believed to be particularly well suited to the natural sciences. The
idiographic method—basically seeking to understand individual
cases—was believed to be more appropriate for human studies such
as history. These distinctions became especially important to the
work of sociologist Max Weber, author of *The Protestant Ethic and
the Spirit of Capitalism.*

But these arguments reached much deeper than simply into the
preferred method for the various fields of study; they involved the
very nature of human beings. The New Enlightenment thinkers saw
the human animal as they saw all natural phenomena—ultimately
subject to the same natural processes as everything else in the universe. The dissenters, both the Romantics and the others, saw
humans as unique and qualitatively different from the other natural
phenomena.

In France philosopher Henri Bergson objected to the mechanistic aspect of the positivist view, laying the foundations for a new
"vitalist" school of thought on the nature of humanity. Bergson
argued that it was intuition, not intellect, that could best serve in the
effort to understand the human being, and that the positivists'
search for deterministic laws was both misdirected and ill-advised.
A most significant—if not in a way prophetic—statement by
Bergson was that the exclusion of value and freedom from the
human formula would lead inevitably to moral irresponsibility.

Mention must also be made of George Bernard Shaw, the
English Fabian socialist and playwright who in 1903 wrote *Man and
Superman.* Again in direct opposition to the mechanism of the scientific positivists, Shaw carried Bergson's vitalism a step further by
positing a raw life force that both motivates and directs the course
of evolution. As in earlier aeons the human animal had evolved
physically, in modern times humanity was in the process of evolv-
ing a new kind of mind, producing higher and higher individuals
toward the final emergence of the superman. As such, Shaw's ideas
can be seen as consistent with the older Enlightenment humanistic

optimism, but with a rather Romantic rejection of the mechanistic determinisms of the scientific positivists.

Certainly no Romantic but nevertheless a rather violent critic of the widespread smug progressivism was German philosopher Friedrich Nietzsche. Somewhat of a loose cannon in European intellectual circles, Nietzsche wrote much that was hostile to all three of the major streams of thought being discussed here. Like Shaw, Nietzsche believed in a kind of superman that would rise above the rest; but Nietzsche's superman was far different from Shaw's philanthropic rationalist. In Nietzsche's thinking the superman would rule over others through superior intelligence and ruthless power. Democracy and humanitarianism were seen as the irrational protection of the weak, cowardly, and inferior. These ideas directly laid the groundwork for the fascism that would soon sweep across Europe and draw the world into war.

Nietzsche had much to say about Christianity as well. Obviously any doctrine that advocated the relinquishment of power and the turning of the other cheek he would find contemptible. Then of course there was the famous "death of God" controversy, in which Nietzsche made his triumphal proclamation that humanity now existed in a world completely devoid of deity. His 1886 book *Beyond Good and Evil* made it clear that he well understood the moral consequences of such a godless worldview—that purely secular ethics must lead in the end to pragmatic brutalism.

THE CHRISTIAN STREAM

Unlike the two streams of thought already discussed, Christian thought has always had certain moorings to which it remains tied—albeit with longer and shorter lifelines at different times and places—even as it develops. Traditionally these moorings have been recognized widely in Christendom as the Holy Scriptures, the church, and the unique revelations or means of guidance of the Holy Spirit. Though controversies have raged over the relative merits and authority of each of these standard sources, there has nevertheless remained over the centuries a remarkable degree of consensus with regard to the basics of Christian orthodoxy.

In order to understand the Christian stream of thought at the time of C.S. Lewis's birth, we need to mention at least briefly the basics of orthodox Christian doctrine and then the particular turns of religious thought and theology in nineteenth-century England. We can begin with a look at the more generic foundations of Christian orthodoxy in the West before the Reformation, paying special attention to ideas on the nature of God and the nature of human beings.

The traditional orthodox Christian position on the nature of God is that of an omnipotent Creator of all that exists. This God is seen as the same as the Yahweh in ancient Jewish tradition as revealed in the Old Testament, as well as the Triune God—consisting of the Father, the Son, and the Holy Spirit—revealed in the Old and especially in the New Testament. As early as the fifth Christian century, Augustine of Hippo had established the Trinity as the orthodox standard in defining the Christian God.

Another important attribute of the Christian God as defined by the apostle Paul and then Augustine four centuries later was God's transcendent, mystical character. This metaphysical "otherness" of God was asserted consistently in Christian doctrine through the early centuries, reiterated by Thomas Aquinas in the thirteenth century, and preserved in the more traditional theologies—both Catholic and Protestant—to the present day.

Another basic idea in Christian thought is that human beings, men and women, were specially created by God in the image of their Creator. The implications of this special genesis are many, but relevant here is the notion that as the Creator is a creative, intelligent, free, self-willed, and spontaneous being, it follows that these created human copies are meant to possess those characteristics as well. On this matter, then, Christian thought can be seen as consistent with that of the nineteenth-century Romantics, some of whom—for example, William Blake and Robert Browning—were indeed Christians themselves.

An important implication of the special creation of human

beings is that there is a qualitative, spiritual difference between the human creature and the other creatures. This unique and purposeful creation gives humanity and human life an intrinsic significance, a cosmic meaning, reaching far beyond the bounds of a single lifetime in a given time and place in history. Such a conception stands, of course, in direct contradiction to the evolutionary idea of the human animal as one among many accidental mutations that incidentally proved to be the most fit to survive. It also serves as a pillar in the edifice of the Christian ethics of charity, in that every person—be it king or beggar—is entitled to that level of justice and mercy befitting a soul that is very special to the Creator.

With regard to ethics, it is important to point out another basic Christian belief: God is the absolute good, and therefore there exists an absolute, non-relative standard of good and evil. Again we easily see the sharp contradiction of the relative ethics of the New Enlightenment. Recall the various attempts to derive ethical standards from biological imperatives, or survival value, or cultural norms, or even the scientific method itself. On the other hand, traditional Christian doctrine held that right and wrong were not dependent upon nature, nor culture, nor any artifact of humanity; instead, they were defined and fixed by God, the absolute good.

Yet another major issue wherein Christian doctrine differed sharply from both the New Enlightenment ideas and those of the humanistic arm of Romanticism concerns the perfectibility of humanity. The pseudo-scientific optimism of the nineteenth century held that humans could and would use their sciences to control their destiny and achieve perfection. There were also various evolutionary and other utopian models that spoke of a gradual and inevitable "progress" of humankind toward its perfection. All of these models held in common a belief that human efforts could achieve the desired goals.

The Christian reply to the question of human perfectibility seems at first to be pessimistic but in the end becomes more optimistic than even the wildest utopia imaginable. It is a mixed reply, consisting of a denial that humanity is capable of perfecting itself, but then a promise that there is a way to ultimate perfection and glory. The traditional doctrine of the Fall and of original sin states that humans were created good but that through their own self-will they chose to rebel against God and thereby brought upon themselves the consequences of their rebellion: the fall into sin and error. As such, then, there is no hope for humanity to achieve perfection through evolution or through science or through any other human means. Christian doctrine holds that human perfection will come, but that it will come only through the door called Jesus of Nazareth, the Christ of the Triune God.

We have seen here several essential points at which traditional Christian doctrine contradicts the basic tenets of the New Enlightenment and some of the popular ideas from the Romanticist school as well. There is, of course, a great deal more to be said on this subject, but for now we shall have to leave the discussion in the far more capable hands of C.S. Lewis and others. Our purpose here has been to give only the briefest sketch of traditional Christian orthodoxy.

By the mid-eighteenth century western Christendom had fragmented not only into the major division between Protestant and Roman Catholic doctrines, but even into the smaller and more distinct categories represented by the Jansenists, the Anglicans, the French Jesuits, the English Methodists, the German Pietists, and many others. This multiplicity of sometimes-antagonistic movements and denominations led many to conclude that Christianity itself was disintegrating as an untenable and indefensible position in the face of the overwhelmingly popular Enlightenment ideas.

Even many theologians themselves were swayed by the call of rational empiricism. In 1730 Thomas Woolston argued in his *Discourses on the Miracles* that the biblical miracles were merely hoaxes, calling for a rejection of revealed religion and a "return" to the religion of nature. In a similar vein Matthew Tindal and later William Wollaston reflected the materialist temper of the times in their attempts to purge religion of all "mystery and superstition."

Meanwhile, the great philosophers had much to say on the subject of God as well. While the deist Voltaire had argued the existence of God based on design in nature, Hume was busy attacking on logical grounds all arguments for God's existence. Immanuel Kant stated that God is "speculatively unknowable" but deduced God's existence from the moral nature of humanity. Rousseau consistently argued for a natural religion in which intuition and introspection were the way to find God.

It was Kant who gave a clear definition to delineate between a deist and a theist. A deist is one who believes in a God that created all things but is inactive now. The God of the deist is not found in revealed religion but can be deduced from nature. A theist, on the other hand, is one who believes in a living, active, revealed God. Voltaire's "critical deism" amounted to a frontal attack against organized religion and particularly Christianity, which Voltaire held responsible for the superstitions, fanaticisms, massacres, and wars that plagued the world.

In 1780 German theologian Gotthold Lessing in his *Education of the Human Race* held that humanity's religious consciousness was moving upward through progressive revelations. The ancient Jews conceived of a unitary God for themselves only. Christianity conceived of a universal God and personal immortality. And now humanity was destined to grow and understand rationally what was once only revealed. It is not difficult to see the Enlightenment influences in Lessing's theology, or the basic underpinnings for modern process theology.

By the dawning of the nineteenth century, then, western European intellectual thought had reached an apex of hostility toward Christian doctrine. As historian Franklin Baumer explains:

> This is what really happened in the eighteenth century, not only for some few freethinkers and skeptics but for many people who still called themselves Christians. A great many people . . . lost their sense of the miraculous, the sacred and the transcendental, with the predictable result that Christian

revelation receded in importance and even began to seem outmoded or fraudulent.[3]

While the natural theology of the deists thrived, there was a
widespread belief that reason had triumphed over revelation in religious matters.

But as the nineteenth century began to unfold, the Romantic
reaction seemed to touch off a religious revival of sorts. Inspired perhaps by a deep sense of metaphysical loss, some of the Romantics
became Roman Catholics, some became Protestants, and others
such as William Blake took more innovative paths back toward
Christianity. In 1833 Thomas Carlyle wrote in reference to the eigh-
teenth-century philosophers:

> The philosophers went far wrong, however, in this, that
> instead of raising the natural to the supernatural, they strove
> to sink the supernatural to the natural.[4]

Consistent with the Romanticists' deep sense of mystery and meaning beyond the empirical, a new generation of philosophers and theologians sought to interpret the God behind the natural phenomena.

The Roman Catholic apologist Chateaubriand in 1802 wrote
The Genius of Christianity, offering no logical proofs of God, nor
even a restatement of Christian doctrine. Instead Chateaubriand
appealed to the human heart—to the passions, joys, and fears of
humanity—in interpreting Christianity. Also, in direct contradiction
of the famous historian Gibbon, Chateaubriand discussed the great
Christian contributions to civilization—for example, a superior
kind of morality and the many excellent works of art and literature
in the Christian tradition.

It must be noted here that Roman Catholic theology remained
remarkably unified and stable even through this tumultuous nineteenth century. In 1869 the Vatican Council solidified the
supremacy of the Roman bishop by declaring the doctrine of papal
infallibility. This doctrine was powerfully defended by the Catholic

scholars Joseph Marie de Maistre, Louis de Bonald, and Hugues de Lamennais, as well as by the powerful order of Jesuits within the church.

But perhaps the most important action by the Roman Catholic Church in the nineteenth century was Pope Leo's declaration that the work of Thomas Aquinas would be the standard for Catholic instruction. In the thirteenth century Aquinas had brilliantly applied logical principles to Christian doctrine, establishing the logic of Catholic orthodoxy for centuries to come. This declaration of Aquinas as the standard effectively forestalled the liberalism that would so influence Protestant theology during the nineteenth and twentieth centuries.

At about the same time in Germany, Protestant theologian Friedrich Schleiermacher offered a "theology of feeling," writing of a precognitive state in which humans "thirst for the infinite." Again consistent with Romantic ideas, Schleiermacher's theology made much of individuality, as opposed to the Enlightenment ideas of inexorable forces driving the masses.

Meanwhile, the forces of the Enlightenment were busy attacking Christianity, though they were far from trying to abolish religion. Rather, there developed in the nineteenth century a new movement that might best be called the Religion of Humanity. This new religious development rejected the Christian God and looked to anthropology for the basis of its faith.

Perhaps the most famous spokesman for the Religion of Humanity was sociologist Auguste Comte, whose proposed religion worshiped a "Great Being," collective humanity itself. Comte even went so far as to form a new secular church—which, incidentally, no one ever joined—complete with priests and rituals and saints' days. There were also the Young Hegelians, who sought to humanize God, claiming that the real Christ was all of humanity and that God is in a process of becoming as humanity plays out its history.

This century was the setting for the new higher criticism, which subjected the Bible and all Christian doctrines and practices to scientific scrutiny. This higher criticism not only questioned the authenticity and reliability of the Scriptures, but it also urged people to think of religions historically—as myths bound to particular times and places. These ideas were particularly supported by the works of early anthropologists such as E.B. Tylor and Sir James Frazer, who claimed to have traced all religions back to primitive practices and beliefs. In the context of the scientific enthusiasm prevalent in the nineteenth century, the proponents of higher criticism had a profound effect on western European thought both inside and outside the church.

The German theologian David Friedrich Strauss interpreted the life of Jesus as a myth or a social product arising from a great need for a messiah. In 1841 Ludwig Feuerbach synthesized theology and anthropology, claiming that all religion is simply human nature objectified. Religion, he said, merely reflects the degree to which humans are alienated from themselves, and ideas of deity originate in self-projection. In other words, humanity creates its gods in its own image.

One of the most influential names in the field of emerging liberal theology was that of Albrecht Ritschl. This famous German theologian rejected the doctrine of original sin, stating instead that evil is remediable. Again seeking to synthesize Christian doctrine and modern scholarship, Ritschl applied the popular methods of historical criticism to the study of the primitive Christian community and the historical Jesus. Though Ritschl held the Old and New Testaments in high esteem as historical documents, he rejected any notion that metaphysical or supernatural beliefs were necessary to the Christian truth. Following in Ritschl's liberal tradition were the works of other influential Protestant theologians such as Wilhelm Herrmann and Adolf von Harnack, as well as the "history of religions" school advanced by Ernst Troeltsch.

To set the more immediate stage for our subject C.S. Lewis, however, we need finally to take a brief look at the developments in and around the Anglican Church in the nineteenth century. The dominant feature of British Christianity at the dawn of the century was the great evangelical revival that swept across England. Both the Evangelicals inside the church—known as the "low-church party"—

and the Methodists outside the church experienced a great renewal of spirit and vigor early on, and as the century unfolded there grew a wave of non-conforming movements including Congregationalists, Baptists, Presbyterians, Quakers, and Unitarians.

As distinct from the low-church and non-conformist movements, there grew within the Anglican fold a more liberal "broad-church" movement that attempted to reconcile church doctrine with contemporary science and historical criticism. Some of the shining stars in this broad-church movement were Charles Kingsley and Alfred, Lord Tennyson. Their numbers never grew great, but their influence on English Christianity proved to be substantial.

A very significant development within the Anglican Church in the nineteenth century was the "Oxford movement"—also called the "Tractarian movement"—out of which eventually developed the Anglo-Catholic party of the church. This movement began as discussions among a group of young clergy at Oriel College, Oxford, involving a renewed interest in many of the "Catholic usages" that Protestantism had rejected. Some of the major names associated with this movement were Richard Hurrell Froude, Hugh James Rose, John Keble, John Henry Newman, and later Edward Pusey. Eventually John Henry Newman led hundreds of followers out of the Anglican Church and into the Roman Catholic Church, thus reviving the Roman church in England for the first time since the Reformation.

The consequences of the Oxford movement and Newman's defection were many. For one, Roman Catholicism gained a new foothold in England, and there soon followed a series of reforms indicating more religious tolerance in government and public life. Another result was the growth of the Anglo-Catholic party within the Anglican Church under the leadership of Edward Pusey. Greater Anglo-Catholic influence brought not only a richer kind of liturgy into the church, but a renewed zeal to help the poor and unchurched among the populace. These propensities for more Catholic ritual and liturgy are sometimes referred to as the "high-church" movement in Anglicanism.

Other developments in English Protestantism in the last half of the nineteenth century were influenced by the Second Great Evangelical Awakening spurred by the work of American evangelist Dwight Moody. There soon followed the founding of Edward Irving's new Catholic Apostolic Church, seeking to restore the "gifts" of the apostolic age; the establishment of John Nelson Darby's Plymouth Brethren churches, emphasizing the priesthood of all believers; and the growth of William Booth's Salvation Army, engaging in street evangelism and philanthropic work.

By the end of the nineteenth century, Christianity in England reflected an array of approaches to theology and Christian doctrine. The broad-church perspective reflected the widespread liberal endeavors to synthesize religion and the dominant secular philosophies and science. The high-church view and the activities of the Anglo-Catholic party had revivified the Anglican Church by bringing more elaborate liturgy and ritual into its practices. The low-church movement of the Evangelical party and the various non-conformist movements placed more emphasis on personal salvation, evangelism, and missions. Both the high- and low-church movements and many of the non-conformist groups took a great interest in applying the Christian moral truths to social concerns and charitable activities.

A NEW CENTURY DAWNS

As the nineteenth century came to its conclusion and western Europeans looked forward—some with optimism and hope, some with pessimism and despair—to the dawning of the twentieth century, the intellectual stage had been set for the controversies and arguments in which C.S. Lewis would grow to immerse himself. It is probably fair to say that the major tenor of the age was set by the New Enlightenment stream of thought, featuring its enthusiasm for science and an upbeat belief that the wheels of progress promised a better future with humanity in control of its own destiny.

But as we shall see, C.S. Lewis was a man who would grasp his intellectual environment and wrestle with it. He would come of age as a fairly typical reflection of his time and social class. He would obtain a very uneven education in schools both public and private. As a young man he would experience as a soldier the horrors of World War I. He would return to the academic life at Oxford University. But in midlife he would make a discovery that would change the course of his life and his intellectual contributions radically and forever.

A little past one hundred pages into his scholarly masterpiece *The Allegory of Love*, C.S. Lewis gives his readers an explanation for the great amount of preparatory comment they have so far endured. He writes:

> The reader who has followed—if any has followed—my first two chapters may well feel that he has been taken on a long journey through scenery more various than agreeable, and may pardonably ask why such a circuitous approach to our subject was needed.[5]

This may be the dominant question in the mind of the reader of this chapter as well. But Lewis goes on to explain that in order to understand the issues and arguments of a certain era and its writers, it becomes necessary to "remount the stream of time"—that is, to go back and revisit the argument as it leads into the issues at hand. The purpose of this chapter and the one following is to take Lewis's advice and "remount the stream of time" in order to understand the life and work of this remarkable man, C.S. Lewis.

3

ENTER C.S. LEWIS

Even as the tumultuous nineteenth century surrendered its final years to the record of history, Albert and Flora Lewis of Belfast, Ireland, found that they were about to have another child. When on November 29, 1898, Flora gave birth to their second son in three years, the new arrival was named Clive Staples Lewis—a name that Lewis would grow to reject almost as soon as he began to speak. A story is told that even as a toddler, Clive gave himself the nickname "Jack," and he was known as Jack by his family and friends forever thereafter.

In his book *Surprised by Joy* C.S. Lewis describes his father as a passionate, volatile Welshman whose emotions rose and fell rather wildly with the tides of his fortunes. Albert Lewis was a solicitor—an official in the courts of law—and a natural orator and storyteller who relished his hours of narrating and gesticulating among family and friends. If he had chosen to pursue such a course, he might have been a good politician. Albert was a high churchman, which at that time denoted a rather liturgical and non-metaphysical religiosity. When Flora died of cancer in 1908, the grief-stricken Albert withdrew from the boys, and his relationship with his sons appears never to have recovered from the schism. C.S. Lewis speculates that these events imprinted in his own mind a lifelong distrust of emotion.

For the first ten years of his life Jack Lewis enjoyed the strong, loving guidance of his mother. Flora Lewis was in some ways the opposite of her husband. For example, while Albert wrestled with wild emotions, Flora remained a steady, pleasant force in the boys' lives while she lived. Having graduated with a degree in mathematics from Queen's College, Flora gave the boys their beginning instruction in Latin and French. She was not, however, an overtly religious woman.

Both of Lewis's parents were very intelligent and well-read, though neither showed any interest in fantasy or Romanticism in literature. On this subject Lewis writes:

> What neither he nor my mother had the least taste for was that kind of literature to which my allegiance was given the moment I could choose books for myself. Neither had ever listened for the horns of elfland. There was no copy of either Keats or Shelley in the house, and the copy of Coleridge was never (to my knowledge) opened. If I am a romantic my parents bear no responsibility for it.[1]

Of course we learn later that C.S. Lewis would become not only a very important contributor to the Romantic stream of thought, but also a major force in the literature of fantasy.

A third great influence in Jack Lewis's early life was his elder brother Warnie. Though Warnie was three years his senior, Jack knew his brother as his closest companion and friend. When their mother died and their father withdrew from them, the boys pulled together and formed a bond that would last a lifetime. They lived together for most of their lives, and it was Warnie who sat at Jack's bedside when he died sixty-five years later.

Even before little Jack could read or write, both of the boys spent their time creating imaginary worlds. Jack's world was animal land; Warnie's was a fictional place he called India. Both boys made elaborate drawings of their characters and environments, and both developed complete histories and geographies of their lands. C.S. Lewis reports that between the ages of six and eight he lived almost entirely in his imagination.

Some of the readings that delighted young Jack were Swift's *Gulliver's Travels*, E. Nesbit's fantasy trilogy, and the Beatrix Potter books. It was in the latter that Lewis felt his first delight in beauty, the beginnings of an experience that he would later come to call "Joy." Lewis writes with regard to this Joy:

> . . . an unsatisfied desire which is itself more desirable than any other satisfaction. I call it Joy, which is here a technical term and must be sharply distinguished both from Happiness and from Pleasure. Joy (in my sense) has indeed one characteristic, and one only, in common with them; the fact that anyone who has experienced it will want it again.[2]

This longing for longing becomes a C.S. Lewis trademark, so to speak, as this Joy becomes the essential concept in his development toward conversion to Christianity later in his life.

But Lewis's journey toward Joy was soon interrupted by the traumatic death of his mother—an event that seemed to initiate a period of brutal and unhappy experiences during his adolescent years. The first source of pain was the behavior of his father Albert. Lewis explains:

> If I may trust my own experience, the sight of adult misery and adult terror has an effect on children which is merely paralyzing and alienating. . . . His nerves had never been of the steadiest and his emotions had always been uncontrolled. Under the pressure of anxiety his temper became incalculable; he spoke wildly and acted unjustly. Thus by a peculiar cruelty of fate, during those months the unfortunate man, had he but known it, was really losing his sons as well as his wife.[3]

Lewis would later describe himself and his brother during this period as ". . . two frightened urchins huddled for warmth in a bleak world."[4]

His schooling was also troublesome. Lewis's descriptions of his experiences in school comprise an almost unrelenting series of unpleasantries, including the harsh cruelties of the schoolmasters, the unchecked bullying by the older pupils, and the unproductive pedagogy found in most of his early schools. Echoes of these unhappy times appear repeatedly in Lewis's fiction, particularly in the Chronicles of Narnia.

By the time young Jack began his teenage years, he had already come to the conclusion that he did not like the world in which he lived. In *Surprised by Joy* he writes: ". . . but I had very definitely formed the opinion that the universe was, in the main, a rather regrettable institution."[5]

As he moved into the upper classes at a school he calls Chartres, Jack came to drop whatever remnants of Christian faith he may have held and instead poured his energies into becoming a showy sophisticate. He recalls:

Up till now I had committed nearly every other sin and folly within my power, but I had not yet been flashy.[6]

Under the influence of an older boy, Lewis began to dress in the most faddish ways and to act with the swaggering distinction of those in the know. "I began to labor very hard," he writes, "to make myself into a fop, a cad, and a snob."[7]

And yet, despite all of this ingrained pessimism and shallow folly Lewis again experienced something unexpected and extraordinary—a recurrence of ". . . the stab, the pang, the inconsolable longing."[8] Though in his school days his journey toward Joy had been abandoned and forgotten, finally through his reading, his old desire was suddenly reawakened.

The vehicle of Lewis's personal renaissance was the discovery of Wagner and an illustrated volume of *Seigfried and the Twilight of the Gods*. Lewis himself explains the incident:

Pure "Northernness" engulfed me: a vision of huge, clear spaces hanging above the Atlantic in the endless twilight of

Northern summer, remoteness, severity . . . and almost at the same moment I knew that I had met this before, long, long ago. . . . And with that plunge back into my own past there arose at once, almost like heartbreak, the memory of Joy itself. . . .[9]

And so "Northernness" became yet another term Lewis used in his story to convey that unendurable sense of desire and loss that would come to dominate his life.

In his preface to the third edition of *The Pilgrim's Regress*, Lewis explains the general structure of his allegory by reference to the sequence of his own intellectual development over the years. He writes:

On the intellectual side my own progress had been from "popular realism" to Philosophical Idealism; from Idealism to Pantheism; from Pantheism to Theism; and from Theism to Christianity.[10]

What we have seen so far in Lewis's life story is the "popular realism" he inherited from his parents and then honed to an obnoxious conformity during his school days. On the other hand, we have seen at least the seeds of philosophical idealism in the imaginary worlds of Jack and Warnie, followed eventually by a full immersion in the idealism and pantheism of Wagner and "the twilight of the gods."

As the war in Europe began to heat up, Warnie Lewis was called into military service. Meanwhile, the younger Jack was sent to Bookham to study under an extraordinary teacher named Mr. Kirkpatrick—also affectionately called "Kirk" or "the Great Knock." It was from this venerable old pedagogue that Lewis learned his logical clarity, and it was under Kirkpatrick's tutelage that Jack began his first serious studies of the Greek and Latin classics. As his teacher was an anthropological atheist, the young Lewis came to lean in that direction during this period of his life as well.

Even so, Lewis was not unaware of the opposite poles doing

battle in his mind all along. He had already tasted too much of "the twilight of the gods" and the literary Romantics to throw his mind and soul in wholeheartedly with the materialist skeptics. In retrospect he would recall:

> Such, then, was my position: to care for almost nothing but the gods and heroes, the garden of the Hesperides, Launcelot and the Grail, and to believe in nothing but atoms and evolution and military service. At times the strain was severe. . . .[11]

But then the young Lewis discovered the supernaturalism of William Butler Yeats. What was so stunning to Lewis at the time was that Yeats actually believed in the magic that he wrote about. Here was an otherwise-rational poet, a non-Christian, ". . . who believed in a world behind, or around, the material world."[12] And again Lewis found himself being drawn beyond his latent idealism and into a kind of pantheism.

The next important step that Lewis reports in his intellectual development was his accidental introduction to the writings of George MacDonald. Without his understanding of the change that was being wrought even as he read MacDonald's *Phantastes*, Lewis was being drawn through his vague pantheism toward a clearly defined theism. Lewis remembers:

> It is as if I were carried sleeping across the frontier, or as if I had died in the old country and could never remember how I came alive in the new. For in one sense the new country was exactly like the old. I met there all that had already charmed me in Malory, Spenser, Morris and Yeats. But in another sense all was changed. I did not yet know (and I was very long in learning) the name of the new quality, the bright shadow, that rested on the travels of Anodos. I do now. It was Holiness.[13]

Later Lewis adds, "That night my imagination was, in a certain sense, baptized; the rest of me, not unnaturally, took longer."[14] The seed was at least planted, though it would still be some time before Lewis's pantheism would grow into theism.

In the winter of 1916 Lewis took his scholarship exams at Oxford University, and by Christmas he had learned of his acceptance. However, after only one term at University College, he enlisted in the armed forces. Arriving at the front lines in France on his birthday in 1917, Lewis was wounded five months later. While convalescing in a military hospital, he happened to pick up a little book of essays by G.K. Chesterton—of whom he had never heard before—and the result was something totally unexpected. Lewis recalls:

> In reading Chesterton, as in reading MacDonald, I did not know what I was letting myself in for. A young man who wishes to remain a sound Atheist cannot be too careful of his reading. There are traps everywhere. . . . God is, if I may say it, very unscrupulous.[15]

It was during this time also that Lewis discovered the vitalist Bergson and from thence ". . . learned to relish energy, fertility, and urgency; the resource, the triumphs, and even the insolence, of things that grow."[16]

Before the war, one of Jack's best friends had been Paddy Moore. Knowing that they would both see military service, and knowing that one or both of them might not survive the war, Jack promised to take care of Paddy's mother in the event that Paddy did not return. When Paddy was indeed killed in the war, Lewis returned home and kept his promise by moving in as Mrs. Moore's "adopted son" and caretaker. This promise and responsibility Lewis kept faithfully until Mrs. Moore's death some thirty years later.

In the year 1919 Lewis finally returned to resume his undergraduate studies at Oxford. This was a time of interregnum with regard to Lewis's growth toward Christianity. It was a time in which many forces influenced him to retreat from the very "romantic longings and unhealthy speculations"[17] that had once been his greatest concern. For a time he entered once again into the mainstream of skepticism that dominated university life.

On the other hand, during that same year he published his first book of poetry, *Spirits in Bondage*, under the pseudonym Clive Hamilton. And among his new friends were remarkable men such as J.R.R. Tolkien, who was a Roman Catholic and who dabbled in romantic fantasies. There was also Owen Barfield, whose interminable arguments with Lewis brought the latter to understand a whole new perspective on history. Under Barfield's influence, Lewis came to reject the widely practiced "chronological snobbery" that so dominated the dogmas of the intelligentsia. Lewis defined this snobbery as:

> . . . the uncritical acceptance of the intellectual climate common to our own age and the assumption that whatever has gone out of date is on that account discredited. You must find why it went out of date. Was it ever refuted (and if so by whom, where, and how conclusively) or did it merely die away as fashions do? If the latter, this tells us nothing about its truth or falsehood.[18]

This line of questioning would come to take center stage in much of Lewis's later scholarly works—particularly in *English Literature in the Sixteenth Century—Excluding Drama*. Perhaps more importantly, this method would become a cornerstone in Lewis's basic apologetic works as these questions would be applied to the popular rejection of Christian doctrine in the nineteenth and twentieth centuries.

Another consequence of Lewis's friendship with Barfield, Tolkien, and others was that he came to believe in the existence of "the Absolute." As Lewis himself tells it:

> And so the great Angler played His fish and I never dreamed that the hook was in my tongue. But two great advances had been made. Bergson had showed me necessary existence; and

from Idealism I had come one step nearer to understanding the words, "We give thanks to thee for thy great glory."[19]

And suddenly Lewis found himself again standing on the threshold of theism.

At this point in his story, Lewis found yet another dear friend, Nevill Coghill, whom Lewis discovered to be clearly the most intelligent man in the class and yet a "thorough-going supernaturalist," and even a Christian! Like Barfield, Coghill managed to turn Lewis's historical prejudices on their heads. For the first time Lewis was forced to consider seriously the possibility that it was our ancestors who were civilized, and we in fact are barbaric.

Near the end of his years as an Oxford student, Lewis served as a substitute instructor of philosophy at University College at Oxford. While teaching philosophy Lewis began to say "God" for the Absolute, but he still hastened to add that by this he meant a "philosophical God" rather than the God of Christianity. But again he came up against G.K. Chesterton. Having read *The Everlasting Man*, Lewis saw for the first time the whole Christian outline of history, and he found that he had to admit that it all made sense to him. This new conception of God in actual history served to force Lewis's hand. He recalls:

> I was to be allowed to play at philosophy no longer. It might, as I say, still be true that my "spirit" differed in some way from "the God of popular religion." My Adversary waived the point. It sank into utter unimportance. He would not argue about it. He only said, "I am the Lord"; "I am that I am"; "I am."[20]

Over the next several years Lewis would struggle with the fact of God, trying his best to avoid the unwelcome idea that God might be who the Christians said He is.

Meanwhile, Lewis's reputation as a first-rate scholar was growing steadily as his essays continued to win awards at the university and he earned his way into the highest class at University College. Though his overt interests tended toward philosophy, it was during this period that Lewis began working on a long, mythological, narrative poem called *Dymer*, which he would publish some years later under his favorite pseudonym, Clive Hamilton.

Finally in 1925 Lewis was accepted as a Fellow in English at Magdalen College in Oxford. There he began a long and fruitful career as a scholar in medieval and renaissance English literature; and there he would come to write his remarkable, scholarly masterpiece *The Allegory of Love*, his science fiction trilogy, his popular *Screwtape* fantasy, most of his Narnia stories, his basic apologetics, and other important Christian writings.

Readers who are familiar with modern western history will recall the famous "Lost Generation" of artists, writers, and intellectuals who emerged in Europe and America after World War I. Famous names in this movement include the Englishmen D.H. Lawrence and Aldous Huxley, the Irishman James Joyce, the German Thomas Mann, the Frenchmen Marcel Proust and Andre Gide, and the Americans Ernest Hemingway and Eugene O'Neill. Disillusioned with the great war and its dubious results, these writers and many others wondered if civilization were merely a thin veneer to hide man's basic savagery. In 1922 T.S. Eliot published his famous poem *The Waste Land*, which included these lines:

> *But red sullen faces sneer and snarl*
> *From doors of mudcracked houses.*

What interests us especially here is how C.S. Lewis remained largely immune to the rather hopeless and cynical views of the "Lost Generation." And this apparent immunity would bear important implications for Lewis's career and scholarship. Lewis had dreamed of being a poet, and his *Spirits in Bondage* and his later *Dymer* were his inaugural efforts in that direction. However, Lewis's poetry was that of a different era—a passing era of narrative poetry with regular meter and rhyme. In the early twentieth century the fashion in poetry had shifted radically, and the ascendant stars were men such as Ezra Pound and T.S. Eliot.

To understand the radical nature of the change that had taken place in poetry, we need only to compare form in specimens of poetry by C.S. Lewis and T.S. Eliot. First consider these lines from "The Satyr" in Lewis's *Spirits in Bondage*:

> *When the flowery hands of spring*
> *Forth their woodland riches fling,*
> > *Through the meadow, through the valleys*
> *Goes the satyr carolling.*

Now compare the form and language in the following lines from T.S. Eliot's *The Waste Land*:

> *"What is that noise?"*
> *The wind under the door.*
> *"What is that noise now? What is the wind*
> > *doing?"*
> > *Nothing again nothing.*
> *"Do*
> > *You know nothing? Do you see nothing?*
> > *Do you remember*
> > *Nothing?"*

Furthermore, there was a lot more going on in the 1920s besides disillusionment with western civilization. Romanticism itself was again under attack on two formidable fronts—from "above" and from "below," as Lewis put the matter. From above the heart, the idea of spirits and "immortal longings" was besieged by a surge of humanist and materialist sentiments, particularly in America. From below the belt, there came attacks from Sigmund Freud and D.H. Lawrence, who sought to reduce all human passions to primal sexual urges. Meanwhile, as we have seen, C.S. Lewis continued undaunted on his private journey through Romanticism toward Christianity.

In 1929 Lewis was still struggling with God, but God was winning the battle. Lewis relates:

> In the Trinity Term of 1929 I gave in, and admitted that God was God, and knelt and prayed: perhaps, that night, the most dejected and reluctant convert in all England.[21]

But even still, Lewis makes it clear that this conversion was to theism, not to Christianity. The final leg of his journey would take about two more years and—perhaps characteristically for Lewis— would follow the path of the intellect rather than of the emotions.

Ever since reading Chesterton's *The Everlasting Man*, Lewis had been haunted by the idea that the pagan religions might have been the incomplete and often inaccurate anticipations or premonitions of the true religion. In Lewis's words, the question became, "Where has religion reached its true maturity?"[22] As the ancient myths had anticipated many of the Bible's stories, the vague idea of a "dying god" had anticipated the life and death of the Christ. But what Lewis found unique to Christianity was ". . . the summing up and actuality of them all"[23] in the actual, historical person of Jesus of Nazareth.

This final intellectual step brought Lewis to the precipice of faith. And then one day in 1931 Lewis was on his way to visit the Whipsnade Zoo. He tells what happened:

> I know very well when, but hardly how, the final step was taken. I was driven to Whipsnade one sunny morning. When we set out I did not believe that Jesus Christ is the Son of God, and when we reached the zoo I did.[24]

And so by this confession of faith in Jesus Christ, Lewis completed the journey that he would retrace in allegorical form two years later in *The Pilgrim's Regress*.

Before we proceed into Lewis's subsequent life as a Christian believer, we should mention The Kilns. Shortly before his conversion

Jack, Warnie, and Mrs. Moore purchased a house near the woods by Oxford. This house was a typical English cottage, but it was unusual in that two brick kilns stood in the yard; thus, The Kilns became the nickname for their new home. Both C.S. Lewis and Mrs. Moore would live at The Kilns until their deaths, but after Jack's death Warnie would find other quarters.

At The Kilns developed an informal coterie of intellectual friends who came to be known as the Inklings. Meeting every week over a period of roughly fifteen years, this group of men shared ideas, read aloud the latest work on their various projects, and generally gave each other advice and encouragement. It was among the Inklings that J.R.R. Tolkien hammered out much of his famous *Lord of the Rings* trilogy. Other regular Inklings were Owen Barfield, Hugo Dyson, Nevill Coghill, Adam Fox, Robert Havard, and later, Charles Williams. The Inklings developed into a very close group that concerned itself not only with the work of its members, but with university politics as well.

The publication of Lewis's *The Pilgrim's Regress* in 1933 managed to raise a few eyebrows among the Oxford dons, but the book drew relatively little attention on the whole. When three years later Lewis produced *The Allegory of Love*, however, the academic world sat up and took notice. Here at last was a piece of first-rate scholarship that seemed to keep the promise of Lewis's genius as an undergraduate student. With the publication of this book Lewis established himself as a widely respected scholar of medieval and renaissance English literature.

In *The Allegory of Love* one found the fruit of Lewis's voracious reading and his keen insight into the implications of what he read. But even more startling was the quality of his exposition. For here was a scholar who paid every proper attention to thoroughness, accuracy, and detail, and yet whose text carried the style of a Romantic story. In this, his first great scholarly work, Lewis set the standard for the clear, understandable, and entertaining prose that would grace his writings for the rest of his life.

During this same period of time, Lewis became one of the most popular lecturers at Oxford University, and the lecture halls were packed with students eager to hear his rich and witty presentations. His series of lectures on medieval and Renaissance literature were eventually collected and published under the title *The Discarded Image*, a book that still stands as perhaps the most enjoyable of Lewis's scholarly works. In this book we find some of his best explications of the assumptions and perspectives of the writers in centuries past. Here we also find some of Lewis's most basic arguments against the misconceptions and prejudices in the New Enlightenment rendition of European history.

If Lewis's conservative and humanistic colleagues had hoped that *The Allegory of Love* signaled the end of Lewis's embarrassing forays into Romantic fantasy and Christian apologetics, they were soon to become disappointed. For in 1938 he published *Out of the Silent Planet*—the first installment of his space trilogy—followed by two other Christian works, *The Problem of Pain* in 1940 and *The Screwtape Letters* in 1942. Neither of the first two were particularly well-received, even among Lewis's friends. However, *The Screwtape Letters* became a huge success among the public, much to the chagrin of the Oxford dons. By academic standards it had been bad enough that Lewis had publicly dabbled in science fiction, and even more unfortunately in Christian apologetics. But to have written a religious fantasy—about Satan, of all things—of which the public so enthusiastically approved would be considered as something akin to pandering to the lowest tastes in return for popularity.

Meanwhile, there was another world war going on. Though C.S. Lewis did not serve in the military during the Second World War, he was very much involved in the war support activities on the Oxford campus. For a time children were housed at The Kilns as protection against the German bombings of London. This arrangement inspired part of the plot of Lewis's story *The Lion, the Witch and the Wardrobe* almost a decade later. But the most important of Lewis's activities during the war may have been his series of talks on basic Christian doctrine given to the troops. In these Lewis the scholar did a remarkable job of distilling and simplifying rather complicated ideas so that even the uneducated men could understand. In 1941 the British Broadcasting Corporation (BBC) asked Lewis to give these talks on the radio, and these broadcast talks were published in book form the next year. There followed two more sets of radio talks, published as *Christian Behaviour* and *Beyond Personality*. Ten years later these wartime lectures would be collected and published under the title *Mere Christianity*.

Despite the war, Lewis thrived at Oxford, lecturing and producing an impressive number of books. During this time he wrote his *Preface to Paradise Lost*, an excellent introduction to Milton's great poem and a very good starting point for the reader interested in Lewis's scholarly books. In two years he finished his space trilogy with *Perelandra* and *That Hideous Strength*, and in 1943 he published one of the century's most important books of Christian apologetics, *The Abolition of Man*. Finally, as World War II came to a close, Lewis wrote the delightful fantasy *The Great Divorce* and his apologetic *Miracles*.

Although this great outpouring of creative and religious work endeared C.S. Lewis to the reading public and to Christians in particular, the general reaction of the Oxford campus was far from endearment. The widespread academic prejudices against popular and Christian works were only part of the story. There were political maneuvers in which the Inklings pulled together and had their way at the expense of the established Oxford dons. There was Jack Lewis's rather aggressive and boisterous behavior in the local pubs. And there was the Socratic Club.

The Socratic Club was founded in 1941 by a group of Christians including C.S. Lewis. Its purpose was to establish a forum for orderly and rational debate between intellectual opponents—especially atheists versus Christians. Lewis served as the club's first president and of course one of its most active combatants on the Christian side. Many of Lewis's best preserved speeches originated in the debates of the Socratic Club. But the complaint was that Lewis was often a bully—that he dealt so harshly and thoroughly with his opponents that a considerable amount of resentment developed.

When in 1948 an Oxford philosopher named Elizabeth Anscombe trounced the undefeated C.S. Lewis in a debate, it is said that more than a few onlookers felt that Lewis had it coming to him.

Mid-century brought many changes into Lewis's life. By then his long-time friendship with J.R.R. Tolkien had definitely cooled. Resentments among the Inklings had grown to such proportions that they had quietly disbanded by 1949. Then in 1951 Mrs. Moore died, ending years of very unpleasant scenes as her health and congeniality had deteriorated. And all the while, Warnie struggled with a debilitating problem of alcoholism.

Ever since *The Screwtape Letters* had rendered C.S. Lewis a famous Christian in the public's eye, he had received a steady flow of letters from around the world. Most of these letters were from people seeking his advice or asking questions about his writings. The remarkable thing in this situation is that Lewis made it a point to write a reply to every letter he received. Over time he developed a regular correspondence with an amazing number of people, particularly in England and the United States.

One such correspondent was an American woman named Joy Gresham, the wife of a novelist and an aspiring author herself. Joy began writing to Lewis in 1950. Two years later—after a painful divorce from her husband—she moved to England. The story of the romance that developed between Joy (Gresham) Davidman and C.S. Lewis is dramatized in the stage play called *Shadowlands* and has been subsequently made into two motion pictures. Of these two movies, the earlier BBC version is by far the best, as it does not completely obliterate Lewis's Christian beliefs as the newer version does.

To recount the story briefly, during the five years following the death of Mrs. Moore, C.S. Lewis—though in his early fifties—experienced the greatest romance of his life with Joy Davidman. It was indeed a late romance, and it was a whirlwind romance that ended as abruptly as it had begun. For in 1956 Joy was diagnosed as having terminal cancer. Aware then that he loved her very deeply, Lewis married Joy in actuality shortly before she died in that same year. There followed for Lewis a period of grief, bitterness, and questioning of God, some of which came to be published years later in *A Grief Observed*.

But during those years with Joy, Lewis produced a generous stream of writing, including the seven books of the Chronicles of Narnia as well as another substantial scholarly work, *English Literature in the Sixteenth Century—Excluding Drama*. With the release of the Narnia stories, Lewis's fame as a writer of fantasy stories surged as the world's children joined the ranks of his many admirers. But of course there was a price to be paid as well.

His popularity among his colleagues on the Oxford campus had reached an all-time low—partly due to his rough personality, partly due no doubt to jealousy, and partly due to the nature of much of his written work. The great penalty at a university is non-promotion. By then Lewis had served for nearly forty years as one of the university's most popular lecturers and as a recognized foremost authority on the older English literature; yet he had never been granted the rank of Professor. By the mid-fifties Lewis understood that he would likely never be granted his deserved promotion.

Consequently, when in 1954 the nearby rival Cambridge University offered Lewis a more prestigious position, he sadly left his alma mater forever. Not only did Cambridge offer Lewis a promotion, but they created a new Chair with Lewis's qualifications written into its description. They called it the Chair of Medieval and Renaissance English Literature, and the significance of that title was discussed by C.S. Lewis in his inaugural address, "De Descriptione Temporum" (see *They Asked for a Paper*).

Lewis's new college at Cambridge University was called Magdalene College. At Oxford he had served at Magdalen College. At Cambridge he wrote his autobiographical *Surprised by Joy*, and he finished the last two of his Chronicles of Narnia. In 1956 he also finished the remarkable *Till We Have Faces*, a retelling of the Psyche and Eros (Cupid) myth; this book was considered by many to be Lewis's literary masterpiece.

After Joy's death, Lewis's publications included some collections of essays, *A Grief Observed* as mentioned earlier, and his famous study of affection, friendship, erotic love, and charity, *The Four Loves*. The final publication before Lewis's death was a broad collection of essays called *They Asked for a Paper*.

Lewis's death came about after some years of prostate trouble, urinary infections, and problems with a weak heart. He and Warnie were still living at The Kilns, but in June of 1963 C.S. Lewis had a heart attack and was taken to the hospital. It was believed that he would die, and he was given extreme unction. Unable to cope with what was happening, Warnie went on a drinking binge and was hospitalized himself. However, Jack recovered and was sent home under the care of a nurse. When Warnie came home, the brothers spent a few months together for the last time. Finally, on Friday, November 22, 1963—the same day that American President John F. Kennedy was assassinated in Texas—Warnie found his brother slumped in his chair and put him to bed. That evening C.S. Lewis died in his bedroom, reportedly calm and cheerful to the end.

4

THE CHRONICLES OF NARNIA

The series of seven books of Narnia stories for children is possibly C.S. Lewis's most famous body of writing. For a half-century now these delightful chronicles have been read and reread by millions of children and adults worldwide, and their impact in conveying basic Christian underpinnings to successive generations has been immeasurable. To read the Chronicles of Narnia is to follow a master storyteller into a different world where the stories of God and the created universe are played out in ways unique to those other times and places. It is to follow the author's fantasies in and out of Earth time, and thereby to gain wonderful new perspectives on the meaning of the Christian faith in universal terms.

Professor Lewis wrote these fantasies from 1950 to 1956, well after his reputation had been firmly established as a foremost scholar in medieval and Renaissance literature. At the publication of the Narnia stories there was considerable surprise—and some disapproval—that a serious scholar would engage in such a frivolous enterprise as writing stories for children, for the mores of higher education declare that one simply does not publish outside one's own academic field. Furthermore, a university scholar does not write children's stories nor science fiction—both of which C.S. Lewis loved and wrote prolifically. Consequently, Lewis soon enough found himself in the unenviable position of gaining popular fame for activities that many of his academic colleagues found laughable, if not offensive.

But I think it reflects well on Professor Lewis's character that he pursued the writing he loved nevertheless, fully aware that a great many of his colleagues condemned not only his chosen genres, but to an even greater extent the Christian doctrine embedded in his stories and fantasies. For even in Lewis's day the great universities had fallen under the spell of what historian Page Smith has called "academic fundamentalism,"[1] or the toleration of only a narrow, scientific materialist approach to everything from physics to literature. In our refracted view through Lewis's subsequent fame, it is easy to underestimate the degree of integrity and courage Lewis exercised in thus swimming against the academic stream.

It was important to C.S. Lewis that his readers understand that the Narnia stories were not meant as allegories. In allegories the characters and events stand for something other than what they are. For example, in John Bunyan's classic *The Pilgrim's Progress* the various characters and places can be understood to represent the various helps and pitfalls in living the Christian life. Many readers mistakenly approach the Chronicles of Narnia in the same frame of mind, attempting to decipher the exact theological or doctrinal referent for every character and situation in the stories.

But Lewis insisted that the Narnia stories are not meant as allegories. The obvious parallels are there, to be sure. Aslan, the great lion, throughout the stories clearly fulfills the role of Jesus in Christian doctrine, and the eschatology of the stories is markedly consistent with the biblical accounts. But Lewis did not want his readers spending their time decoding his stories and coming to such conclusions as, for example, that a given event indicates the author's belief in the doctrine of purgatory.

Instead, Lewis wanted his stories to be enjoyed as art and understood intuitively as children tend to understand stories. Rather than attempting to make an allegory for the Christian doctrine of Jesus and His church in the world, Lewis imagined how the story might have gone in another world and another time. Given the attributes of God and the nature of the creation, what are some of the stories that might have been true in worlds other than our own?

The author's denial of allegory is important for two reasons. For one, it frees Lewis and those who study Lewis from the task of defining and defending every detail of the Chronicles in view of specific Christian doctrines. For another, it frees the casual reader to enjoy the stories for what they say, without having to worry over hidden meanings that only a select few intellectual Lewis scholars can decipher. The Chronicles of Narnia were written for the pure enjoyment and intuitive understanding of children and those fortunate others who are capable of seeing the world through the eyes of a child.

Fans of Lewis's Chronicles of Narnia will be interested in Paul F. Ford's *Companion to Narnia*[2], a virtual encyclopedia of the people and places mentioned in the Narnia stories. As C.S. Lewis so often pointed out, good literature bears reading again and again, each time in a different way and on a different level. Ford's companion can be a handy reference during one's first reading of the Chronicles, but even more an essential tool for those readers who return for a deeper reading.

While some of the more recently published sets of the Chronicles of Narnia place the stories in an alternative order[3], we will discuss the seven stories in the traditional order in which they appeared in print during Lewis's lifetime. Following the sequence as each was published, the stories are:

1. *The Lion, the Witch and the Wardrobe* (1950)
2. *Prince Caspian* (1951)
3. *The Voyage of the "Dawn Treader"* (1952)
4. *The Silver Chair* (1953)
5. *The Horse and His Boy* (1954)
6. *The Magician's Nephew* (1955)
7. *The Last Battle* (1956)

Here we will look at each story in its turn.

The Lion, the Witch and the Wardrobe

The major setting for this story is Narnia during the time when the former Queen Jadis of Charn has managed to establish herself as the malevolent Queen of Narnia. In establishing her reign of terror, she has cast a spell over the land, wherein it is "always winter and never Christmas."[4] Both for her icy complexion and her cruel ways, she is widely known among her subjects as the White Witch.

The protagonists of this story are the four Pevensie children—Peter, Susan, Edmund, and Lucy—who are sent to stay in a large country house to escape the bombing of London during World War II and who soon discover that an old wardrobe is in fact a doorway into another world. The first to discover Narnia is Lucy, who encounters and befriends the faun Tumnus during her first visit. Later all four of the siblings stumble into Narnia, where the great adventures of this story unfold.

The Lion, the Witch and the Wardrobe is rich in imagery, which C.S. Lewis uses to contrast the death-producing effects of the White Witch with the life-producing effects of the lion Aslan. There is the stark, cold winter already mentioned, as contrasted with the warm spring that arrives when Aslan comes to Narnia. There are the stone statues in the Witch's courtyard—living beings whom she has turned to stone. Later Aslan breathes into them the breath of life. In general, there is the Witch's cruelty and Aslan's kindness.

Much of the appeal in C.S. Lewis's stories comes from his insights into the human heart. The character Edmund illustrates this point well. In his disgruntled state he falls easy prey to the Witch's false offers of prestige and power. He falls as well into the age-old trap of letting his appetites skew his judgement.

> But he still wanted to taste that Turkish Delight again more than he wanted anything else.
>
> "Who told you that stuff about the White Witch?" he asked.
>
> "Mr. Tumnus, the Faun," said Lucy.

"You can't always believe what Fauns say," said Edmund, trying to sound as if he knew far more about them than Lucy.[5]

And so in Edmund we see ourselves, too often letting our desires and passions determine what we consider rational action.

Another strong thematic element in *The Lion, the Witch and the Wardrobe* is the role of prophecy. C.S. Lewis masterfully weaves the idea of prophecy and its fulfillment into the tapestry of his story in such a way that the reader hardly notices the instruction that is taking place. Early in the story there are numerous references to the significance of the children being four in number, two boys and two girls. Eventually it is Mr. Beaver who explains the significance:

> "Because of another prophecy," said Mr. Beaver. "Down at Cair Paravel—that's the castle on the sea coast down at the mouth of this river which ought to be the capital of this whole country if all was as it should be—down at Cair Paravel there are four thrones and it's a saying in Narnia time out of mind that when two Sons of Adam and two Daughters of Eve sit on those four thrones, then it will be the end not only of the White Witch's reign but of her life, and that is why we had to be so cautious as we came along, for if she knew about you four, your lives wouldn't be worth a shake of my whiskers!"[6]

Consequently, the story's suspense and resolution—which I will not here reveal—depends greatly upon whether or not the old prophecies are indeed true. In this tale C.S. Lewis is clearly illustrating the kind of role that prophecy plays in the Christian Bible.

I cannot resist mentioning as well the matters of logical thinking and materialist philosophy. These are issues that C.S. Lewis explores more completely in the later Chronicle *The Silver Chair*, but here in *The Lion, the Witch and the Wardrobe* the old professor raises the issue several times, asking himself, "Why don't they teach logic at these schools?"[7] What I find most interesting is that the context of these professorial complaints is the children's appeal to what would widely be considered rational-empirical methods of determining truth. Here the professor's comment amounts to a not-so-subtle turning of the tables on strict materialist thinking.

In the story Peter and Susan have appealed to the professor because they fear that Lucy is losing her mind. Their concern is based upon Lucy's claim that she and Edmund have visited another world, while Edmund denies and ridicules the very idea. Witness the following conversation:

> Then Susan pulled herself together and said, "But Edmund said they had only been pretending."
>
> "That is a point," said the Professor, "which certainly deserves consideration; very careful consideration. For instance—if you will excuse me for asking the question—does your experience lead you to regard your brother or your sister as the more reliable? I mean, which is the more truthful?"
>
> "That's just the funny thing about it, Sir," said Peter. "Up till now, I'd have said Lucy every time."
>
> "And what do you think, my dear?" said the Professor, turning to Susan.
>
> "Well," said Susan, "in general, I'd say the same as Peter, but this couldn't be true—all this about the wood and the Faun."
>
> "That is more than I know," said the Professor, "and a charge of lying against someone whom you have always found truthful is a very serious thing; a very serious thing indeed. . . ."
>
> "But do you really mean, Sir," said Peter, "that there could be other worlds—all over the place, just round the corner—like that?"
>
> "Nothing is more probable," said the Professor, taking off his spectacles and beginning to polish them, while he muttered to himself, "I wonder what they do teach them at these schools."[8]

In those few words—"That is more than I know . . ."—Lewis draws his battle line with materialist philosophy. The professor is pointing out that the claim that alternate, non-empirical realities are "impossible" is ultimately an unsupportable claim. Logically speaking, it is more than we can know. The professor's subsequent comment, "Nothing is more probable," is Lewis's reminder that some of the most widely accepted notions about being and reality are arguably less probable than some of the most widely rejected notions. In other words, the materialist point of view is affirmed by neither logic nor probability.

A final thematic issue to be mentioned here is Lewis's ideas on the "Deep Magic" and the "Deeper Magic" with regard to Aslan's sacrifice at the Stone Table. Again without attempting to pin the author down to precise allegorical identifications, we can recognize that Lewis is giving one theory of atonement as found in Christian doctrine. In this case we see the obvious parallel between the Stone Table and the whole configuration of the old covenant, the Law, and the wages of sin as death; and then we see the "Deeper Magic":

> "It means," said Aslan, "that though the Witch knew the Deep Magic, there is a magic deeper still which she did not know. Her knowledge goes back only to the dawn of Time. But if she could have looked a little further back, into the stillness and the darkness before Time dawned, she would have read there a different incantation. She would have known that when a willing victim who had committed no treachery was killed in a traitor's stead, the Table would crack and Death itself would start working backwards."[9]

And so again C.S. Lewis has taken his readers to another time and place to explore the basic ontological and doctrinal questions. How might the meaning of Jesus' death and resurrection have been played out in this setting? Though the episode is not intended as a direct metaphor, it can certainly serve as a help in understanding the complicated issue of atonement.

There are many interesting and gratifying things to look for in reading *The Lion, the Witch and the Wardrobe*. Look for a fine adventure story, where children can be heroes. Notice the life-death motif as imbedded in the imagery. Look for Lewis's insights into humanity—on temptation, on perception, on ego, on rationalizing, and on the inner spirit. Watch for the role of prophecy in the story.

The more philosophically inclined will enjoy Lewis's treatment of materialism, empiricism, skepticism, and rationalism included in the old professor's comments. There are also many fascinating references to the internal effects of Aslan—and even the mere mention of Aslan's name—on the various characters. And finally, look for that wonderful C.S. Lewis sense of humor, particularly in his treatment of the animal characters and the giant near the end of the story.

Prince Caspian

When we last saw Narnia, the country was still under the benevolent rule of King Peter, King Edmund, Queen Susan, and Queen Lucy. But then, as we know from the final events of *The Lion, the Witch and the Wardrobe*, the four children were returned through the wardrobe to their former life in England. The story *Prince Caspian* begins with these same children waiting in an English train station on their way back to school, when they are suddenly pulled back to Narnia once again.

The children discover in Narnia that hundreds of years have passed since their reign, and the country has long since fallen into the hands of invading Telmarines. The children soon learn that the ruling King Miraz is a vain and wicked man who has murdered his brother and usurped the throne. As long as Miraz was childless, he was content to raise his brother's son Caspian to succeed him on the throne. But when a son was born to Miraz, he sought to kill the boy Caspian to ensure his son's succession.

When the four Pevensie children reenter Narnia, they find that Caspian has managed to escape into the woods and has begun to raise a ragtag army of talking beasts. They soon discover as well that

Miraz has mustered a formidable army and has entered the forest to destroy Caspian and his band of rebels. The suspense through much of the story concerns, first, whether the Pevensie children will reach Caspian in time, and, second, what exactly they will be able to do if they do reach him.

One of the several fascinating themes in *Prince Caspian* is that of materialist skepticism versus mystical religion. When King Miraz first learns that Caspian's nurse has told the boy about Aslan and the history of Narnia, the king is outraged:

> "That's all nonsense, for babies," said the king sternly. "Only fit for babies, do you hear? You're getting too old for that sort of stuff. At your age you ought to be thinking of battles and adventures, not fairy tales."[10]

Here is the voice of materialism scoffing at everything beyond its pale, calling anything spiritual or non-empirical "nonsense" and "fairy tales."

What is especially effective in *Prince Caspian* is the way Lewis illustrates the deadening pall that materialist thinking casts over the entire country. The effects spread like cancer, rendering people unable to see what they could see before and unable to believe what they had believed before. These effects are portrayed on several levels. There is the widespread skepticism reflected in the comments of even Narnia's talking beasts. As Trumpkin the red dwarf says:

> . . . I think the Horn—and that bit of broken stone over there—and your great King Peter—and your Lion Aslan— are all eggs in moonshine. . . . There's no good raising hopes of magical help which (as I think) are sure to be disappointed.[11]

The effects of the materialist view spread even into the nature of things themselves. Fewer of the Narnian beasts are now talking beasts. The trees, the Dryads and Hamadryads, have become sense-less vegetation. And the people have become as beasts, believing in nothing greater than themselves and seeking nothing more than their own advantage.

At one point in the story Lucy is moved by the thought of such regression to the level of beasts:

> "Such a horrible idea has come into my head, Su."
>
> "What's that?"
>
> "Wouldn't it be dreadful if some day in our own world, at home, men started going wild inside, like the animals here, and still looked like men, so that you'd never know which were which?"[12]

Indeed, written in the year 1951, Lucy's speculation now seems prophetic, and C.S. Lewis is deliberately drawing a direct link between a widespread materialist skepticism and the lowering of humanity to the level of beasts. This idea is developed more fully in the nonfiction setting of Lewis's *The Abolition of Man*.

Another important theme in *Prince Caspian* is that of providence, the power of Aslan, and human responsibility. Here Lewis raises some of the perennial human questions concerning God's interventions in history and the role of human efforts in that context. In this story C.S. Lewis illustrates two sides of the coin.

First there is providence, God's influence in the flow of events and the outcomes of history. Early in the story we find Peter, Susan, and Lucy recovering the gifts they had been given in *The Lion, the Witch and the Wardrobe*. But here an apparent problem arises:

> Susan's gift had been a bow and arrows and a horn. The bow was still there, and the ivory quiver, full of well-feathered arrows, but—"oh Susan," said Lucy. "Where's the horn?"
>
> "Oh, bother, bother, bother," said Susan after she had thought for a moment. "I remember now. I took it with me the last day of all, the day we went hunting the White Stag.

It must have got lost when we blundered back into that other place—England, I mean."

Edmund whistled. It was indeed a most shattering loss; for this was an enchanted horn and, whenever you blew it, help was certain to come to you, wherever you were.

"Just the sort of thing that might come in handy in a place like this," said Edmund.[13]

Later in the story we find old Cornelius surreptitiously handing an ancient object to the boy Caspian:

> He put in Caspian's hands something which he could hardly see but which he knew by the feel to be a horn.
>
> "That," said Doctor Cornelius, "is the greatest and most sacred treasure of Narnia. . . . It is the magic horn of Queen Susan herself which she left behind her when she vanished from Narnia at the end of the Golden Age. It is said that whoever blows it shall have strange help—no one can say how strange."[14]

Finally the children learn from Trumpkin the dwarf that it had been Caspian's desperate blast on Susan's horn that had suddenly pulled them from the English railway station back into Narnia. And so we discover after all that Susan's loss of her horn was all part of Aslan's plan to intervene in the flow of Narnian history even centuries after the horn was lost.

On the other hand, Aslan does not simply take on all of the children's problems and clear the way using his superior powers. There is a great struggle required even of those who choose to follow Aslan's lead. As the High King Peter explains the situation before the great battle:

> We don't know when he will act. In his time, no doubt, not ours. In the meantime he would like us to do what we can on our own.[15]

Here in a nutshell is C.S. Lewis's theology of human responsibility. God, Lewis says, can and does influence the flow of history, sometimes even in a dramatic way. Yet those who would follow God cannot sit on their hands and expect God to overpower the world on their behalf. On the contrary, God requires of us difficult decisions and decisive actions to the best of our gifts and abilities.

Prince Caspian is yet another story in which C.S. Lewis glories in animal interaction. Indeed, the army of the Narnian rebels consists of a menagerie of talking beasts, each kind specializing in its peculiar gift. We meet the reliable badger Trufflehunter, the talkative squirrel Patterwig, the valiant mouse Reepicheep, the violent dwarf Nikabrick, the Three Bulgy Bears, the Seven Brothers of Shuddering Wood, and a host of others. Again Lewis displays his mastery at weaving the many animal characteristics into the fabric of his story, and the result is a delightful time for the reader.

There is much to look for while reading *Prince Caspian*. There is, of course, the materialist pall versus the things of the spirit. There is providence and human action. But look as well for the role of joy, revelry, and celebration in Aslan's plans. Here and elsewhere we find that Lewis is no straitlaced ascetic, no teetotaler, nor an enemy of dance and bodily frolic in times of celebration. Witness his description of Aslan's procession near the end of the story:

> "You'll stay with us, sweetheart?" said Aslan.
>
> "Oh, may I? Thank you, thank you," said Gwendolen. Instantly she joined hands with two of the Maenads who whirled her round in a merry dance and helped her take off some of the unnecessary and uncomfortable clothes that she was wearing.
>
> Wherever they went in the little town of Beruna it was the same. Most of the people fled, a few joined them. When they left the town they were a larger and a merrier company.
>
> They swept on across the level fields on the north bank, or left bank, of the river. At every farm animals came out to join them. Sad old donkeys who had never known joy grew

suddenly young again; chained dogs broke their chains; horses kicked their carts to pieces and came trotting along with them—clop-clop—kicking up the mud and whinnying.[16]

Watch for Lewis's thoughts on faith and obedience as shown particularly in Lucy's interactions with Aslan and her elder siblings. Look for those ubiquitous C.S. Lewis ironies, especially in the marvelous scene where King Miraz' treacherous counselors goad him into combat against Peter. And finally, of course, look again for a great adventure story packed with suspense and meaning and humor.

The Voyage of the "Dawn Treader"

Before the adventure begins in *The Voyage of the "Dawn Treader,"* we are introduced to a most disagreeable child named Eustace Scrubb, who makes a habit of bullying and complaining and making other people miserable whenever he can. We discover as well that the two youngest Pevensie children, Edmund and Lucy, have been handed the unfortunate plight of having to spend the summer with their obnoxious cousin Eustace while their parents are away visiting America.

Upon his cousins' arrival, Eustace wastes no time before proving himself unpleasant. However, he soon finds himself in for a very great surprise. A picture of a Narnian ship on the wall of Lucy's bedroom turns out to be enchanted, and it suddenly draws all three children into its seas, where they are rescued by King Caspian and the crew of the *Dawn Treader*. And thus the next Narnian adventure begins.

The children learn that Caspian and his men have set sail toward the east, where they hope to explore the Lone Islands and beyond. The setting is three Narnian years after the children last visited, and the purpose of the voyage is to discover what has happened to the seven Narnian lords whom the usurper Miraz had banished into the eastern seas. But we soon find that there is at least one on board, Reepicheep the mouse, who hopes as well to set foot on Aslan's country itself.

As in all of the Narnian chronicles, there is wonderful adventure and suspense. And as in all of my synopses I will reveal here as little of the surprises and outcomes as I can. There are two themes, however, that beg some scrutiny.

The first theme is conversion. Early in the book C.S. Lewis goes to great lengths to show how very self-centered, small-minded, and mean-spirited his character Eustace Scrubb really is. Later we find that these revelations are necessary, because the story of Eustace is a story of conversion. It is a story illustrating the painful process by which one must peel away the layers of evasions, excuses, and self-justifications before the renewed, better self can emerge.

In revealing Eustace's thoughts, Lewis does an amazing job of laying bare the workings of the self-centered mind. The entries in Eustace's journals are most telling. Though Scrubb is clearly being treated with utmost fairness and respect, his descriptions tend to read like this:

> Very short rations for dinner and I got less than anyone. Caspian is very clever at helping and thinks I don't see! Lucy for some reason tried to make up to me by offering me some of hers but that interfering prig Edmund wouldn't let her.[17]

Recall that in the previous Narnian stories Lewis made the point that a certain kind of thinking produces a certain kind of person and eventually a certain kind of world. In *The Voyage of the "Dawn Treader"* Eustace's self-centered greed ends in his being transformed into a greedy dragon hoarding his trove of treasures. Lewis writes:

> He had turned into a dragon while he was asleep. Sleeping on a dragon's hoard with greedy, dragonish thoughts in his heart, he had become a dragon himself.[18]

But the problem for Eustace is that he then discovers how very lonely he really is. The wisdom in Eustace's discovery is that being granted at last what he had always wanted—wealth and the power to terrorize—brings him to see how his own desires and actions inevitably lead to the most wretched loneliness of all.

When Aslan appears, Eustace's conversion can begin. It begins with the dragon Eustace pulling off his own scales, but he soon finds there are more scales underneath, and then more, and then more. Finally he has to let the Lion peel them away with his terrible claws. As Eustace later describes it:

> The very first tear he made was so deep that I thought it had gone right into my heart. And when he began pulling the skin off, it hurt worse than anything I've ever felt. The only thing that made me able to bear it was just the pleasure of feeling the stuff peel off.[19]

This scene is much like the episode in Lewis's *The Great Divorce* where the man allows his counselor to tear the lizard off his shoulder. Clearly, Lewis considers self-knowledge and pain to be an essential part of conversion.

Christian readers will immediately identify the basic doctrine of repentance and renewal in the story of Eustace Scrubb. They will recognize the dire consequences of getting exactly what one desires, the consequent feelings of wretchedness and loneliness, the fear of the undiluted truth, the pain of confessing one's faults, and finally the release and renewal as the scales of sin and guilt are stripped away.

But Lewis hastens to add that conversion is not immediate and complete. It is instead a process, though one that requires an abrupt turnaround before it can begin. He writes of the renewed Eustace Scrubb:

> It would be nice, and fairly nearly true, to say that "from that time forth Eustace was a different boy." To be strictly accurate, he began to be a different boy. He had relapses. There were still many days when he could be very tiresome. But most of those I shall not notice. The cure had begun.[20]

Here is a realistic view of conversion, recognizing that as long as we remain human we remain fallible, and that the kingdom of God is always in a state of becoming.

Another strong theme in *The Voyage of the "Dawn Treader"* is temptation itself. The captain, crew, and passengers of the "Dawn Treader" face continuous temptations—including the water that turns everything to pure gold, the island where all dreams come true, and in the end the temptation to abandon all else for a chance to find Aslan's country.

But the most poignant episode of all is perhaps Lucy's temptations in the great book of magic. At first she is sorely tempted to use the magic that would make her the most beautiful woman in the world. She has almost fallen for this temptation when Aslan appears and saves her from it. Later she does fall to the temptation to hear what her friends are really saying about her, and she is rewarded with pain for her efforts. Afterward, Aslan reprimands her:

"Child," he said, "I think you have been eavesdropping."

"Eavesdropping?"

"You listened to what your two schoolfellows were saying about you."

"Oh that? I never thought that was eavesdropping, Aslan. Wasn't it magic?"

"Spying on people by magic is the same as spying on them in any other way. And you have misjudged your friend. She is weak, but she loves you. She was afraid of the older girl and said what she does not mean."

"I don't think I'd ever be able to forget what I heard her say."

"No, you won't."

"Oh dear," said Lucy. "Have I spoiled everything? Do you mean we would have gone on being friends if it hadn't been for this—and been really great friends—all our lives perhaps—and now we never shall."[21]

In the end both of these themes represent a unity, because to Eustace and Lucy and all the others the issue repeatedly is whether they will get what they desire. When they are headstrong and pursue what their own appetites suggest, they find imprisonment and ruin. But when they pursue the purposes that Aslan has for them, they find their desires more than met. The theme of *The Voyage of the "Dawn Treader"* is well summed up in the New Testament verse, "But seek ye first the kingdom of God and his righteousness; and all these things shall be added unto you."[22]

In reading *The Voyage of the "Dawn Treader"* look for the interplay of human desires and submission to God's leading. Watch for the ironies in Eustace's adventures and the stages of his conversion. Pay close attention to the many temptations presented in the story, as well as to the ways of overcoming them. Again monitor Lucy's faith throughout, and learn more of human frailty and God's grace. Look for adventure, suspense, and marvelous imagery as C.S. Lewis, the master storyteller, paints his pictures of the eastern seas and the worlds beyond.

The Silver Chair

Possibly the most powerful, if not the most haunting, of the Narnian tales is *The Silver Chair*. This story is one of my personal favorites because of Lewis's clever treatment of the issues of empirical skepticism and relativist philosophy. The story also features one of the Chronicles' most memorable characters, Puddleglum the Marshwiggle, whose gloomy and pessimistic exterior hides a solid core of hope and joy that comes through to sustain the children through their terrible ordeal.

The children in this story are a schoolgirl named Jill Pole and a rather humbled and improved version of the same boy Eustace Scrubb whom we met already in *The Voyage of the "Dawn Treader"*. This adventure begins as Jill and Eustace are hiding in the school yard from their malevolent peers when the two are suddenly taken away to another world. There in Narnia the children soon find that they have been called to rescue the lost Prince Rilian. As Rilian's father, King Caspian, is very old and ready to die, the children must restore Rilian to Narnia if the kingdom is to survive.

Early in the story we find an interesting bit of C.S. Lewis's theology in the initial exchange between Jill Pole and the great lion Aslan. Jill is extremely thirsty, but she is afraid to approach the water with the lion standing so near.

> "I'm dying of thirst," said Jill.
>
> "Then drink," said the Lion. . . .
>
> "Will you promise not to—do anything to me, if I do come?" said Jill.
>
> "I make no promise," said the Lion.
>
> Jill was so thirsty now that, without noticing it, she had come a step nearer.
>
> "Do you eat girls?" she said.
>
> "I have swallowed up girls and boys, women and men, kings and emperors, cities and realms," said the Lion. . . .
>
> "I daren't come and drink," said Jill.
>
> "Then you will die of thirst," said the Lion.
>
> "Oh dear!" said Jill, coming another step nearer. "I suppose I must go and look for another stream then."
>
> "There is no other stream," said the Lion.[23]

A great deal of the doctrine and even the imagery of the New Testament is perfectly clear in this conversation, as Lewis portrays the terrible dilemma of having to give up one's life in order to save it.

A short time later we find as well a C.S. Lewis version of the doctrine of election. Here Jill is questioning whether Aslan has mistaken her for someone else:

> "I was wondering—I mean—could there be some mistake? Because nobody called me and Scrubb, you know. It was we who asked to come here. Scrubb said we were to call to—to Somebody—it was a name I wouldn't know—and perhaps

the Somebody would let us in. And we did, and then we found the door open."

"You would not have called to me unless I had been calling to you," said the Lion.[24]

In this way Lewis illustrates the doctrine that God calls certain people specifically for certain tasks, and that those chosen people become instrumental in forming the course of history.

After Jill is given a series of "signs" to memorize and to use in the search for Prince Rilian, the children soon meet Puddleglum the Marsh-wiggle. This lanky, web-footed character serves through the rest of the adventure as the children's guide and loyal companion, though at times they grow weary of his pessimistic outlook. Here is a bit of their conversation soon after meeting:

"Good morning, Guests," it said. "Though when I say good I don't mean it won't probably turn to rain or it might be snow, or fog, or thunder. You didn't get any sleep, I dare say."

"Yes we did, though," said Jill. "We had a lovely night."

"Ah," said the Marsh-wiggle, shaking his head. "I see you're making the best of a bad job. That's right. You've been well brought up, you have. You've learned to put a good face on things."

"Please, we don't know your name," said Scrubb.

"Puddleglum's my name. But it doesn't matter if you forget it. I can always tell you again."[25]

This exchange typifies the Marsh-wiggle's manner throughout the story, and yet at the critical moment it is he who manages to break through the witch's spell and to assert the hopeful point of view after all.

For after many dangers and adventures the children find themselves captured by the same witch who has enchanted and imprisoned Prince Rilian in her dark underground world. There comes a time in the story when all seems lost, as the attractive and convincing witch casts her spell over the children, the Marsh-wiggle, and the Prince, almost convincing them that their memories of Narnia are merely a construct of their imaginations.

> "Narnia?" she said. "Narnia? I have often heard your Lordship utter that name in your ravings. Dear Prince, you are very sick. There is no land called Narnia."
>
> "Yes there is though, Ma'am," said Puddleglum. "You see, I happen to have lived there all my life."
>
> "Indeed," said the Witch. "Tell me, I pray you, where that country is?"
>
> "Up there," said Puddleglum, stoutly, pointing overhead. "I—I don't know exactly where."
>
> "How?" said the Queen, with a kind, soft, musical laugh. "Is there a country up among the stones and mortar of the roof?"[26]

Later the Prince attempts to describe the sun by comparing it to the lamp hanging nearby.

> ". . . Now that thing which we call the sun is like the lamp, only far greater and brighter. It giveth light to the whole Overworld and hangeth in the sky."
>
> "Hangeth from what, my lord?" asked the Witch; and then, while they were all still thinking how to answer her, she added, with another of her soft, silver laughs, "You see? When you try to think out clearly what this sun must be, you cannot tell me. You can only tell me it is like the lamp. Your sun is a dream; and there is nothing in that dream that was not copied from the lamp. The lamp is the real thing; the sun is but a tale, a children's story."[27]

Here we find C.S. Lewis's ingenious portrayal of the most popular paradigm of the twentieth century. Here we see the *a priori* psychological notion that belief in the supernatural is a sign of a sick mind or a childish dream. Here we find the amused triumphalist assumption that the only reality is empirical reality. Here we notice hints of the relativist philosophy that reality is subjective and dependent on our individual perceptions. And here we encounter the widespread claim that our beliefs and religious ideas are merely copies, or projections from material reality. Thus in this one episode Lewis manages to represent the dominant psychoanalytic and anthropological approaches to the Christian religion.

In the story the witch uses her logic, her attractiveness, and her green, powdery enchantments to convince the others that her Underworld is the only true reality, until the Marsh-wiggle suddenly breaks her spell by stepping into the fire. And then, as the children and the Prince are awakened from the fog of the witch's enchantment, Puddleglum delivers his excellent soliloquy:

> Suppose we have only dreamed, or made up, all those things—trees and grass and sun and moon and stars and Aslan himself. Suppose we have. Then all I can say is that, in that case, the made-up things seem a good deal more important than the real ones. Suppose this black pit of a kingdom of yours is the only world. Well, it strikes me as a pretty poor one. And that's a funny thing, when you come to think of it. We're just babies making up a game, if you're right. But four babies playing a game can make a play-world which licks your real world hollow. That's why I'm going to stand by the play world. I'm on Aslan's side even if there isn't any Aslan to lead it. I'm going to live as like a Narnian as I can even if there isn't any Narnia.[28]

Do we find here a refutation of the philosophical claims at hand? No. Do we find a logical proof of Narnia or Aslan or God or anything else? No. But in Puddleglum's response Lewis has captured something essential to the human spirit: the need for beauty, the need for freedom, and the need for God.

I have already revealed more of this story than I ought, but there is still greater suspense and adventure awaiting the reader of *The*

Silver Chair. In reading this story, look for the author's insights on the Christian life as revealed in the interactions between Aslan and Jill Pole. Pay particular attention to the issue of her duty to "remember the signs," comparing these insights to the Old Testament emphasis on remembering.

Many other themes and images suggest themselves as well. There are of course the obvious issues of empiricism, relativism, and skepticism. There is the less obvious issue of interplay between philosophical atheism and demonic enchantment, as also explored in all three of Lewis's science fiction novels. Look as well for the relationship between material comforts and Aslan's leading. And finally, look for a great adventure story, complete with hidden signs, talking beasts, giants, underground worlds, and a great deal about life, truth, and faith.

The Horse and His Boy

In his fantasy stories C.S. Lewis has a knack for capturing the essence of the various animals—at least as they appear to us humans—and incorporating that essence into their behavior and speech. The next story, *The Horse and His Boy*, is one of Lewis's best in showing his mastery at portraying his talking animals.

For example, employing a reversal reminiscent of Swift's portrayal of the Houyhnhnms in *Gulliver's Travels*, Lewis creates Bree, a horse who is more learned and clever than his human companion, the boy Shasta. Throughout the story it is Bree who displays the pride, courage, and intelligence that one almost expects when one sees a fine, strong horse prancing along confidently in a parade.

Bree is a noble warhorse trained and ridden by the great Tarkaan Anradin of Calormen. Through most of the story Bree maintains his noble manner and aloof air, often reminding his low-born rider of their difference in status. When the horse Bree is first teaching the boy Shasta how to ride, the horse is heard to say:

Now sit up and remember what I told you about your knees. Funny to think of me who has led cavalry charges and won races having a potato-sack like you in the saddle![29]

The mare Hwin is also a talking horse from Narnia and a cultured, well-mannered animal. But in Hwin there is a graciousness and gentility that is somewhat lacking in Bree. Unlike her noble counterpart, Hwin has no problem in deferring to others at times, but neither does she shrink from asserting her opinions when the time is appropriate. In reading the interactions of these horses and their people, one cannot help forming a mental picture of each; and the trick of Lewis's genius is that in those pictures these talking beasts seem not human, but in a sense even more horse-like than ever.

During Shasta's short stay in the Narnians' apartment, he meets the Faun Tumnus—whom we met in a previous story—and a talking Raven who advises King Edmund:

> "Sire," said the Raven. "You shall hear no better plot than the Faun's though we sat in council for seven days. And now, as we birds say, nests before eggs. Which is as much as to say, let us all take our food and then at once be about our business."[30]

Much of the delight in C.S. Lewis's animal stories is that the birds are always doing and saying the perfect birdisms, the horses are always saying and doing the perfect horsisms, and so on.

And so, much of the humor in this story is carried by Bree's occasional pokes at the shortcomings of his human companions. For example, as Bree and Shasta are planning their escape, the horse observes:

> This is the chance for both of us. You see if I run away without a rider, everyone who sees me will say "Stray horse" and be after me as quick as he can. With a rider I've a chance to get through. That's where you can help me. On the other hand, you can't get very far on those two silly legs of yours

(what absurd legs humans have!) without being overtaken. But on me you can outdistance any other horse in this country. That's where I can help you.[31]

For another example, later when Shasta and Aravis are arguing:

"What quarrelsome creatures these humans are," said Bree to the mare. "They're as bad as mules. Let's try to talk a little sense."[32]

However, the main thematic issue in *The Horse and His Boy* is that of conceit and snobbery. In the end both the Tarkheena Aravis and the warhorse Bree are compelled to face this issue and to learn their lessons with regard to prejudices and true character. In the lessons learned we find some of C.S. Lewis's most clearly revealed thoughts on the pretensions of the upper classes.

From the moment of their initial meeting, Bree makes a point of reminding Shasta of their different class backgrounds. When at one point in the presence of Aravis and Hwin, Bree said, "Shasta, don't display your ignorance,"[33] the boy began to feel that he was being snubbed by the other three travelers. Similarly, through most of the story we find Bree pleasantly but incessantly flaunting his nobility, and this class vanity becomes the basis for his immediate affinity to the young Tarkheena.

The girl Aravis is also quick to make her claims to nobility and to criticize the boy Shasta for his poor upbringing and rude manners. Speaking to Bree:

"Look here," said the girl. "I don't mind going with you, Mr. War-Horse, but what about this boy? How do I know he's not a spy?"

"Why don't you say at once that you think I'm not good enough for you?" said Shasta.

"Be quiet, Shasta," said Bree. "The Tarkheena's question is quite reasonable. I'll vouch for the boy, Tarkheena."[34]

In telling the story Lewis is careful to make his readers like the characters Bree and Aravis, and yet to allow an uneasy feeling that both may be a bit too vain after all.

Indeed in the end their conceit does become an issue for each in turn as a result of their encounters with the great lion Aslan. For Bree it is the Hermit who lays the issue on the line:

> "It's all very well for you," said Bree. "You haven't disgraced yourself. But I've lost everything."
>
> "My good Horse," said the Hermit, who had approached them unnoticed because his bare feet made so little noise on that sweet, dewy grass. "My good Horse, you've lost nothing but your self-conceit. No, no, cousin. Don't put back your ears and shake your mane at me. If you are really so humbled as you sounded a minute ago, you must learn to listen to sense. You're not quite the great horse you had come to think, from living among poor dumb horses. Of course you were braver and cleverer than them. You could hardly help being that. It doesn't follow that you'll be anyone special in Narnia. But as long as you know you're nobody very special, you'll be a very decent sort of Horse, on the whole, and taking one thing with another."[35]

The proud Tarkheena Aravis requires more drastic measures—nothing less than having her flesh torn by the lion and finally coming to understand that her life was saved by the courage of the very boy whom she had held in contempt.

> "I know," said Aravis. "I felt just the same. Shasta was marvellous. I'm just as bad as you, Bree. I've been snubbing him and looking down on him ever since you met us and now he turns out to be the best of us all. But I think it would be better to stay and say we're sorry than to go back to Calormen."[36]

When the four runaways are leaving Calormen, we see a princess and a warhorse both full of their own nobility and importance. In the end as the four prepare to enter Narnia we see a very different picture. The new Aravis has been humbled by the events of her journey and has gained a new awareness of what is really important in human character. The new Bree has faced his vanity—which is not to say that he has conquered it—and looks forward with some anxiety as to whether he will "measure up" among the other talking horses of Narnia.

Of course, the attentive reader has already recognized the larger, biblical theme that the greatest shall be the least, and the least greatest.[37] This theme is certainly what C.S. Lewis is about in *The Horse and His Boy*. If the idea can be seen in the cases of Aravis and Bree, it is illustrated perfectly in the cases of the proud Calormene Prince Rabadash and the poor orphan boy Shasta. Again I shall leave this point somewhat vague so as not to spoil the suspense of the story, but Lewis's choice of a title for his final chapter, "Rabadash the Ridiculous," fairly reveals the picture.

For me the key statement in the story is Aravis's, "But I think it would be better to stay and say we're sorry than to go back to Calormen."[38] Here is an important foundation in Christian doctrine. Here is the doctrine of repentance and renewal, the idea that it is better to confess and move on than to return to the slavery of one's sins. Lewis's story illustrates clearly that pride is the greatest roadblock to freedom.

In other words, those who puff themselves up with imaginings of their own importance and virtue will in the end be brought down; those who are humble and serve others will be lifted up. Again C.S. Lewis's fantasy story explores the question, how might this principle be played out in another time and place? And again an essential biblical truth is illustrated.

In reading *The Horse and His Boy* look for the delightful interplay of animal characteristics and personalities. Watch for what the author is saying about class and privilege. Notice especially Aslan's role in the story, paying particular attention to his actions and effects on each character in the story. And of course look for those trademark C.S. Lewis ironies and see what they illustrate with regard to

Christian doctrine. *The Horse and His Boy* is a great story to be understood for its insights and enjoyed for its sheer entertainment.

The Magician's Nephew

The story that reaches farthest back into Narnian time is *The Magician's Nephew*. Here the story takes the children Digory and Polly away to a time when the great lion Aslan first creates the land of Narnia. Indeed, as we read the other chronicles, we find that Digory later grows up to be Professor Kirke, that Queen Jadis later becomes the White Witch, that the sprouting lamppost becomes a permanent feature of Lantern Waste, and that Digory's magic apple seed grows into a tree from which the famous Wardrobe is made.

But this story begins with two children playing in the attics and service corridors of their homes, and then their transportation by means of magic rings to the world of Charn. There they meet the malevolent Queen Jadis, and there begin the adventures sweeping from Charn to Narnia to the children's home on Earth. It is a story that in many ways sets the stage for the later Narnia tales. Without spoiling the suspense by revealing too much detail, I will say that this story contains the kind of beautiful creation imagery that is also found in Lewis's science fiction novel *Perelandra*. Here in *The Magician's Nephew* the children witness the death of an old world, Charn, and then the creation of a new world, Narnia. Typical of the author's creation imagery is this passage in which Aslan is creating Narnia with his songs:

> The Lion was pacing to and fro about that empty land and singing his new song. It was softer and more lilting than the song by which he had called up the stars and the sun; a gentle, rippling music. As he walked and sang the valley grew green with grass. It spread out from the Lion like a pool. It ran up the sides of the little hills like a wave. In a few minutes it was creeping up the lower slopes of the distant mountains, making that young world every moment softer.[39]

C.S. Lewis is always the master at drawing contrasts, and much of his power as a writer is gained by his well-chosen juxtapositions. For example, in this story even as the divine song is spreading life and beauty abroad, the witch Jadis is shrieking her threats and the greedy Uncle Andrew is busy trying to make a fortune from the Narnian abundance. When the uncle has discovered that even metals grow like trees in Narnia, he exclaims:

> The commercial possibilities of this country are unbounded. Bring a few old bits of strab [scrap] iron here, bury 'em, and up they come as brand new railway engines, battleships, anything you please.[40]

In this seminal story we find the foundations for many of the features that make reading the Chronicles of Narnia so gratifying. For example, we are introduced to Narnia's talking animals. Aslan declares:

> Narnia, Narnia, Narnia, awake. Love. Think. Speak. Be walking trees. Be talking beasts. Be divinewaters.[41]

And as soon as the creatures begin speaking, they also discover humor. Of this development Aslan heartily approves:

> Laugh and fear not, creatures. Now that you are no longer dumb and witless, you need not always be grave. For jokes as well as justice come in with speech.[42]

Both C.S. Lewis and his mentor, G.K. Chesterton, were adamant in their insistence that the Christian God is a God of humor, and both authors went to great lengths to include play and laughter in their stories and theologies. For a discussion of Chesterton's theology of joy, the reader may want to see "Hearing God's Laughter" in my book *Battling for the Modern Mind*. In C.S. Lewis's *The Magician's Nephew* the divine mirth is well established, and its presence is felt throughout the entire series of the Chronicles.

An episode of particular importance takes place late in the story when Aslan sends Digory on a mission to retrieve a certain fruit from a special garden. There at the garden gate the boy encounters this message:

> Come in by the gold gate or not at all. Take of my fruit for others or forbear. For those who steal or those who climb my wall shall find their heart's desire and find despair.[43]

And there Digory also encounters the witch, who tempts him to take the fruit for his own purpose.

It is episodes such as these that most tempt the reader to forget the author's admonition that he is not writing allegory. The parallel to the story of Eden is obvious. We find the same strong parallel in the novel *Perelandra*. But again Lewis's purpose is fantasy and speculation. How might that same human dilemma be played out in this new context?

Lewis's purpose in recasting these basic questions goes far beyond a mere borrowing of provocative ideas. What Lewis has done is to illustrate and accentuate some of the eternal questions facing humankind both collectively and individually. Those haunting words, "shall find their heart's desire and find despair," are echoed again in Aslan's statement, "All get what they want: they do not always like it."[44] And this idea, of course, is basic to Christian doctrine.

In reading *The Magician's Nephew* look first for a good fantasy story filled with that great C.S. Lewis sense of humor. Watch for those nuggets of gold buried along the way—those flashes of eternal wisdom that seem to roll so casually off the tongues of the various characters. For example, from Fledge, the talking horse:

> "I'm sure Aslan would have, if you'd asked him," said Fledge.
> "Wouldn't he know without being asked?" said Polly.

"I've no doubt he would," said the Horse (still with his mouth full). "But I've a sort of idea he likes to be asked."[45]

Lewis takes great pleasure in having his ostensibly dull-witted animals give the sensible answer to clever human questions, a technique the author uses prolifically in the story *The Horse and His Boy*. But here from the horse's mouth the reader gets a glimpse of Lewis's doctrine of prayer.

Finally, in reading *The Magician's Nephew* look for the big picture. Notice the scheme of worlds and time and transportation, for these techniques will be used throughout the Chronicles. Resist the appeal to allegory, but release yourself to follow the fantasy and find new light on some of the old questions, as well as new questions to wonder over. Here is one sense in which reading C.S. Lewis can be a cure for smug doctrine and complacent religion. Lewis's stories tend to open up the walls and free the questions of Christian doctrine to be played out again in the vast universe.

The Last Battle

The seventh and final story in the Narnia series is called *The Last Battle*. The setting is about 200 Narnian years later during the reign of King Tirian, the seventh in descent from King Rilian of *The Silver Chair*. In this story the children are not at first introduced. Instead, we are told about an ambitious and crafty ape named Shift and his poor, befuddled sidekick, the donkey Puzzle. We find at once that Shift is clever and manipulative, and that Puzzle is simply not clever enough to understand that he is being taken advantage of.

The reader begins to sense what is coming when the ape talks Puzzle into wearing a lion's skin and pretending to be Aslan. Meanwhile, in order to gain power over the creatures of Narnia, the ape appoints himself Lord Shift, Mouthpiece of Aslan, and begins holding nightly court in front of an old stable. Puzzle is at first very strongly opposed to this plan, but with his limited mentality he is unable to dissuade Shift from this deceptive course of action.

One of the most interesting themes to follow in *The Last Battle* concerns the ape, the false religious leader. This is certainly not the only context in which C.S. Lewis parodies the posturing and pretensions of certain clergymen, and soon enough his character Shift informs the confused and questioning creatures that Aslan "doesn't appear anymore"[46] and that they will thenceforth have to seek Aslan only through his appointed mouthpiece. Here Lewis rather obviously portrays the traditional Roman Catholic doctrine that the church is the only access to God.

Soon enough we begin to see the relativizing, the redefining, and the shifting of emphasis that characterizes much of modern liberal Protestant theology as well. Acting on the assumption that God is open to redefinition, the ape Shift announces first that all religions are equally valid, and second that Aslan is simply synonymous with the Calormene god Tash. Later with the help of his Calormene conspirators, the ape invents the name Tashlan in order to confuse the hapless creatures of Narnia.

Though it is the ape in his cleverness that first instigates the scheme with the Calormenes and Tash, he finds in the end that the whole affair spins out of his control. This is a recurrent theme in C.S. Lewis's stories—that we should be very careful what we ask for, because we will probably get it. Here is a description of Tash:

> In the shadow of the trees on the far side of the clearing something was moving. It was gliding very slowly Northward. At first glance you might have mistaken it for smoke, for it was grey and you could see things through it. But the deathly smell was not the smell of smoke. Also, this thing kept its shape instead of billowing and curling as smoke would have done. It was roughly the shape of a man but it had the head of a bird; some bird of prey with a cruel, curved beak . . . and its fingers—all twenty of them—were curved like its beak and had long, pointed, bird-like claws instead of nails. It floated on the grass instead of walking, and the grass seemed to wither beneath it.[47]

And there is this conversation:

> "It seems, then," said the Unicorn, "that there is a real Tash, after all."
>
> "Yes," said the Dwarf. "And this fool of an Ape, who didn't believe in Tash, will get more than he bargained for! He called for Tash: Tash has come."
>
> "Where has it—he—the Thing—gone to?" said Jill.
>
> "North into the heart of Narnia," said Tirian.
>
> "It has come to dwell among us. They have called it and it has come."
>
> "Ho, ho ho!" chuckled the Dwarf, rubbing its hairy hands together. "It will be a surprise for the Ape. People shouldn't call for demons unless they really mean what they say."[48]

The theme here is our propensity to call on forces for our own uses, only to be overwhelmed and used by those very forces. C.S. Lewis pursues this theme again in both *Perelandra* and *That Hideous Strength*.

But C.S. Lewis is not content in *The Last Battle* to deal only with the two previously discussed aspects of the false church; he deals as well with the widespread skeptical materialism that dominates popular thought outside the church. This secular point of view is personified in the black dwarf Griffle and his cohort. These fellows believe there is no Aslan, there are no other worlds, and there is nothing worth fighting for except their own self-preservation. "The Dwarfs are for the Dwarfs!" they cry repeatedly.

During the great last battle we see the consequences of the points of view portrayed. Eustace and Jill join King Tirian and his warriors to fight for the preservation of Narnia. The Calormenes and the forces of Tash use every kind of treachery to fight for material gain and tyrannical power. The worldly-wise and cynical dwarfs fight against one side and then the other, depending entirely upon their pragmatic view of what will bring them the most gain. Here is a picture of the moral, the immoral, and the amoral as combating forces in human history.

There are indeed surprises at the end of *The Last Battle*, and I have no intention of revealing them here. But I do want to mention an important incident involving the skeptical dwarfs. There is a glorious scene where the children and their allies, the beasts of Narnia, and even the traitorous dwarfs find themselves surrounded by the most wonderful natural beauty imaginable. But much to Lucy's dismay, the stubborn dwarfs refuse to see the truth and keep insisting that they are all trapped inside a dark, foul-smelling stable. She implores the leading dwarf Diggle to open his eyes and see his freedom, but:

> "Well if that doesn't beat everything!" exclaimed Diggle. "How can you go on talking all that rot? Your wonderful Lion didn't come and help you, did he? Thought not. And now—even now—when you've been beaten and shoved into this black hole, just the same as the rest of us, you're still at your old game. Starting a new lie! Trying to make us believe we're none of us shut up, and it ain't dark, and heaven knows what."[49]

Here again we see the genius of C.S. Lewis, as in this one short speech the author captures the essence of the materialist view of Christianity. There are the blinders that make the materialist unable to see the marvelous, the miraculous, the beautiful, and the free all around him. There are the contrived litmus tests to prove the falsity of the faith of others. There is the adamant, even indignant, refusal to be set free.

At Lucy's request even Aslan does what he can to help the dwarfs, but they stick to the prison of their skepticism. In the end all of the dwarfs are saying:

> "Well, at any rate there's no Humbug here. We haven't let anyone take us in. The Dwarfs are for the Dwarfs."

"You see," said Aslan. "They have chosen cunning instead of belief. Their prison is only in their own minds, yet they are in that prison; and so afraid of being taken in that they cannot be taken out."[50]

Using a theme reminiscent of much of G.K. Chesterton's work, Lewis turns many of the Enlightenment assumptions on their heads in claiming that it is belief, after all, that is truly liberating, and skepticism the real prison.

In reading *The Last Battle* look for Lewis's ideas on "worlds" and realities. Observe carefully the relationships between what is happening in one world and its impact in another. Watch what the author does with the enduring question of human efforts and cosmic outcomes.

A close consideration of the fates of Shift the ape, Ginger the cat, Emeth the Calormene, and Puzzle the donkey will bring wonderful insights. The black dwarfs, of course, can be a study in themselves. Finally, look for another great adventure story with plenty of surprises and thought-provoking ideas from the storytelling genius of C.S. Lewis.

5

Science Fiction and Fantasy

Despite the fact of widespread scholarly disdain for science fiction, we are fortunate indeed that C.S. Lewis chose to pursue this, his favorite genre. Some of his most memorable and entertaining writing is found in his books of science fiction and fantasy. It was in 1938, quite early in his tenure as Poetry Chair at Magdalen College, that Lewis launched the space trilogy with *Out of the Silent Planet*. Five years later he completed *Perelandra*, followed in two years by *That Hideous Strength*. During that same time period, Lewis wrote two of his most famous fantasies, first *The Screwtape Letters* and later *The Great Divorce*. Through the early 1950s he devoted his imaginative efforts almost exclusively to the Narnia stories for children, but in 1956 he finished his formidable fantasy novel *Till We Have Faces*. In this chapter we shall visit these products of C.S. Lewis's marvelous imagination.

The Space Trilogy

C.S. Lewis loved the world of fantasy, and this love bore fruit not only in his famous Chronicles of Narnia for children, but also in a set of three science fiction books written for adults. The titles of the space trilogy are *Out of the Silent Planet*, *Perelandra*, and *That Hideous Strength*. As in his children's fantasies, Lewis uses the unusual settings and situations of space to define and illustrate various aspects of Christian theology and doctrine.

I think every Christian should experience a reading of Lewis's space trilogy. Like Milton's classic *Paradise Lost*, the space trilogy takes as its setting the very expanses of the cosmos, its characters being both human and divine, its issues addressing the very fate of Earth and the future of humankind. What Lewis accomplishes in the space trilogy is to carry us outside our earthbound views of Christianity to explore the broad questions of good and evil and salvation on a vast backdrop of time and space. While each of Lewis's science fiction books stands well on its own, the reader who completes the trilogy is rewarded with much broader insights into the place and purpose of human life on a grander scale.

Out of the Silent Planet

C.S. Lewis's first installment in his famous space trilogy is the highly enjoyable novel *Out of the Silent Planet*. In keeping with my promise not to spoil the surprises while discussing Lewis's fiction, here we will look only briefly at the beginning of the story line and dwell instead on the major themes and meanings of the book.

I must say, however, at the onset that this first novel is nothing less than a delight to read. Even more clearly than in his Narnia stories, Lewis demonstrates his mastery of the art of turning a meaning-packed story into a piece of pure entertainment. In the pages of *Out of the Silent Planet* the reader is served a feast of wonderful surprises, breathtaking imagery, fresh new perspectives, and imaginative thoughts, all combined into a story filled with suspense.

Briefly, the story follows a man named Ransom who is kidnapped and taken in a spaceship to Mars—or Malacandra, as the local residents call the red planet. His kidnappers, Weston and Devine, have in mind handing Ransom over to the local sorns, ostensibly as a human sacrifice in exchange for scientific knowledge and gold. The plot of the story beyond that I shall not here divulge.

But as one progresses into the story, one begins to understand what the author is doing with his characters. Weston is a scientific imperialist, and as such he comes to represent the kind of evolutionary progressivism that had captured the popular imagination in Europe and North America by the dawn of the twentieth century. Weston's partner Devine, on the other hand, is the consummate industrialist-opportunist, obviously representing the commercial man reduced to his essential quality of greed. It is near the end of the story that the author makes his warning clear in the words of the great eldil Oyarsa speaking to Ransom.

> But I lay also a command on you; you must watch this Weston and this Devine. . . . They may yet do much evil in, and beyond, your world.[1]

It is this combination of fanatical scientism and unmitigated greed about which the great Oyarsa is speaking, and through him the author similarly warns about the potential dangers in the marriage of science and commerce.

C.S. Lewis scholar Brian Murphy[2] has made an interesting observation on Lewis's stature and reception in the world of science fiction writers. Murphy points out that while the science fiction establishment concedes willingly that Lewis must be listed among the greatest writers in this genre, there is a puzzling tendency to say very little about Lewis's work beyond that. The reason, according to Murphy, is that the underlying meanings of Lewis's science fiction run in direct contradiction to the accepted perspective in the field.

This point is illustrated very clearly in *Out of the Silent Planet*, for Professor Weston indeed embodies and articulates the standard assumptions and beliefs underlying most science fiction writing. This belief is that through science humankind will continue to gain more knowledge and to progress toward greater and greater control over its own destiny, allowing the human species to survive forever and possibly to become masters of the universe. This is the creed of

Doctor Weston in the novel, and it is the unwritten creed of most science fiction writers.

But Lewis's science fiction flies in the face of this "Westonism" and raises the possibility of a very different kind of universe from that of the popular scientific imagination. In Lewis's universe what we call "space" is not an empty, lifeless void, but an all-encompassing realm teeming with significance and vitality. In the protagonist Ransom's thoughts, the idea is expressed thus:

> But already it had become impossible to think of it as 'space.' Some moments of cold fear he had; but each time they were shorter and more quickly swallowed up in a sense of awe which made his personal fate seem wholly insignificant. He could not feel that they were an island of life journeying through an abyss of death. He felt almost the opposite—that life was waiting outside the little iron egg-shell in which they rode, ready at any moment to break in, and that, if it killed them, it would kill them by excess of its vitality.[3]

In Lewis's cosmology the universe is filled with the vitality of the Old One, and it is only Earth that is cut off and silent, due to its temporary occupation by the Bent One—hence the title of the novel: *Out of the Silent Planet.*

Of course, the student of philosophy will see immediately that Lewis has embedded a Christian cosmology into a genre that is traditionally existential in its leanings. As in so much of Lewis's writing in so many forms, Christian doctrine is there to be found. For the Christian the vast universe is not an alien and terrifying void, but the field of the One who gives existence and significance to all that is. In this perspective it is not humanity and its sciences that will determine the fate of our world, but the will of One far beyond our imaginations and control.

And so, in this medium that generally thrives on the scientific prowess of humankind, it comes as an understandably unwelcome thought that the inhabitants of the universe might find their meaning and happiness in humility and submission to a Being greater than humanity. Yet this is the message embedded in C.S. Lewis's science fiction. In his audience before the great Oyarsa and the assembly of the hnau, Ransom is asked many questions about Earth.

> They were astonished at what he had to tell them of human history—of war, slavery and prostitution. 'It is because they have no Oyarsa,' said one of the pupils.
>
> 'It is because every one of them wants to be a little Oyarsa himself,' said Augray.
>
> 'They cannot help it,' said the old sorn. 'There must be rule, yet how can creatures rule themselves? . . . They are like one trying to lift himself up by his own hair—or like one trying to see over a whole country when he is on a level with it. . . .'[4]

Here C.S. Lewis uses the cosmic perspective of science fiction to shed light on a species that has forgotten its place and ever seeks to declare itself to be its own gods.

In contrast to Lewis's cosmology there is Westonism—the novel's representation of the materialist, scientific progressivism that so strongly guides the science fiction of H.G. Wells, Arthur C. Clarke, and others. In *Out of the Silent Planet* this point of view is most directly stated by the character Doctor Weston himself. Speaking of a vague, evolutionary life force or fate, Weston explains:

> She has ruthlessly broken down all obstacles and liquidated all failures and today in her highest form—civilized man— and in me as his representative, she presses forward to that interplanetary leap which will, perhaps, place her forever beyond the reach of death.[5]

Here is a fictionalized statement of the vaguely evolutionary, scientific imperialism that had captured the popular mind and reigned as the dominant creed of science fiction. In his science fiction writing C.S. Lewis holds these ideas up for the scrutiny and satirizing they deserve.

But what the reader should look for in *Out of the Silent Planet* first and foremost is the great adventure of the plot itself. Look for the joy of reading a story superbly told by a master storyteller. Beyond these things, watch for the whole issue of Westonism— Lewis's handling of the popular concepts of progress and science, and the ethics resulting when a research method is turned into a belief. Notice the author's critiques of humankind and its history, particularly with regard to greed, coercion, wars, pride, power, and the exploitation of others.

And lastly, very importantly, when reading *Out of the Silent Planet* look for that marvelous C.S. Lewis sense of humor. The author's humor permeates the book, and it is well worth the reading if for no other purpose than to enjoy a good laugh at the follies and foibles of humankind.

There is a priceless scene near the end of the story where the arrogant Professor Weston is interrogated by the great eldil Oyarsa. Not only is Oyarsa eminently more intelligent and perceptive than the human, but he is also invisible. Being a materialist, Weston naturally refuses to believe in the existence of invisible beings, and so spends the whole conversation addressing himself to an elderly hross nearby who happens to be asleep.

But the imperialist's ludicrous condescension becomes even more laughable when Weston tries to barter with the hnau as if they were childlike savages.

'We kill him,' he shouted. 'Show what we can do. Every one who no do all we say—pouff! bang!—kill him same as that one. You do all we say and we give you much pretty things. See! See!' To Ransom's intense discomfort, Weston at this point whipped out of his pocket a brightly coloured necklace of beads, the undoubted work of Mr. Woolworth, and began dangling it in front of the faces of his guards, turning slowly round and round and repeating, 'Pretty, pretty! See! See!'

The result of the manoeuvre was more striking than Weston himself had anticipated. Such a roar of sounds as human ears had never heard before. . . .[6]

But Weston, the stalwart British imperialist, is not one to be frightened.

'You no roar at me,' he thundered. 'No try make me afraid. Me no afraid of you.'

'You must forgive my people,' said the voice of Oyarsa— and even it was subtly changed—'but they are not roaring at you. They are only laughing.'[7]

Out of the Silent Planet contains great humor and adventure. For those who wish to go deeper, it contains great significance as a critique of the prevailing intellectual fads and as a reminder of an older, more traditional and sensible way of looking at ourselves and our existence. It is a book with several layers of meaning and consequently several avenues for its enjoyment. *Out of the Silent Planet* comfortably bears reading again and again.

Perelandra

The second book in the famous C.S. Lewis science fiction trilogy offers a different kind of reading than that of the first. In *Perelandra* the reader finds much more descriptive imagery in Lewis's detailed depictions of Earth's younger neighbor *Perelandra* (Venus). Indeed, the first few chapters of *Perelandra* consist almost entirely of the protagonist Ransom's sense impressions of how he came to be on Venus and what he encountered once there.

To say that the novel is rich in description is to say that it is rich in both quantity and quality of imagery. It has been observed that C.S. Lewis at one time in his life wanted to be a poet, and here in *Perelandra* we can see clearly how his sense of poetry permeated his works in other genres as well. Here the imagery is powerful and engaging. In his descriptions of Venus, C.S. Lewis engages the reader's every sense in setting the stage for his story.

The examples of Lewis's abundant imagery are legion, but here is a mere taste:

> Over his head there hung from a hairy tube-like branch a great spherical object, almost transparent, and shining. It held an area of reflected light in it and at one place a suggestion of rainbow colouring. . . . He began to examine the nearest one attentively. At first he thought it was moving, then he thought it was not. Moved by a natural impulse he put out his hand to touch it. Immediately his head, face, and shoulders were drenched with what seemed (in that warm world) an ice-cold shower bath, and his nostrils filled with a sharp, shrill, exquisite scent. . . .[8]

This sample is typical of the descriptive power that Lewis sustains throughout this remarkable novel.

The plot in this second story takes a willing Ransom to the planet Perelandra on a mysterious mission of which even he does not at first know the purpose. Once on the planet, he meets the Green Lady and then once again encounters his old nemesis, Professor Weston. In *Perelandra* Weston's plans become even more diabolical than in the earlier story, as he assumes the role of tempter of the innocent Green Lady. And upon the outcome of this attempted seduction hangs the very fate of the planet Perelandra. That is all I will tell here about the plot of the story.

The theme, however, has already been revealed. *Perelandra* is another telling of the biblical story of Adam and Eve as it might have happened in another place and time among other people. Though this story is certainly not an allegory for the Eden story, Lewis does raise once again some of the essential issues involved in the fall of humankind at the dawn of Earth. It is in the exploration of these issues that Christian readers find a depth of understanding beyond the adventure story and the rich imagery.

Again the reader finds Professor Weston defining and asserting the worldview of the evolutionary scientist. Weston explains to Ransom:

> I saw almost at once that I could admit no break, no discontinuity, in the unfolding of the cosmic process. I became a convinced believer in emergent evolution. All is one. . . . The majestic spectacle of this blind, inarticulate purposiveness thrusting its way upward and ever upward in endless unity of differentiated achievements toward an ever-increasing complexity of organisation. . . .[9]

The issue in *Perelandra* becomes that of individual human choice. Professor Weston's view would render the moral choices of one person meaningless. Ransom argues for the Christian doctrine that every choice is eternally significant. In the story the Green Lady is called upon to decide, and the shape of Perelandra's future depends entirely upon her decision.

This theme of the significance of individual choice and will is a consistent concern throughout the novel. In time it becomes clear to Ransom that he has been sent to Perelandra as an advocate, to advise the Green Lady against the diabolical temptations and counsels of the Un-Man who has possessed the body of Weston. But as Ransom begins to realize his own inadequacy for the task, he despairs as to the significance of his efforts at all.

> Very well then. He had been brought here miraculously. He was in God's hands. As long as he did his best—and he had done his best—God would see to the final issue. He had not succeeded. But he had done his best. No one could do more. "'Tis not in mortals to command success." He must not be worried about the final result.[10]

But then Ransom comes to realize that the evasions and excuses will not do.

It snapped like a violin string. Not one rag of all the evasion was left. Relentlessly, unmistakably, the Darkness pressed down upon him the knowledge that this picture of the situation was utterly false. His journey to Perelandra was not a moral exercise, nor a sham fight. If the issue lay in Maleldil's hands, Ransom and the Lady were those hands. The fate of a world really depended on how they behaved in the next few hours.[11]

Much of the power of *Perelandra* comes from its wrestling with the essential issues of the human condition. The book is about human frailty and mortality. It is about the human will and responsibility. It is about the very meaning of the fallen state and its incumbent slavery. In his ruminations over the Green Lady and her impending decision, Ransom complains that:

> . . . the fatal false step which, once taken, would thrust her down into the terrible slavery of appetite and hate and economics and government which our race knows so well, could be made to sound so like the true one.[12]

It is a book about what we are and what we were meant to be.

In reading *Perelandra* look first for the rich imagery in C.S. Lewis's descriptive passages. Better still, immerse yourself in the author's prose, and allow all five of your senses to experience the planet Perelandra as the character Ransom does. Look again for high adventure—a more subtle kind of adventure, but in a sense the highest adventure of all. Look for the diabolical and the ways the Bent One is able to co-opt other causes for his own use.

Finally, look especially for Lewis's treatment of individual human choice. This issue arises repeatedly in the novel, beginning with Lewis's own internal struggles about going to meet Ransom, continuing with Ransom's dilemmas with regard to the Un-Man, and ending with the Green Lady's momentous choice regarding her great temptation. Pay close attention to what Lewis is saying about the significance of every choice and action in our lives.

That Hideous Strength

The third novel in the C.S. Lewis science fiction trilogy takes yet another surprising turn in its presentation, as the first half of the story appears to be concerned with the career aspirations of a young sociologist named Mark Studdock and some unusual events that befall his wife Jane. Indeed, one begins to wonder where is the science fiction, for the bulk of the early story concerns the inner politics and machinations of a small British university and subsequently a progressive new organization called the National Institute of Co-ordinated Experiments (N.I.C.E.).

But the reader soon enough finds that the story is about seduction and conversion, and again about individual choice. Jane Studdock finds herself drawn increasingly toward the traditional beliefs she had rejected as a child. Mark Studdock, on the other hand, finds himself somewhat willingly seduced into the inner circle of a diabolical conspiracy to control the world.

The plot of *That Hideous Strength* follows the establishment of the N.I.C.E. and its efforts to bring about a progressive synthesis of the methods of science and the powers of the state. Lewis writes:

> The N.I.C.E. was the first-fruits of that constructive fusion between the state and the laboratory on which so many thoughtful people base their hopes of a better world.[13]

This application of state coercion to the scientific management of human beings is a theme that C.S. Lewis addressed extensively in his nonfiction *The Abolition of Man*—a book whose reading would be helpful as a preface to *That Hideous Strength*.

Recall that in Lewis's formative years there had been a great amount of public debate as to the benefits of science, and there were a sizable number of progressive thinkers who lamented that government was not under the control of scientific minds. In Lewis's novel this reality finally begins to materialize and is hailed as a triumph by free-thinkers and progressives worldwide. As an enthusiastic Mark Studdock exclaims early on:

> The real thing is that this time we're going to get science applied to social problems and backed by the whole force of the state, just as war has been backed by the whole force of the state in the past. One hopes, of course, that it'll find out more than the old free-lance science did; but what's certain is that it can do more.[14]

And doing much more is precisely what the inner circle at N.I.C.E. have in mind.

At first there is merely the vague talk of progress and the bright future espoused by the Progressive Element among the Fellows at Bracton College. Subsequently the N.I.C.E. effort becomes more clearly defined in terms of taking "control of our own destiny"[15] and scientific solutions to all social problems:

> We expect a solution of the unemployment problem, the cancer problem, the housing problem, the problems of currency, of war, of education. We expect from it a brighter, cleaner and fuller life for our children, in which we and they can march ever onward and onward and develop to the full urge of life which God has given each one of us. The N.I.C.E. is the people's instrument for bringing about all the things we fought for.[16]

Into all of this talk of bright tomorrows, however, there is soon introduced the cynical reality that Lewis discusses elsewhere in *The Abolition of Man*—the fact of the human lust for power. In the novel the idea is first expressed in a passing comment by Lord Feverstone (formerly Dick Devine, last seen in *Out of the Silent Planet*):

> Man has got to take charge of Man. That means, remember, that some men have got to take charge of the rest. . . . You

and I want to be the people who do the taking charge, not the ones who are taken charge of.[17]

Later the scientist Filostrato echoes these same sentiments:

I mean it will then be reduced to one man. You are not a fool, are you, my young friend? All that talk about the power of Man over Nature—Man in the abstract. . . . You know as well as I do that Man's power over Nature means the power of some men over other men with Nature as the instrument. There is no such thing as Man—it is a word. There are only men.[18]

But the real action in the novel begins when the N.I.C.E. scientists in their lust for power strike a deal with the forces of evil. Here as in the previous novel C.S. Lewis uses the Faustian theme of humans bargaining with the powers of darkness and ending up slaves for the effort. As he does in so many contexts, Lewis here warns of the subtle process:

The physical sciences, good and innocent in themselves, had already, even in Ransom's own time, begun to be warped, had been subtly manoeuvred in a certain direction. Despair of objective truth had been increasingly insinuated into the scientists; indifference to it, and a concentration upon mere power, had been the result. . . . Dreams of the far future destiny of man were dragging up from its shallow and unquiet grave the old dream of Man as God.[19]

The "hideous strength" referred to in the novel's title is this unholy synthesis of science and the lust for power that leads to evil.

Even more than the earlier novels, *That Hideous Strength* instructs on the Christian doctrine of repentance and renewal. One of the more enlightening aspects of the novel is found in following closely the separate mental and moral journeys of Jane and Mark

Studdock. It is instructive to see Jane's struggles against abandoning her "modern" and "progressive" prejudices about herself and her relations with others. It is equally interesting to see Mark's seduction into evil by means of his inordinate need to be an "insider." It is enlightening to see exactly how repentance leads to humility and renewal in each character.

Lewis's third science fiction novel is not without its parodies, its ironic moments, and its satirical comments on a variety of topics. Delightful examples abound, but here are a few. Regarding Mark's education and resulting state of mind, Lewis writes:

> It must be remembered that in Mark's mind hardly one rag of noble thought, either Christian or Pagan, had a secure lodging. His education had been neither scientific nor classical—merely "Modern."[20]

At another point Lewis satirizes the scholarly propensity to believe what is written in books by experts even more than the plain truth before one's eyes:

> . . . for his education had had the curious effect of making things that he read and wrote more real to him than the things he saw.[21]

And Lewis has a great deal to say about the slippery slopes of moral compromise that are ventured upon by well-meaning "progressives" at every turn. Early on, a pragmatic official of the N.I.C.E. speaks frankly about his progressive allies among the college Fellows:

> But our two poor friends, though they can be persuaded to take the right train, or even to drive it, haven't a ghost of a notion where it's going to, or why.[22]

And later there is a passing description of one of the progressive professors:

I knew him well; he was an old dear. All his lectures were devoted to proving the impossibility of ethics, though in private life he'd walked ten miles rather than leave a penny debt unpaid.[23]

A major theme in *That Hideous Strength* is the many subtle ways in which progressive thinking and moral ambiguity can be, and very often is, transformed in the end into unmistakable evil.

Finally, it seems that no C.S. Lewis fiction would be complete without the inclusion of very dear animals in the story. In *That Hideous Strength* the reader soon finds that animals of every kind are to be the victims of vivisection and other scientific experiments at the N.I.C.E.. But there is also a comical old brown bear named Mr. Bultitude, who is Ransom's friend and devotee, and upon whom the author spends much enjoyable time delving into the depths of ursine thoughts and motives.

A particularly colorful example appears near the end of the story, when the resurrected Merlin whispers into the bear's ear the suggestion that it ought to attack the Deputy Director of the N.I.C.E.:

He laid his hand on its head and whispered in its ear and its dark mind was filled with excitement as though some long forbidden and forgotten pleasure were suddenly held out to it. Down the long, empty passages of Belbury it padded behind him. Saliva dripped from its mouth and it was beginning to growl. It was thinking of warm, salt tastes, of the pleasant resistances of bone, of things to crunch and lick and worry.[24]

That Hideous Strength is a complex novel, and there are consequently many things to look for. Again, look for an adventure story and the ubiquitous C.S. Lewis sense of humor with regard to the fads and foibles of the intelligentsia. Watch for the development of the major themes surrounding progressivism, moral compromise, and emergent evil. Look again for Professor Lewis's warning about the dangers in trying to turn the scientific method into a basis for ethics or a means to power.

On another level this novel is the story of Jane and Mark Studdock, a thoroughly modern couple with all of the properly sophisticated notions on marriage and children and careers. In the end both man and woman come to some humbling conclusions that the author openly admits are "old fashioned" and yet as true as ever. Look for C.S. Lewis's re-introduction of the much-maligned concept of obedience—as applied to both the male and the female situations—into the vocabulary of human relations; and look for how Lewis's thoughts on repentance, humility, and obedience shed light on the larger picture of God, the universe, and human existence.

OTHER WORKS IN FANTASY

Unlike the space trilogy, C.S. Lewis's other fantasy works discussed here do not present a unified and interacting vision of the cosmos so much as they represent the imaginative play of a great mind pondering specifically Christian problems. This is true particularly with regard to *The Screwtape Letters* and *The Great Divorce*, as both take a somewhat lighthearted look at such topics as heaven and hell, Satan and demons, human frailty and the Christian life. The final entrée of Lewis's fantasy in this chapter is *Till We Have Faces*, his fascinating retelling of the Greek myth of Cupid and Psyche.

The Screwtape Letters and Screwtape Proposes a Toast

A book that brought C.S. Lewis great popularity was *The Screwtape Letters*, an imaginative series of letters from a senior devil to his apprentice concerning the best ways to bring about the destruction of a human soul. That it was this delightful book instead of his more substantial works that brought Lewis's initial notoriety was ever a source of irritation to the scholar, but it is easy to understand why the public would be so drawn to the *Screwtape* works, for they are both as highly entertaining as they are insightful.

In his 1962 preface to *Screwtape Proposes a Toast*, Lewis explains the method used for both of his *Screwtape* works:

> Screwtape's outlook is like a photographic negative; his whites are our blacks and whatever he welcomes we ought to dread.[25]

The words of the senior devil Screwtape, both in the letters and the speech, then, are to be read as what a diabolical mentor might say to his apprentice to bring about as much human misery as possible. By this clever technique Lewis seeks to teach the Christian believer about the many seemingly harmless things that the Tempter can effectively use to draw people under his influence.

This "photographic negative" approach must be understood if one is to appreciate and enjoy *The Screwtape Letters*. Indeed, if there are modern readers who have completely misunderstood the intent and method of Lewis's *Screwtape* books, they are certainly not alone. In his 1960 preface, Lewis himself reports of a clergyman who objected to the editor that much of the advice given in Screwtape's letters "seemed to him not only erroneous but positively diabolical."[26] But of course that is the point; Screwtape is a devil.

In that same preface we find a most succinct statement of what Lewis is about in *The Screwtape Letters*. In a social context in which traditional morality is widely dismissed as a somewhat arbitrary suppression of everything that is fun, Lewis is eager to expose the widespread illusion that evil is somehow liberating. He writes:

> We must picture Hell as a state where everyone is perpetually concerned about his own dignity and advancement, where everyone has a grievance, and where everyone lives the deadly serious passions of envy, self-importance, and resentment.[27]

Here we find the tone and the theme of the *Screwtape* works, as well as the reason why pride is often seen as the deadliest sin of all.

The Screwtape Letters follows the efforts and fortunes of

Wormwood, an apprentice tempter, through the advice and admonitions of his superior and uncle, Screwtape. While the topics discussed range from tearoom manners to formal philosophy, from fads and fashions to concepts of time and eternity, from irritating habits to doctrinal disputes, the underlying purpose of Screwtape's advice is always the same: the capture and destruction of the human soul.

Of the many topics discussed by Screwtape in his letters, one of the most important is prayer. The senior devil is, of course, clear in his advice that Wormwood must do his best to prevent his subject's praying at all. But failing at that, Wormwood is told that he still might be able to turn the prayers to diabolical advantage. Remember, when Screwtape speaks of the Enemy, he is speaking of God. Screwtape writes:

> When the patient is an adult recently converted to the Enemy's party, like your man, this is best done by encouraging him to remember, or to think he remembers, the parrot-like nature of his prayers in childhood. In reaction against that, he may be persuaded to aim at something entirely spontaneous, inward, informal, and unregularised; and what this will actually mean to a beginner will be an effort to produce in himself a vaguely devotional mood in which real concentration of will and intelligence have no part.[28]

Here, through a devil's words, the Christian finds some valuable insight into feelings and prayer. How many believers have been discouraged in their prayers because they have not achieved what they believe to be the proper mood. This is a good example of how C.S. Lewis teaches through the words of Screwtape.

Here is another good example of Screwtape's advice to Wormwood, this time regarding the great value—to Satan of course—of promoting a sense of guilt without repentance:

> If such a feeling is allowed to live, but not allowed to become irresistible and flower into real repentance, it has one invalu-

able tendency. It increases the patient's reluctance to think about the Enemy. All humans at nearly all times have some such reluctance; but when thinking of Him involves facing and intensifying a whole vague cloud of half-conscious guilt, this reluctance is increased tenfold. They hate every idea that suggests Him, just as men in financial embarrassment hate the very sight of a bankbook.[29]

And so the Christian reader learns of the diabolical uses of guilt and consequently the great need for repentance. *The Screwtape Letters* is packed with such insights, and Lewis presents them in a most entertaining way.

The very short work called *Screwtape Proposes a Toast* is often included in the same volume with the letters. The toast is a speech given by the distinguished devil Screwtape to a graduating class of novice tempters. The tone and style are the same as in the letters, but here the topics of concern are democracy and education.

By having Screwtape praise the institutionalized "leveling-effect" in modern English and American education, C.S. Lewis is obviously deploring it. For example, the devil Screwtape gleefully describes "... the vast, overall movement towards the discrediting, and finally the elimination, of every kind of human excellence—moral, cultural, social, or intellectual,"[30] all under the misused name of "democracy." Lewis's theme is that an educational system that works at leveling, or attempting to make everyone the same, is destined to stifle what is the very best in a society. It is a point with far-reaching implications for the policies we see in public education today.

In reading the *Screwtape* works, it is essential that the reader never lose sight of the fact that the letters and speech are presented entirely from a diabolical point of view. The advice is bad advice— or perhaps effective advice given for bad purposes. Lewis describes the devilish point of view that sets the tone for the *Screwtape* books:

The work into which I had to project myself while I spoke through Screwtape was all dust, grit, thirst, and itch. Every trace of beauty, freshness, and geniality had to be excluded. It almost smothered me before I was done.[31]

In this diabolical role-playing, Lewis effectively accomplishes what he set out to do: to expose the lie that there is something more freeing and more fun about doing evil.

Look for the diabolical structure—the relations between ranks of devils, the kinds of controls used, the role of ego and status—and consider its implications for the social structure in which we live. Look for the many useful insights on Christian living—insights on fads and fashions, on our emotions, on prayer, on our desires and pleasures, on our associations, on time and eternity, on politics, on permanence and change, and of course on education. Consider how a knowledge of the diabolical uses of these matters can equip the Christian believer for greater steadfastness of faith. Finally, look for the overall themes concerning freedom and bondage, humility and pride, joy and despair. Here the reader will find a consistency that echoes throughout C.S. Lewis's writings from the Narnia stories, through the science fiction trilogy, through his addresses and essays, and even into his academic works.

The Great Divorce

One of my favorite C.S. Lewis books is *The Great Divorce*. This story is pure fantasy, and it is Lewis the student of human nature at his best. Again the reader is warned not to look for too much direct analogy in the story, as Lewis clearly had no intention that the book should be taken as a theological allegory defining heaven and hell. But one of the author's purposes was obviously to throw more light on some of the follies of the human spirit, and this task he accomplishes in a most enjoyable way.

The story follows its protagonist on a bus ride from hell on earth to the outer regions of heaven. From the very beginning we are taken into Lewis's penetrating satire as the passengers begin to quarrel among themselves even before they embark on the bus. At once we see the crowding and pushing and cheating that ring only too true to our everyday knowledge of life in the modern city. And similarly, throughout the book Lewis portrays fantastic situations in such a way that the reader sees even more clearly into the realities of human absurdity.

Along with the rich physical descriptions of the bus ride and the wonders outside the bus, Lewis holds a series of types of people up for the reader's scrutiny. Thus at the beginning he spends some time with the misunderstood artist, followed by the cynical intellectual, then the belligerent bully, the scientific skeptic, and the man who makes himself miserable demanding his rights when he could have much more.

It is not surprising that Lewis spends an entire chapter on a thoroughly modern, liberal-minded clergyman, for such over-acculturated clerics were always among his favorite subjects for satire. The minister is met at the edge of heaven by his old friend Dick, who tries to dissuade him from his agnostic relativism. Here is a taste of their conversation, beginning with a question from the clergyman:

> "Now that you mention it, I don't think we ever do give it a name. What do you call it?"
>
> "We call it Hell."
>
> "There is no need to be profane, my dear boy. I may not be very orthodox, in your sense of that word, but I do feel that these matters ought to be discussed simply, and seriously, and reverently. . . . No doubt you'll tell me why, on your view, I was sent there. I'm not angry."
>
> "But don't you know? You went there because you are an apostate."
>
> "Are you serious, Dick?"
>
> "Perfectly."
>
> "This is worse than I expected. Do you really think people are penalised for their honest opinions? Even assuming, for the sake of argument, that those opinions were mistaken."[32]

Readers who have encountered a certain species of religious intellectual will immediately sense that Lewis has caught the mode and manner perfectly. Professor Lewis knew well all of the posturing and qualifying and negating and relativizing and sophistry that typify such discussions, and in the end he makes his character Dick confront the basic dishonesty in the whole endeavor. Dick says:

> Friend . . . let us be frank. Our opinions were not honestly come by. We simply found ourselves in contact with a certain current of ideas and plunged into it because it seemed modern and successful. At College, you know, we just started automatically writing the kind of essays that get good marks and saying the kind of things that won applause. . . . Having allowed oneself to drift, unresisting, unpraying, accepting every half-conscious solicitation from our desires, we reached a point where we no longer believed the Faith.[33]

Nowhere have I seen this process of intellectual disenchantment more clearly and honestly portrayed than here in *The Great Divorce*.

But *The Great Divorce* is not primarily about disenchantment and intellectual dishonesty; it is about the larger picture of the many ways people try to convince themselves there is no clear distinction between good and evil. In this regard Lewis laments the popular modern attempt to obscure the difference between right and wrong:

> The attempt is based on the belief that reality never presents us with an absolutely unavoidable "either-or"; that, granted skill and patience and (above all) time enough, some way of embracing both alternatives can always be found; that mere development or adjustment or refinement will somehow turn evil into good without our being called on for a final and total rejection of anything we should like to retain. This belief I take to be a disastrous error.[34]

Here C.S. Lewis has succinctly stated the theme of *The Great Divorce*, reflecting the traditional Christian doctrine of repentance and renewal.

The story line of this fantasy takes the protagonist on a tour, wherein he sees for himself the many and various ways that the people around him try to hang on to what will in the end destroy them. Again Lewis explains himself clearly:

> I do not think that all who choose wrong roads perish; but their rescue consists in being put back on the right road. A wrong sum can be put right: but only by going back till you find the error and working it afresh from that point, never by simply going on. Evil can be undone, but it cannot "develop" into good. . . . It is still "either-or." If we insist on keeping Hell (or even earth) we shall not see Heaven: if we accept Heaven we shall not be able to retain even the smallest and most intimate souvenirs of Hell.[35]

A final note on *The Great Divorce* concerns Lewis's rich imagery. When his bus passengers disembark at the edge of heaven their appearance is very different:

> Now that they were in the light, they were transparent—fully transparent when they stood between me and it, smudgy and imperfectly opaque when they stood in the shadow of some tree.[36]

On the other hand, all of the objects and persons of heaven are much more solid, heavier, and somehow more real. And our protagonist discovers that one becomes more "real" as one moves closer to the center of heaven.

This sense of the falseness, or at least the flimsiness, of our earthly, material world as contrasted with the more substantial realness of the spiritual world is a reflection of the sacramental mysticism that both C.S. Lewis and G.K. Chesterton derived from their readings of George MacDonald, who is, incidentally, the protagonist's personal tour guide in *The Great Divorce*. Briefly, the idea is that what we experience empirically is real, but it is only the "faded backside" of the much richer tapestry of experiences that we do not see. Consequently, our every decision and action holds a great importance as the visible representations of spiritual events beyond the pale of our senses. Thus, as Lewis pointed out earlier, our daily lives become the field for continuous decisions whose consequences reach far beyond what we may perceive. This perspective of sacramental mysticism is summarized in Chapter 8 of my book on G.K. Chesterton[37] and is discussed in detail by Ian Boyd in a "Special C.S. Lewis Edition" of *The Chesterton Review*.[38]

What to look for in reading *The Great Divorce* is first of all a highly enjoyable piece of satire on the human condition. Also enjoy the great imagery not only of the inhabitants of hell, but even more so of heaven. For example:

> The noise, though gigantic, was like giant's laughter: like the revelry of a whole college of giants together laughing, dancing, singing, roaring at their high works.[39]

Look for types. C.S. Lewis was ever the student of human behavior, and his insights into our propensities and habits are invaluable. Look for definitions of good and evil, and especially watch for the author's exposition of the ideas and forces seeking to blur the lines between them. Finally, let Lewis's fantastic story and its imagery stimulate your own imagination toward thoughts and fantasies of heaven.

Till We Have Faces

This imaginative novel—considered by some to be C.S. Lewis's finest literary work—is a reworking and retelling of the ancient Greek myth of Cupid (Eros) and Psyche. It is a book that is profoundly different from Lewis's other works and probably reflects the broadening and maturing influence wrought by his love for Joy Davidman. Critics have suggested that Orual, the main character in Lewis's mythical rendition, is in many ways a portrait of Joy Davidman herself. There are many themes and many levels by which this complex novel can be approached, and my purpose here is merely to suggest a few points for beginning.

C.S. Lewis went to great lengths to insist that *Till We Have Faces* was written as a myth, and not as an allegory. The difference, he once explained, is that in allegory the characters are intended to represent abstract qualities, as we find in Bunyan's classic *The Pilgrim's Progress*. But a myth is a story from which various readers in different times and places can draw a number of meanings. Thus, a myth is far from a story that is untrue; in fact, it may be said to be a story that is even more true than any others.

With these definitions in mind, Lewis considered it entirely legitimate for him to borrow the classical myth of Cupid and Psyche by drawing from it a central, enduring meaning and then retelling the story in such a way as to shed new light on it for modern readers. The classical myth is a story of a beautiful, loving woman named Psyche who is betrayed and apparently destroyed by her jealous sisters. The story involves a marriage of the mortal Psyche to the immortal Cupid, a sacred prohibition, a coercion, a blackmail, and a subsequent disaster for Psyche.

But *Till We Have Faces* is a retelling from the point of view of Orual, Psyche's unattractive eldest sister. In the beginning we find that while the second sister, Redival, is outwardly jealous of Psyche's beauty—both inward and outward—Orual seems to take great delight in Psyche and appears to love her dearly. It is only as the story develops that we begin to see the problems in Orual's love, for it is a love that seeks to possess, consume, and even destroy its object if need be. And this is a central meaning in Lewis's retelling of the myth: to explore this wrong kind of love and to illustrate its destructive power.

As Orual's narrative unfolds, the reader begins to catch glimpses of the problem to come. One sees hints in Orual's selfish complaints when Psyche is to be sacrificed to the cruel goddess Ungit:

"Oh cruel, cruel!" I wailed. "Is it nothing to you that you leave me here alone? Psyche, did you ever love me at all?"[40]

And later when Orual finds Psyche living joyfully with Eros on the mountain, again it is not Psyche's happiness that is Orual's chief concern. Orual complains:

> For the world had broken in pieces and Psyche and I were not in the same piece. Seas, mountains, madness, death itself, could not have removed her from me to such a hopeless distance as this. Gods, and again gods, always gods . . . they had stolen her. They would leave us nothing. A thought pierced up through the crust of my mind like a crocus coming up in the early year. Was she not worthy of the gods? Ought they not to have her? But instantly great, choking, blinding waves of sorrow swept it away and, "Oh!" I cried. "It's not right. It's not right. Oh, Psyche, come back!"[41]

Even the evidence that Psyche is happy and where she belongs does not deter Orual from her lamentations.

If Orual's possessive love for Psyche is perhaps understandable at first, Orual's narrative eventually reveals the radical lengths to which this "love" will go. "If there is no other way, I will kill her!" she says.[42] Rather than leave Psyche to a fate that Orual cannot understand, she tells herself that even killing Psyche would be an act of love. And so, after yet another ". . . memory of Psyche in the mountain valley, brightface, brimming over with joy,"[43] Orual's possessive love compels her to use whatever means necessary to reveal Psyche's secret. In the end she uses Psyche's love for her to blackmail Psyche into deceiving her divine husband and thereby bringing misery upon herself.

What is the point of this illustration of a possessive, devouring kind of love? On one level Lewis is showing the difference between two kinds of love: that of devotion versus that of possession. One meaning of the myth is simply that selfish, possessive love is destructive to its object. In the end the reader sees Orual's passion for her sister as greedy and dehumanizing—using Psyche as an object for her own gratification rather than as an independent spirit.

On another level *Till We Have Faces* deals with the theme of death in the transformation of natural love into *agape* love. The real story here is not that of Psyche's apparent death. Psyche, in fact, is portrayed as a kind of natural Christian from the onset. The real story is Orual's story: that painful, rebellious, agonizing pilgrimage from natural love to *agape* love. In the end we begin to understand the several kinds of death that Orual's transformation requires, and we see the power of repentance. Finally Orual reports:

> "Oh Psyche, oh goddess," I said. "Never again will I call you mine; but all there is of me shall be yours. Alas, you know what it's worth. I never wished you well, never had one self-less thought of you. I was a craver."[44]

The story contains much that sheds light on the meanings of death and resurrection, repentance and renewal.

In *Till We Have Faces* C.S. Lewis does in fiction much of the same kind of work he does in nonfiction in *The Abolition of Man* and *Mere Christianity*. By this I mean that Lewis is doing what might be called pre-Christian foundation work. There are certain stages or preconditions that people go through—speaking both historically and individually—that predispose them to accept Christianity. An example would be the rejection of the narrow materialism that precludes the acceptance of the numinous, awe-inspiring realms of the spirit. In this regard Lewis makes the rather surprising observation that even a belief in pagan gods brings us closer to the truth than does materialist skepticism. In the words of the novel's repentant Greek, called the Fox:

> I am to blame for most of this, and I should bear the punishment. I taught her, as men teach a parrot, to say, "Lies of poets," and, "Ungit's a false image." I made her think that

ended the question. . . . I never told her why the old Priest got
something from the dark House that I never got from my trim
sentences. . . . Of course, I didn't know; but I never told her
I didn't know. I don't know now. Only that the way to the
true gods is more like the house of Ungit. . . .[45]

What C.S. Lewis is about in much of his writing is exploring these
pre-Christian gropings, and much of his intellectual work on myth
and legend is focused on their role as early approximations of the
truth.

This aspect of C.S. Lewis's work is puzzling to many Christians,
perhaps particularly to those of more strictly fundamentalist leanings. All of this talk of gods and pre-Christian types of religions as
containing seeds of truth might even seem dangerous in view of the
First Commandment in the Old Testament. But it is important to
realize that Lewis is not advocating the legitimacy of pagan gods.
What he does suggest in several contexts is that there were many
hints—inaccurate and ill-conceived and even ignorantly blasphe-
mous as they may have been—at the truth of Jesus long before the
historical event of Jesus' life took place. It is as if in ancient mythology we find humankind's dark gropings toward a truth that would
come to be revealed with increasing clarity over time.

It is a point worth pondering, for a favorite tactic of the atheist
intellectual is to point out the strong similarities between biblical stories and pagan myths from an earlier date. The argument is that, for
example, if the story of the Great Flood and the Ark is found to be
predated by a Hittite story of a great flood and a boat, then the biblical story obviously plagiarized or at least borrowed from the other
source. Many a college sophomore has stumbled over this very argument and others like it. But what Lewis is about in this regard is to
point out that cultural diffusion is not the only logical explanation
of why similar ideas appear in various times and places. It can be
argued with equal force that the truth exists outside time and place,
that it is forever seeking to break through to human consciousness,
and that it does break through now here, now there in various man-

ifestations, by various symbols, and with varying degrees of accuracy. Therefore, C.S. Lewis the Christian is quite comfortable with the ancient myths, whether or not they bear a similarity to biblical accounts.

In his novel *Till We Have Faces*, then, Lewis recognizes a body of pre-Christian truths and proceeds to hammer them into a shape more recognizable as consistent with Christian doctrine. The result is a story affirming many of the basic underpinnings of Christian theology—for example, the need for sacrifice, the true meanings of love, the value of humility, the issues of justice and mercy, and the power of repentance. These are all important themes to look for while reading this novel.

There are many other fascinating aspects to Lewis's story, and—truly characteristic of the myth—each reader will find in it meanings that perhaps few others have perceived. But as an aid to the beginner, let me suggest a few topics worth watching. Notice the interplay of Glome versus Greece, Bardia versus the Fox, pagan religiosity versus rational materialism. Follow Orual's path from self-deception to self-knowledge, from rebellion to submission, from pride to humility, from accusation to repentance, from ugliness to beauty. Note how Psyche's remarkable physical beauty comes to be eclipsed by her inner beauty as expressed in her compassion, honesty, acceptance, forbearance, faith, and hope. Pay attention to the author's treatment of materialist philosophy as preached by the Fox, as embraced by Redival and Orual, and as it affects Orual's ability to see and understand the fate of her beloved Psyche.

Finally, the reader may wonder about the meaning of the novel's title, *Till We Have Faces*. Our clue is found late in the story in the context of Orual's ruminations after making her complaint to the gods:

> The complaint was the answer. To have heard myself making it was to be answered. . . . I saw well why the gods do not speak to us openly, nor let us answer. Till that word can be dug out of us, why should they hear the babble that we think

we mean? How can they meet us face to face till we have faces?[46]

The image is reminiscent of the scene in *The Great Divorce* where the people in their natural state are nearly invisible but then begin to gain a solidity as they are drawn nearer to God. As long as we cling to the falseness of our natural state, we have not even sufficient substance, or face, to address the supernatural. Until we encounter the reality of ourselves, we cannot begin to encounter the reality that is God.

6

BASIC
APOLOGETICS

If by apologetics we mean argumentation designed to demonstrate the truth and sense of Christian doctrine, then it is true that most of Lewis's works in both nonfiction and fiction can be seen basically as apologetic works. Indeed, from the moment Lewis was converted to Christianity, he wrote tirelessly to try to convince others of the historical verity, the rational soundness, and the moral importance of orthodox Christian doctrine in modern life.

We have seen the larger intellectual stage upon which C.S. Lewis strode and argued, and we have located his works roughly within the Romantic and Christian streams of thought flowing into and through our century. We have looked as well at his children's stories and his science fiction and other fantasies. We turn in this chapter to three of Lewis's most basic books in Christian apologetics: *The Pilgrim's Regress, The Abolition of Man,* and *Mere Christianity.*

The Pilgrim's Regress

The first book that C.S. Lewis wrote after becoming a Christian was an allegory inspired by the classic *The Pilgrim's Progress* by John Bunyan. Lewis's *The Pilgrim's Regress* is not among his easiest to understand and is therefore recommended to readers who already have some background in Lewis's writings. In fact, in his own preface to the third edition, Lewis accuses himself of "needless obscurity" as well as an "uncharitable temper" in some of his metaphors and characterizations.

The story follows its protagonist, John, through a land where the places and people represent various human characteristics and schools of thought. For example, he passes through a city named Thrill, representing the life given over entirely to sensual pleasures; and he passes another city named Claptrap, representing the formidable body of pseudo-scientific and intellectual foolishness passed freely among a people fittingly called the Clevers.

As C.S. Lewis explains, his allegory is meant to retrace his own intellectual journey from popular realism to philosophic idealism to pantheism to theism and finally to Christianity. While he had written *The Pilgrim's Regress* as perhaps a companion or guide for others, he later lamented that there are relatively few who actually follow the same sequence of changes and discoveries that eventually led him to Christianity. "I still think this is a very natural road," he wrote, "but I now know that it is a road very rarely trodden."[1] Nevertheless, one needs not be a sojourner on Lewis's special road in order to enjoy and benefit from his insights into the various points of view represented along the way.

In the beginning many Christian readers are surprised and confused by the portrait of the Landlord and his Steward. For the author is clearly referring to God and the clergy, and the emerging picture is one of an unreasonable ogre and his hypocritical representative. There is a scene early on when the boy John is taken by his parents to the Steward, who at first acts friendly but then dons a mask and begins to question the boy.

> "I hope," said the Steward, "that you have not already broken any of the rules." John's heart began to thump, and his eyes bulged more and more, and he was at his wit's end when the Steward took the mask off and looked at John with his real face and said, "Better tell a lie, old chap, better tell a lie. Easiest

for all concerned," and popped the mask on his face all in a flash.[2]

This surprising behavior and the fact that the card of rules contains on its back an alternative set of rules negating those on the front are Lewis's way of portraying the contradictory and even hypocritical ways that God and Christian doctrine are often presented to a child. Thus with childlike clarity Lewis shows the effects of compromise and insincerity in religion.

Another potentially puzzling issue early in the book is that of the brown girls. In the space of only three consecutive sentences the protagonist, John, meets and fornicates with a brown girl, and then within the next page he discovers that his pleasures have produced a host of daughters. Upon discovering there are serious consequences to his sins, John simply flees.

Here Lewis has portrayed the young man in his natural, irresponsible state, suddenly surprised to learn that his own actions always yield very real consequences. John's flight is the common human flight from responsibility, and Lewis's story contains the author's comment on this propensity to blind ourselves to the effects of our own excesses and follies. This theme occurs throughout the book, perhaps most noticeably in the later revelations about the real infrastructure supporting the Clevers.

But one of the most interesting aspects to *The Pilgrim's Regress* is its treatment of John's desire for the far-off Island. In this book Lewis used the term "romance" to denote this sense of longing, but he later regretted the term because of its many, sometimes disparate and distracting popular meanings. The issue is indeed a very particular kind of desire, as the author explains:

> But this desire, even when there is no hope of possible satisfaction, continues to be prized, and even to be preferred to anything else in the world, by those who have once felt it. This hunger is better than any other fulness; this poverty better than all other wealth.[3]

It was this desire—and the desire for the desire—that Lewis later chose to call Joy and to pursue further in his autobiographical *Surprised by Joy*.

For those readers with the patience for allegory, *The Pilgrim's Regress* is full of rewards. Along the way John encounters a series of unforgettable people, each of which rings true to a type in real life. There are the urbane, sophisticated Clevers, who sneer at tradition and congratulate each other for their free-floating iconoclasm. There is the psychologizing Giant, who claims to see below the surface into the subconscious causes of all behavior. There is the endlessly-equivocating Mr. Sensible, whose formidable storehouse of misquotes and half-truths tend to render all decisive or moral action as rash or ill-advised. And there are many, many more characters the reader cannot help but recognize.

Near the end of the book when John experiences his new perspective on the world he had left behind, he sees many things more clearly than he had before. Using this device of renewed vision, C.S. Lewis provides some of his finest critiques of our civilization. Here is but one example:

> Their labor-saving devices multiply drudgery; their aphrodisiacs make them impotent; their amusements bore them; their rapid production of food leaves half of them starving, and their devices for saving time have banished leisure from their country.[4]

In the great tradition of Swift's *Gulliver's Travels* and Bunyan's *The Pilgrim's Progress*, C.S. Lewis's allegory provides unusual insights into the fads and foibles of modern men and women.

In reading *The Pilgrim's Regress* one does not look for a fast-moving plot loaded with action, but for the meanings of the people and places that the protagonist encounters. Look for the logic behind the rhetoric as each person seeks to convince John of a given truth with regard to his Island dream. Look for C.S. Lewis's web of associations among characters and places, paying close attention to the maps provided in the book.

It can be especially instructive to watch the relationship between John and his companion Virtue, for here Lewis has deliberately set up two very different kinds of seekers pursuing basically the same goal. Look for the meaning behind Virtue's "northern" propensities, as contrasted with John's "southern" bent. Pay special attention to what is required of them each in the end. And finally, of course, explore the ways in which the fate of John and Virtue speak to your own life.

The Pilgrim's Regress bears reading and re-reading not only because of its "obscurity," but because it is a book that lends itself to different levels of understanding by different readers or the same reader at different points in his or her life. It is a book packed with insights and perspectives that are essential to an understanding of Christian faith in the larger milieu of the popular ideas of the twentieth century.

The Abolition of Man

The Abolition of Man is not an easy book for the casual reader. But it is an important book, and one need not be an intellectual or philosopher to understand its arguments. The author's subtitle for the book indicates its subject to be "reflections on education," but its scope is much broader and its reach much deeper than that. In fact, matters of pedagogy are discussed relatively little and only as a point of departure into the true subject of the book. *The Abolition of Man* is really about the trends in modern thinking that seek to subordinate the human mind and soul to the processes of natural phenomena, thus bringing about the abolition of humanity as we know it.

Many readers will find Lewis's approach to the problem somewhat unusual, if not troubling. No doubt this will be particularly true of the reader who is looking for the kind of Christian apologetics found in Lewis's *Mere Christianity*. But here Lewis is not specifically defining or defending Christian doctrine; rather, he is doing more foundational work in philosophy. In other words, in *The Abolition of Man* Lewis digs into the bedrock of modern popular philosophy and lays some of the foundations upon which religious arguments can be made. That is why Lewis draws his illustrations and data from various ancient traditions including the Hindu, Confucian, Egyptian, Babylonian, Hebrew, Platonic, Aristotelian, and Christian.

For convenience of argument Lewis develops a concept that he calls the Tao. He defines the Tao as the compendium of those bedrock beliefs about right and wrong found in all major religions. The Tao includes such ideas as that all human beings possess an intrinsic value entitling them to at least a minimal measure of justice, that it is wrong to take another's life, that it is good to give respect to one's parents, that it is wrong to steal or to lie, that widows and orphans should be taken care of, and that one should not abandon one's spouse and children.

These and many other bedrock moral criteria Lewis sees as basic to the traditional understanding of human existence. He writes:

> This conception in all its forms, Platonic, Aristotelian, Stoic, Christian, and Oriental alike, I shall henceforth refer to for brevity simply as 'the Tao.' . . . But what is common to them all is something we cannot neglect. It is the doctrine of objective value, the belief that certain attitudes are really true, and others really false, to the kind of thing the universe is and the kind of things we are.[5]

Lewis correctly calls objective value a doctrine because it can be neither proved nor disproved. It is an assumption that can be accepted or rejected. The most popular modern philosophies reject it.

In the first chapter, "Men Without Chests," Lewis presents a picture of modern "value-free" intellectual skeptics as people with heads but no hearts. His opening comments on education reveal a concerted effort in the schools to train young minds to reject any notions of value as somehow unreal as compared to facts. This popular but false separation of value and fact is responsible, according to Lewis, for a great amount of folly in modern society as well as for the emergence of a peculiar kind of learned experts—men without chests.

> It is an outrage that they should be commonly spoken of as Intellectuals. This gives them the chance to say that he who attacks them attacks Intelligence. . . . It is not excess of thought but defect of fertile and generous emotion that marks them out. Their heads are no bigger than the ordinary: it is the atrophy of the chest beneath that makes them seem so.[6]

We have become, writes Lewis, a society that claims to accept no values, but only facts. But in seeking to reject all values we place ourselves in the tragic and ironic position of needing leaders and people with the very qualities we reject. While there is a popular cry for the qualities of "the chest" or the heart—such as courage, magnanimity, sentiment, honesty, and the like—the prevailing philosophy seeks to reject these qualities as unreal.

The result, in Lewis's words, is this:

> And all the time—such is the tragi-comedy of our situation—we continue to clamour for those very qualities we are rendering impossible. . . . In a sort of ghastly simplicity we remove the organ and demand the function. We make men without chests and expect of them virtue and enterprise. We laugh at honour and are shocked to find traitors in our midst. We castrate and bid the geldings be fruitful.[7]

The second chapter of *The Abolition of Man* is called "The Way," and here Lewis advances his case against the "values-free" philosophy of modern education. Here he takes up the issue of "debunking" or ostensibly "seeing through" the values hidden in other people's thoughts. This debunking motif has always been a favorite ploy of the intellectual and has even since Lewis's time enjoyed considerable academic prestige under the banner of the sociology of knowledge.

But Lewis hastens to point out that such debunking of values tends to be used rather selectively.

> Their scepticism about values is on the surface: it is for use on other people's values: about the values current in their own set they are not nearly sceptical enough. . . . A great many of those who 'debunk' traditional or (as they would say) 'sentimental' values have in the background values of their own which they believe to be immune from the debunking process. They claim to be cutting away the parasitic growth of emotion, religious sanction, and inherited taboos, in order that 'real' or 'basic' values may emerge.[8]

This self-serving selectivity and immunity in the values-debunking process tends to hide the fact that all schools of thought, all forms of knowledge, and all methods of study and models of rationality contain hidden values that give them their sense and coherence. This is the point Lewis develops in his second chapter.

Through much of this second chapter Lewis discusses the concept of instinct as the widely proposed replacement for traditional values. The popular idea among the evolutionists was that once we rid ourselves of the arbitrary and archaic values passed along to us from the traditional religions, we can turn to the basic human instincts—such as the survival instinct—to create new, more realistic values.

But Lewis attacks this argument on two fronts. First, he demonstrates how human instinct leads either back to the bedrock values of the Tao or to no values at all. Second, he points out that such appeals to human instinct can easily lead into the Nietzschean morality of power as its own justification. The point is that when "realism" is set up as the standard of morality as opposed to the Tao, the standard is both a lie and an imminent danger to human decency.

The third and final chapter, called "The Abolition of Man," takes up the idea of "man's conquest of nature," which was so popular among the early apologists of science. This self-flattering concept no doubt drew its popularity from the image of men and women everywhere seizing control of their lives and mastering the forces of nature for their own betterment, comfort, and happiness.

But Lewis uses the examples of the airplane, the radio, and contraceptives to point out that such a vision of "man's conquest of nature" is a gross exaggeration at best. He writes:

> What we call Man's power is, in reality a power possessed by some men which they may, or may not, allow other men to profit by. Again, as regards the powers manifested in the aeroplane or the wireless, Man is as much the patient or subject as the possessor, since he is the target both for bombs and for propaganda.[9]

In other words, what is commonly called "man's conquest of nature" often turns out to be the power that some exercise over others using nature as the instrument.

Once we have understood this basic deception in the idea of "man's conquest of nature," we are able to see the relevance and prescience of Lewis's vision in *The Abolition of Man*. Though he first presented these ideas in the 1940s, subsequent intellectual and technological developments have borne the very fruit that Lewis predicted.

Much of Lewis's argument in the final chapter is concerned with the scientific control of human behavior. Those who consider such ideas to be merely a remote possibility or the idle dreams of cranks and utopians are urged to take another look, for such behavioral and social control has long been advocated by highly respected scholars in both psychology and sociology.

Most notably in the field of psychology, behaviorist B.F. Skinner has for many years promoted a new kind of society in which scientific planners control human behavior through stimulus-response mechanisms. Skinner's desired society can be found in his book *Walden Two*. His rationale is argued in his 1971 book *Beyond Freedom and Dignity*. Here Skinner contends that the only thing preventing us from gaining complete control over human behavior is those "traditional prescientific views" that need to be swept away. He writes:

> Freedom and dignity illustrate the difficulty. They are the possessions of the autonomous man of traditional theory, and they are essential to practices in which a person is held responsible for his conduct and given credit for his achievements. A scientific analysis shifts both the responsibility and the achievement to the environment.[10]

Professor Skinner could hardly have been more clear in revealing the motives, methods, and objective that he desires.

In the field of sociology the banner is carried most notably in the work of the positivist George A. Lundberg, who clarified his ideas in a little book called *Can Science Save Us?* Like Skinner, Lundberg calls for the scientific management of human behavior, similarly basing his arguments in the successes of the natural sciences. In Lundberg's version:

> The dominant thoughtway of our time as regards social problems is a legalistic-moralistic, "literary" orientation which has been largely abandoned in coming to terms with our physical environment.[11]

And indeed throughout the field of sociology the dominant assumption is that human behavior is primarily a function of either natural or historical phenomena.

It is in this arena that C.S. Lewis is making combat, and it is in this context that *The Abolition of Man* is such an important book. For here Lewis does no less than to challenge the most basic foundational assumptions of the most popular social sciences. Here Lewis questions the establishment of behavioral and social control, the advocacy of what has come to be called "genetic engineering," and the very appropriateness of naturalism as a theoretical model for the study of human beings.

Regarding the efforts of scientific planners to control human behavior, Lewis asks the essential question: to what end? In other words, what are the desired results of such control? An answer to such a question necessarily invokes certain values, whether they be some vague conceptions of fairness or equality or basic human rights or whatever. But the important point to Lewis is that such answers inevitably amount to little more than secularized versions of the Tao. And so the very people who reject the Tao as "prescientific" end by appealing to the Tao's guidance for their scientific efforts.

One of the major points Lewis is making in *The Abolition of Man* is that there are certain basic values that define us—human beings—as distinct from the other animals. Try as we may, we can never manage to escape those values without in fact becoming something that is not human. Lewis writes:

> Stepping outside the Tao, they have stepped into the void. Nor are their subjects necessarily unhappy men. They are not men at all: they are artefacts. Man's final conquest has proved to be the abolition of Man.[12]

Lewis warns us that in our scientific attempts to submit ourselves to value-free controls, we unwittingly abolish the very uniqueness that defines us as human beings.

Lewis also has much to say regarding eugenics, the efforts to produce desirable people through selection and manipulation of human genes. Here again is Lewis's prescience borne out in the rising concerns over what we now call "genetic engineering." In this regard Lewis writes:

> I am only making clear what Man's conquest of Nature really means and especially that final stage in the conquest, which, perhaps, is not far off. The final stage is come when Man by

eugenics, by pre-natal conditioning, and by an education and propaganda based on a perfect applied psychology, has obtained full control over himself. Human nature will be the last part of Nature to surrender to Man. The battle will then be won. . . . But who, precisely, will have won it?[13]

One begins to see that all of these efforts to subordinate humanity to impersonal forces larger than themselves ignore a consistent consequence wherein humanity is no longer humanity.

This point leads logically into Lewis's final observations concerning naturalism as the dominant perspective on the human being. The term *naturalism* is used here to mean looking at all phenomena—including ourselves and the meaning of our lives—through the idealized perspective of the natural scientist. Lewis summarizes this naturalist perspective thus:

Nature seems to be the spatial and temporal, as distinct from what is less fully so or not at all. She seems to be the world of quantity, as against the world of quality: of objects as against consciousness: of the bound, as against the wholly or partially autonomous: of that which knows no values as against that which both has and perceives value: of efficient causes (or, in some modern systems, of no causality at all) as against final causes. Now I take it that when we understand a thing analytically and then dominate and use it for our own convenience we reduce it to the level of 'Nature' in the sense that we suspend our judgements of value about it, ignore its final cause (if any), and treat it in terms of quantity.[14]

Here Lewis describes the widespread tendency, particularly in the natural sciences, to deny values, to ignore final causation, and to define everything in terms of classification and quantity.

While the naturalist perspective has been arguably effective and useful in understanding and manipulating the physical world, *The*

Abolition of Man argues that applying the naturalist view to human beings is a formula for disaster. Lewis explains:

> But as soon as we take the final step of reducing our own species to the level of mere Nature, the whole process is stultified, for this time the being who stood to gain and the being who has been sacrificed are one and the same.[15]

In his final warning Lewis likens the prospect to the selling of our souls, adding to the above comment: "It is the magician's bargain: give up our soul, get power in return."

Concerning these matters Lewis is serious and literal. The very souls of human beings are at stake, he says, and when we deny our souls we abolish our humanity. *The Abolition of Man* is a call to reverse the philosophical trends of our times and to stop pretending that humanity can be understood and managed without reference to those traditional, basic values that Lewis calls "the Tao." It is a wake-up call to a modern generation that has dedicated itself to its own demise.

In reading *The Abolition of Man* look for Lewis's argumentation against the major modern critics of Christian doctrine, particularly the materialist skeptics and the debunkers of religious beliefs. Look for his definition of what it means to be human and his observations on the major forces seeking to dehumanize humanity. Consider Lewis's idea of the "Tao" and its significance for understanding what it means to be human.

Pay attention as well to C.S. Lewis's arguments concerning humankind's alleged "conquest of nature." Look for the lie embedded in this Enlightenment notion, and consider which side of the argument the events of the twentieth century appear to support. Finally, very importantly, ponder the issue of values and the positivist call for "value-free objectivity" in human affairs. Follow Lewis's logic and questions regarding the probable results of pursuing such a perspective.

Mere Christianity

One of C.S. Lewis's most popular books is *Mere Christianity*. This compilation of lectures delivered on the radio in the 1940s includes some of Lewis's most memorable descriptions of Christian doctrine and theology in a manner that is witty and enjoyable.

While there are disadvantages in turning a series of lectures into a book, the great advantages are that the style of the public lecture tends to be more informal, and the arguments tend to be reduced to their simplest statements. And these advantages work very well in Lewis's *Mere Christianity*, as the four sections contain some of the most cogent and concise explanations of Christianity to be found anywhere.

Lewis's expressed purpose in setting down his thoughts and arguments is to present the very basics of Christian beliefs that are held in common by virtually all of the mainline denominations of the church. Consequently, he assiduously avoids sectarian controversy whenever possible, always referring the reader to the experts in matters of denominational differences. Prefacing his discussions with the observation that the various Christian denominations have much more in common than in disagreement, Lewis seeks only to bring the outsider into the vestibule of the church. In this regard he writes:

> I hope no reader will suppose that "mere" Christianity is here put forward as an alternative to the creeds of the existing communions. . . . It is like a hall out of which doors open into several rooms. If I can bring anyone into that hall I shall have done what I attempted. But it is in the rooms, not in the hall, that there are fires and chairs and meals.[16]

Mere Christianity is a book of Christian apologetics, and yet it is probably read more widely among Christian believers than among atheists or agnostics. The reasons for this are many, but one outstanding reason is that Christians find in this little book a great measure of encouragement and strengthening of faith. Like G.K. Chesterton before him, Lewis argues for the rational basis for Christian faith in a world that has turned increasingly to irrational irreligion.

The first section of *Mere Christianity* is called "Right and Wrong as a Clue to the Meaning of the Universe." Here Lewis takes up some of the same arguments presented in *The Abolition of Man* concerning those certain, basic moral ideas that appear to be intrinsic to human consciousness. Foregoing this time the reliance on the concept of "the Tao" that so many readers have found distracting, Lewis writes here of "the Law of Human Nature" as those basic ideas of decent behavior, of right and wrong, of morality shared almost universally among the moral systems in the human world of time and space.

But in this argument Lewis adds another dimension: the fact that people do not behave in the ways that their moral systems tell them they ought to behave. It is from this foundation of humanity's basic morality and yet failure to act morally that Lewis derives his discussions in *Mere Christianity*. He writes:

> These, then, are the two points I wanted to make. First, that human beings, all over the earth, have this curious idea that they ought to behave in a certain way, and cannot really get rid of it. Secondly, that they do not in fact behave that way.... These two facts are the foundation of all clear thinking about ourselves and the universe we live in.[17]

From this beginning Lewis proceeds to demonstrate that right and wrong are not merely relative to one's culture or perspective; that what varies from culture to culture is not the basic moral code, but a few superficial matters of custom within the basic values. "Think of a country," he writes, ". . . where a man felt proud for doublecrossing all the people who had been kindest to him. You might just as well try to imagine a country where two and two make five."[18] With this analogy Lewis is saying that just as certain mathematical relationships are given in the nature of things, certain moral ideas are given in the nature of people.

Lewis turns his attention next to theories of what the universe is and how it came to be there. There are basically two kinds of theories: the materialist view and the religious view. The materialist view is the dominant philosophy of modern, urban-industrial, western societies, and it has become so prevalent that even a great many among the religious leaders have fallen prey to its spell.

The materialist view is that matter and space have always existed, though nobody knows why. In addition, matter behaves in certain fixed ways. Lewis continues:

> By one chance in a thousand something hit our sun and made it produce the planets; and by another thousandth chance the chemicals necessary for life, and the right temperature, occurred on one of these planets, and so some of the matter on this earth came alive; and then, by a very long series of chances, the living creatures developed into things like us.[19]

And so, the theory goes, by some incredible cosmic fluke unintelligent matter managed to become intelligent, sensing, feeling, reasoning creatures called human beings.

The religious view, on the other hand, is widely dismissed as irrational and unscientific. According to this view, what is behind the universe is something very close to what we would call a mind: it is conscious, it has purposes, and it displays preferences. In this theory, space and matter are created by an intelligent motive force, and the dynamics are not based on chance, but on purpose.

Lewis argues that the materialist view may appear to work well when studying nonliving matter such as rocks or chemicals, but the perspective becomes increasingly problematic as our attention moves up through the life forms and especially to human beings. For here we find self-conscious individuals possessing all kinds of emotional states and creative imaginings and carrying within them those two troublesome, intrinsic thoughts—that they ought to act in certain ways, and that they do not act in those ways.

And so, reasons Lewis, we humans have cause to be uneasy. For if we do in fact believe in an absolute goodness, then our own human shortcomings become all the more problematic. Lewis explains:

> For the trouble is that one part of you is on His side and really agrees with His disapproval of human greed and trickery and exploitation . . . we know that if there does exist an absolute goodness it must hate most of what we do. That is the terrible fix we are in.[20]

Only after a person comes to understand the fix we are in does Christianity begin to talk, for these are the questions that Christianity claims to answer. As Lewis summarizes: "Goodness is either the great safety or the great danger—according to the way you react to it. And we have reacted the wrong way."[21]

Having laid these foundations, Lewis launches into the second section of *Mere Christianity*, the discussion called "What Christians Believe." Here Lewis begins a sort of process of elimination whereby he delineates what Christian orthodoxy does and does not include. The first question is whether or not God exists at all. Christians naturally join the many others whose answer is affirmative.

But those who believe in a God can also be divided between those who believe that (1) God is beyond the categories of good and evil or that (2) God is good. In the former category Lewis places the pantheists, including the followers of Hegel and the Hindus. Pantheists tend to believe that the universe is God, and therefore every thing and every person is part of God.

But Jews, Muslims, and Christians belong to the latter category, believing that God is good. These monotheistic religions claim that God is one and that God is the very definition of good. It is also an essential distinction that God created the universe and everything that is in it. Therefore, in direct opposition to the God of the pantheists, the one God is distinct and separate from all other existence.

At this point in Lewis's argument he takes up the issue of evil. Clearly rejecting the dualism that claims two equal, independent powers of good and evil, Christian doctrine reiterates that all things were made by the one good God. Among these created beings were angels and people, both of whom were especially endowed with a free will—that is, the ability to know and to choose between right and wrong behavior. It is free will that has made evil possible.

But why, it is sometimes asked, would a good God allow evil to exist? If free will is the culprit, then why were we given a free will in the first place? Lewis's answer is instructive:

> Because free will, though it makes evil possible, is also the only thing that makes possible any love or goodness or joy worth having. A world of automata—of creatures that worked like machines—would hardly be worth creating. The happiness which God designs for His higher creatures is the happiness of being freely, voluntarily united to Him and to each other in an ecstasy of love and delight compared with which the most rapturous love between a man and a woman on this earth is mere milk and water. And for that they must be free.[22]

Yes, free will allows us to do evil, but it also allows us the true ecstasy of choosing to love God and each other.

Here again we benefit especially from Lewis's literary vision, for he brings his step-by-step, rational argument to the point where he suddenly draws a mental picture of "an ecstasy of love and delight" incumbent in choosing the good. And we can be certain that Lewis was fully aware of the several standard catechisms that begin with the question and answer, "What is the chief purpose of man? To love God and enjoy Him forever."

It was important for Lewis to bring the fact of joy into his apologetics because of the popular misconception of God as the great cosmic killjoy. Lewis often reminds his readers that a great amount of the petty self-righteousness that passes as Christian morality is actually anti-Christian. "That is why," he states in another context, "a cold, self-righteous prig who goes regularly to church may be far nearer to hell than a prostitute."[23] To Lewis it is important to establish that the real Christian morality is in the long run and in the larger picture something that brings joy to those who choose it.

The remaining chapters, on "Christian Behavior," concern various aspects of biblical morality. There is a chapter on Christian marriage that includes a great amount of important and sensible discussion on adultery and on "falling in love." Perhaps the best among these gems is:

> But, of course, ceasing to be "in love" need not mean ceasing to love. Love in this second sense—love as distinct from "being in love" is not merely a feeling. It is a deep unity, maintained by the will and deliberately strengthened by habit; reinforced by . . . the grace which both . . . ask, and receive, from God.[24]

In contrast to the popular but false assumption that if we marry the right person we shall go on "being in love" forever, here is the more accurate and sensible view of the depth of love in a true marriage.

Love is the subject of the following chapter as well, but in this case in the context of "love thy neighbor" and "forgive thy enemy." Lewis argues that loving one's neighbor does not mean feeling fond of him or finding him attractive or even thinking him nice. Establishing that it can and must be acceptable to loathe the things a person does, Lewis brings his logic to the point of the old Christian aphorism: hate the sin but not the sinner.

So the point to Lewis is that we love other sinners as we love ourselves. He explains:

> Consequently, Christianity does not want us to reduce by one atom the hatred we feel for cruelty and treachery. We ought

to hate them. . . . But it does want us to hate them in the same way in which we hate things in ourselves: being sorry that the man should have done such things, and hoping . . . that somehow, sometime, somewhere, he can be cured and made human again.[25]

Suddenly "love thy neighbor as thyself" is seen in a fresh light.

The subject of Christian love is brought up yet again in a later chapter on "Charity." Here Lewis makes the highly valuable observation that such love is an act of will, rather than being an emotion. Recognizing that it can seem impossible simply "to manufacture affectionate feelings"[26] for another person, Lewis gives the practical advice to apply one's will to loving acts toward that person. He adds:

> The rule for all of us is perfectly simple. Do not waste time bothering whether you "love" your neighbor; act as if you did. As soon as we do this we find one of the great secrets. When you are behaving as if you loved someone, you will presently come to love him.[27]

Lewis goes on to explain that feelings are not what God principally cares about. "Christian love, either towards God or towards man, is an affair of the will."[28]

What Lewis is suggesting is radically different from the widespread notion that love is a feeling over which we have very little control. It is also an important departure from the popular love that is contingent on the lovability of the other. Most importantly, though, Lewis's conceptions suggest a way out of the emotional gridlock of guilt for not having the proper feelings for other people.

The final chapters of "Christian Behavior" contain more of Lewis's clear logic and illustration with regard to pride, hope, and faith. Each of these chapters is well worth reading, but here we shall look briefly at his comments regarding faith as our final subject for this section.

Faith, according to Lewis, is certainly not a matter of suspending our rational faculties, nor of simply believing something on the basis of another person's authority. It was always important to Lewis to insist that Christian doctrine is defensible both rationally and experientially. In fact, a central purpose of the book *Mere Christianity* was to establish that rational foundation for the creed.

But Lewis's conception of faith does call for a certain measure of stability and durability in one's beliefs once established. For no one gets much of anywhere by riding on every passing intellectual breeze and floating from cause to cause as each becomes popular. As Lewis puts the matter:

> Now Faith, in the sense in which I am here using the word, is the art of holding on to things your reason has once accepted, in spite of your changing moods . . . unless you teach your moods "where they get off," you can never be either a sound Christian or even a sound atheist, but just a creature dithering to and fro, with its beliefs really dependent on the weather and the state of its digestion.[29]

Consequently, what may at first appear to be merely an obstinate refusal to consider reason may in reality be the kind of faith that refuses to let a mountain of evidence be toppled by a spade full of contrary evidence.

The final section of *Mere Christianity* bears the title "Beyond Personality: or First Steps in the Doctrine of the Trinity." As the title promises, what Lewis offers here is a practical theology, explaining and illustrating various aspects of the Triune God.

But before launching into specifics, Lewis answers the charge that theology is something unreal, while practical religion is something real. Using an analogy of theology as a map, he argues:

> The map is admittedly only coloured paper, but there are two things you have to remember about it. In the first place, it is based on what hundreds and thousands of people have found out by sailing the real Atlantic. . . . In the second place,

if you want to go anywhere, the map is absolutely necessary.[30]

Theology, then, is not God; it is only a map of God. But the map is
based on the real experiences of hundreds of people who really were
in touch with God. When we rely on our own feelings and notions
of God, we very often become hopelessly confused. "Consequently,"
Lewis concludes, "if you do not listen to Theology, that will not
mean that you have no ideas about God. It will mean that you have
a lot of wrong ones. . . ."[31]

Lewis begins his discussion of the Trinity by delineating between
that which is created and that which is begotten. Briefly, that which
God creates is not God; that which God begets is God. Here is the
essential distinction between speaking of a man as a son of God (created) as distinct from Jesus Christ as the Son of God (begotten).
While human beings are made in the image of God, they are still created beings. But Jesus as the incarnation of God is a begotten being,
very man and very God.

But the central issue of this last section is "how human souls can
be taken into the life of God and yet remain themselves—in fact, be
very much more themselves than they were before."[32] In this fascinating discussion Lewis deals with time and eternity, with prayer,
with cause and effect, with the Incarnation and the Resurrection.
And in the end Lewis's lucid logic leads back to the way in which
putting on Christ takes us "beyond personality" as a new person
altogether.

And yet, says Lewis, we do not become more like one another,
but even more unlike. Borrowing the metaphor of salt from the New
Testament, Lewis explains:

> . . . suppose a person knew nothing about salt. You give him
> a pinch to taste and he experiences a particular strong, sharp
> taste. You then tell him that in your country people use salt
> in all their cookery. Might he not reply, "In that case I sup-
> pose all your dishes taste exactly the same: because the taste

of that stuff you have just given me is so strong that it will kill the taste of everything else." But you and I know that the real effect of salt is exactly the opposite. So far from killing the taste of the egg and the tripe and the cabbage, it actually brings it out. They do not show their real taste till you have added the salt.[33]

And so, the fear of losing ourselves when we commit to Christ is really based on an illusion; our real selves are there waiting for us in Him.

In this way Lewis concludes *Mere Christianity* with a challenge to throw off our old selves and to become even more of what we are meant to be. "The more," he writes, "we get what we now call 'ourselves' out of the way and let Him take us over, the more truly ourselves we become."[34] In the end, this "mere Christianity" consists in nothing less than a complete transformation from the old self-centered being to a new kind of person as salted by Jesus Christ.

In reading *Mere Christianity* look again for Lewis's clear arguments in defining what is and what is not Christian doctrine. Look for the foundational ideas from *The Abolition of Man* and then the building of the logical structure of specific Christian doctrines on that basis. Enjoy the author's masterful and methodical process of elimination as he delineates the beliefs that make Christianity unique among the religions of the world.

Look for the many useful insights concerning such matters as love of neighbor, love of spouse, and love of God. The chapter on faith is well worth reading even without the rest of the book. Finally, follow closely Lewis's discourse on the self—on individuality, on losing the self, on going beyond the self—as an essential part of the Christian life.

The books *The Abolition of Man* and *Mere Christianity* contain C.S. Lewis's most clearly stated arguments in philosophy and theology. Both are written in straightforward language that makes them accessible to the unscholarly reader and interesting to a broad audience. Each, but especially *Mere Christianity*, should serve well the apologetic effort to explain and convince the interested agnostic of the logic of Christian doctrine. However, each can serve to strengthen and encourage Christian believers in their own faith as well. In today's intellectual milieu, which is increasingly hostile to faith of any kind, C.S. Lewis's clear and patient instruction is needed more than ever.

7

ON PAIN, LOVE, AND MIRACLES

Some of C.S. Lewis's most insightful work is found in his studies of specific topics. We have seen that his general apologetics often touched on pain, love, and miracles, but in time Lewis felt a need to pursue these subjects in greater depth. We are indeed fortunate that he did, for in these books we find the answers to some of the questions that arose in our minds as we pondered his more basic works. For example, why do good people so often suffer pain? Are religious platitudes really comforting in times of grief? What is the real relationship between Christian charity and erotic love? Why do we see so few miracles these days?

In this chapter we will visit four of C.S. Lewis's most powerful books. In *The Problem of Pain* Lewis explores the many theoretical questions surrounding pain in the context of Christian theology, and in *A Grief Observed* he deals with his own pain after the death of his beloved wife. His book *The Four Loves* takes a fascinating—if somewhat controversial—look at affection, friendship, eros, and charity. Finally, *Miracles: A Preliminary Study* contains some of Lewis's most important insights on the materialist perspective, modern philosophical assumptions, and the rational approach to miracles.

The Problem of Pain

In 1940 C.S. Lewis was asked by a publisher to contribute to a series of popular theological works focusing on various topics in Christian living. Lewis's assigned topic was "the problem of pain," and the result was a book by that same title. It is a typical Lewis analysis of the questions surrounding personal pain, and it contains many of the same arguments found elsewhere, most notably in *The Abolition of Man* and *Mere Christianity*.

Here Lewis approaches the topic of pain by asking the basic question of why a loving God allows us to suffer:

> "If God were good, He would wish to make His creatures perfectly happy, and if God were almighty, He would be able to do what He wished. But the creatures are not happy. Therefore God lacks either goodness, or power, or both."
> This is the problem of pain in its simplest form.[1]

This is the question that Lewis attacks head-on, but his reply is prefaced with a reiteration of the very basic perspectives of all religions in general and then Christianity in specific.

All religions, writes Lewis, include an experience of awe and dread as well as some kind of morality, or ideas of good and evil. With the Jewish religion came the development that the awesome and dreaded being is also the guardian of morality. With Christianity came the added historical event of Jesus and the new gospel of redemption. Basic to Lewis's answers to the problem of pain is the essential question, who was this Jesus? It is in this context that C.S. Lewis wrote his now-famous assertion:

> The claim is so shocking—a paradox, and even a horror, which we may easily be lulled into taking too lightly—that only two views of this man are possible. Either he was a raving lunatic of an unusually abominable type, or else He was, and is, precisely what He said. There is no middle way.[2]

Why is the fact of Jesus important to Lewis's arguments concerning human pain? Because the life, death, and resurrection of Jesus are the very events that bring some sense into the riddle of human suffering. Lewis's logic here takes several steps.

The first premise in Lewis's logic is simply that the very nature of matter determines that everyone cannot be pleased at once:

> If a man travelling in one direction is having a journey down hill, a man going in the opposite direction must be going up hill.[3]

So, then, why not have everybody travel in the same direction? The answer here lies in the free will of the human being. Lewis contends that without free will we do not have a life at all—or at least not a life in the sense that we experience human life. And given the finite nature of matter, the very presence of free will makes some suffering for some people a surety. Lewis writes:

> Try to exclude the possibility of suffering which the order of nature and the existence of free wills involve, and you find that you have excluded life itself.[4]

And so Lewis's first conclusion on the problem of pain is that a certain amount of suffering is the price to be paid for having free wills of our own.

The next question arises, however, when we ponder what it means to be Christians—to be God's people. Why, then, doesn't God simply make bad people suffer and let good people escape from pain? If God is a loving God, why are God's people so often subjected to pain and suffering? The greater part of Lewis's *The Problem of Pain* develops his several answers to this question.

One of the most compelling replies is that in asking this question we betray an important misunderstanding of the word *love*. Love is not the same thing as kindness. But in our unexamined feelings we tend to desire not a God of love, but a God of kindness:

We want, in fact, not so much a Father in heaven as a grand-father in heaven—a senile benevolence who, as they say, "liked to see young people enjoying themselves," and whose plan for the universe was simply that it might be truly said at the end of each day, "a good time was had by all."[5]

But of course, given the nature of matter and free will, we ask for the impossible.

Lewis points out that a God of love is a very different thing from a God of kindness, and nowhere in the Bible are we offered a mere God of kindness. Reminding us that "Love is something more stern and splendid than mere kindness,"[6] Lewis goes on to lay out a more realistic portrait of the loving God:

> You asked for a loving God: you have one. The great spirit you so lightly invoked . . . is present: not a senile benevolence that drowsily wishes you to be happy in your own way, not the cold philanthropy of a conscientious magistrate, nor the care of a host who feels responsible for the comfort of his guests, but the consuming fire Himself, the Love that made the worlds, persistent as the artist's love for his work and despotic as a man's love for a dog, provident and venerable as a father's love for a child, jealous, inexorable, exacting as love between the sexes.[7]

And so, Lewis concludes, we think of our pain as a philosophical "problem" only if we attach a trivial meaning to the word *love*. To love and to be loved is to expect pain, and to be loved by the true God is to suffer God's correction.

This theme of correction, or of being perfected, is strong in Lewis's discussions of pain. The idea is that if we are God's people, then God is forever training us, seeking our improvement, in a sense rubbing us to make us shine. The rubbings of God are often—but not always—painful. And though we might at times wish that God would leave us alone and stop trying to improve us, our wish is unrealistic if God is really God. Lewis explains:

> To ask that God's love should be content with us as we are is to ask that God should cease to be God: because He is what He is, His love must, in the nature of things, be impeded and repelled by certain stains in our present character, and because He already loves us He must labour to make us lovable.[8]

God's laboring to make us lovable becomes the central concept in C.S. Lewis's analysis of the problem of pain; it illuminates and informs his subsequent chapters dealing with the Fall, hell, heaven, and other matters.

C.S. Lewis's *The Problem of Pain* is not a book that I would recommend to a person who is currently in the throes of deep grieving or pain. It was obviously not written for that purpose. But I think it is a good equipping book, in the sense that a Christian would be better equipped to deal with painful situations after reading it. The book also deals quite clearly and sensibly with various issues that might concern the curious agnostic—issues such as God's omnipotence, God's goodness, social action, animal pain, and heaven and hell.

In reading *The Problem of Pain* look for C.S. Lewis's characteristic logic and clarity in argument. Pay special attention to his delineations between love and kindness, as well as the destructive role of pride in the human experience. Notice Lewis's reiteration of the basic connections among self-surrender, humility, sadness, and joy. Don't overlook the insight that the acceptance of pain is not the same thing as the denial of pain, nor the same as seeking pain in masochism.

The power of this and other C.S. Lewis nonfiction efforts lies partly in his excellent logic, but partly as well in his marvelous sense of human reality. It is this practical sense that leads Lewis to those unforgettable illustrations that seem to seize our minds and never let go. I will close here with one such illustration that Lewis uses in answering why our tribulations must never cease:

Thus the terrible necessity of tribulation is only too clear. God has had me for but forty-eight hours and then only by dint of taking everything else away from me. Let Him but sheathe that sword for a moment and I behave like a puppy when the hated bath is over—I shake myself as dry as I can and race off to reacquire my comfortable dirtiness, if not in the nearest manure heap, at least in the nearest flower bed.[9]

A Grief Observed

Only four years after his marriage to Joy Davidman at age fifty-eight, C.S. Lewis found that the love of his life was suddenly taken from him by cancer. Perhaps this loss was even more painful for Lewis because of the intensity of this late-life romance, as well as its brevity. In the wake of Joy's death, Lewis experienced some of the most severe testing that his Christian faith would encounter, and there were those who wondered if he might lose his faith altogether. During those difficult times Lewis kept a journal, recording his feelings and thoughts about his loss, and these were later published under the title *A Grief Observed*.

This book is short , and it is not a comfortable one to read. It is a work born of pain and struggle, and it contains the questions of an intelligent man in his agony. It is not a place to look for the cool analysis of the disinterested intellectual, nor for the easy platitudes of the armchair apologist. It is C.S. Lewis in great pain attempting to come to grips with his loss. It is a book not particularly recommended for the weak in faith.

The first issue that Lewis deals with is the apparent absence of God in times of great need. He writes:

When you are happy, so happy that you have no sense of needing Him, so happy that you are tempted to feel His claims upon you as an interruption, if you remember yourself and turn to Him with gratitude and praise, you will be— or so it feels—welcomed with open arms. But go to Him when your need is desperate, when all other help is vain, and what do you find? A door slammed in your face, and a sound of bolting and double bolting on the inside. . . . Why is He so present a commander in our time of prosperity and so very absent a help in times of trouble?[10]

Lewis speaks briefly about some of the answers often given for this problem, but he does not come to an easy conclusion.

Throughout the book Lewis struggles with the platitudes that well-meaning others offer him during his grief. For example:

It is hard to have patience with people who say, "There is no death," or, "Death doesn't matter." There is death. And whatever is matters. . . . She died. She is dead. Is the word so difficult to learn?[11]

And there are many other troubled statements, such as:

Talk to me about the truth of religion and I'll listen gladly. Talk to me about the duty of religion and I'll listen submissively. But don't come talking to me about the consolations of religion or I shall suspect that you don't understand.[12]

And then:

Aren't all these notes the senseless writhings of a man who won't accept the fact that there is nothing we can do with suffering except to suffer it?[13]

But as one moves along with Lewis through *A Grief Observed*, one begins to see a change in tone. The bitterness begins to ebb, and the reason behind Lewis's faith begins to flow once more. One begins to see statements such as:

We were even promised sufferings. They were part of the program. We were even told, "Blessed are they that mourn," and I accepted it. I've got nothing that I hadn't bargained for.[14]

And along the same lines:

The more we believe that God hurts only to heal, the less we can believe that there is any use in begging for tenderness.[15]

Finally after all of the bitterness, questioning, and agonizing, C.S. Lewis is able to write:

I have gradually been coming to feel that the door is no longer shut and bolted. Was it my own frantic need that slammed it in my face? The time when there is nothing at all in your soul except a cry for help may be just the time when God can't give it: you are like the drowning man who can't be helped because he clutches and grabs. Perhaps your own reiterated cries deafen you to the voice you hoped to hear.[16]

So in the end the reader finds once again the C.S. Lewis so well known in his other nonfiction books—the patient faith, the pure analysis, the clear communication. And as we have journeyed through *A Grief Observed*, we have followed the thoughts and feelings of this great Christian through the dark night of his pain and then again into the light of his faith in God's grace and providence.

In reading *A Grief Observed* look for the very real encounter of an intelligent man with death, pain, and loneliness. Notice the honesty that refuses the easy way out or the simple answer. Look for the C.S. Lewis severity—that unyielding clarity and moral strength that gives no quarter to fuzzy logic or emotional platitude. Pay attention to Lewis's grieving through time and the way his conclusions come ever so slowly as a process of healing. Finally, look at the substance of Lewis's conclusions, and notice that the underpinnings of his Christian faith remained solid even through this, the most terrible event of his life.

The Four Loves

In this book the author reveals—perhaps more than in any of his other writings—a personal depth of experience and contemplation on the many aspects of love. *The Four Loves* is a candid and sober look at four kinds of love: affection, friendship, eros, and charity. The first three types Lewis calls the "natural" loves, for each is grounded in human nature, and each can be realized in human interaction by human means. But charity contains a touch of the divine. Indeed, says Lewis, humans are capable of being charitable only by virtue of that "Divine energy" that is God's love.

But far from dismissing the three natural loves in favor of God's charity, Lewis's book offers a greater appreciation of all the kinds of love and an encouragement to allow that "Divine energy" to immerse the natural loves in charity. Lewis explains:

> Divine love does not substitute itself for the natural—as if we had to throw away our silver to make room for the gold. The natural loves are summoned to become modes of Charity while also remaining the natural loves they were.[17]

In *The Four Loves* we learn both what is right and what is wrong in the natural loves, but we end by appreciating each in its place and by desiring that even greater dimension of charity in all our loves.

Lewis begins, however, with some working definitions. Before discussing the four kinds of love, the author delineates between what he calls "Gift-love" and "Need-love." To define the former, Lewis states bluntly that "Divine love is Gift-love."[18] Later he elaborates:

> Let us here make no mistake. Our Gift-loves are really God-like; and among our Gift-loves those are most God-like which are most boundless and unwearied in giving. . . . Their joy, their energy, their patience, their readiness to forgive, their desire for the good of the beloved—all this is a real and all but adorable image of the Divine life. In its presence we are right to thank God "who has given such power to men."[19]

It is Gift-love by which the Father gives all to the Son, and the Son gives all to the Father. Gift-love does not in any way originate in need.

Need-love, on the other hand, is born of poverty. Lewis is quick to point out that Need-love is a consciousness that truly reflects our nature. He explains:

> We are born helpless. As soon as we are fully conscious we discover loneliness. We need others physically, emotionally, intellectually; we need them if we are to know anything, even ourselves.[20]

Thus a great amount of need is endemic to the human condition. It is no surprise, then, that most of the human loves are Need-loves.

But Lewis cautions us against calling the Need-loves "mere selfishness" or denying that they are loves at all. He points out, for instance, that no one calls a child selfish for turning to her mother for comfort, nor a man for turning to his fellows for company. We cannot and should not dismiss Need-love, because we really do need each other and we really do need God. A person's love for God is certainly a Need-love. In this regard Lewis writes rather comically:

> It would be a bold and silly creature that came before its Creator with the boast, "I'm no beggar. I love you disinterestedly."[21]

Consequently, our love for God is a human Need-love that is the greatest of all. Here is the paradox that we can come nearest to God when we are in this sense least like God.

In his ensuing discussions of the dimensions of the natural loves—affection, friendship, and eros—Lewis visits and revisits the darker side of the natural loves, the ways in which these loves can also become "complicated forms of hatred."[22] Consequently, many of the discussions in *The Four Loves* seem to dwell on the negative side of things. In the book there are many examples of "love" that really amount to tyranny, jealousy, manipulation, and attempts at control. Lewis's examples have a ring of truth that can only come from painful personal experience, and it is this ring of truth that gives this book much of its power. The reader knows that here is not merely the cloistered intellectual speculating about love; here is an intelligent and sensitive observer who has soared in the sunlight and plunged into the shadows of the natural loves.

The first kind of love that Lewis examines is called affection. The broadest and least discriminating of the four loves, affection is based on familiarity. The objects of affection can be people or animals or things or even ideas—but they must be comfortable and predictable. The good side of affection, says Lewis, is that it ". . . opens our eyes to goodness we could not have seen, or should not have appreciated without it."[23] He illustrates by saying:

> The dog barks at strangers who have never done it any harm and wags its tail for old acquaintances even if they never did it a good turn. The child will love a crusty old gardener who has hardly ever taken any notice of it and shrink from the visitor who is making every attempt to win its regard.[24]

Affection prefers the familiar. It suffers long and forgives much.

But then there is the dark side of affection. "Nearly all the characteristics of this love are ambivalent," Lewis writes. "They may work for ill as well as for good."[25] He speaks of our unreasonable needs for affection, even our expectation of it regardless of our unlovable behavior. He discusses how the very same sentiments that make affection possible also make an unreasonable hatred possible. There is a lengthy discussion of jealousy and the pleasures of resentment. What is the point of all this dwelling on the perversions of affection? Lewis answers: "That is the whole point. If we try to live by Affection alone, Affection will 'go bad on us.'"[26] Affection is a wonderful kind of love, but it needs something more to guide it into the right course.

The chapter on friendship Lewis describes as a "rehabilitation," for here he argues strongly for the return of true friendships. He begins by pointing out that in modern life friendship is largely a lost art. Friendship is the least natural or organic of the loves; we do not need it in the sense that we seem to need affection and eros. Friendships are freely chosen on the basis of a common interest. Lewis explains:

> It may be common religion, common studies, a common profession, even a common recreation. All who share it will be our companions; but one or two or three who share something more will be our Friends. . . . The man who agrees with us that some question, little regarded by others, is of great importance can be our Friend. He need not agree with us about the answer.[27]

Another way of saying this is that ". . . friendship must be about something."[28]

One cannot read Lewis's discussion of friendship without understanding and feeling the deep satisfaction the scholar Lewis derived from his times with his beloved Inklings. Savor this picture from Lewis's pen:

> Especially when the whole group is together, each bringing out all that is best, wisest, or funniest in all the others. Those are the golden sessions; when four or five of us after a hard day's walking have come to our inn; when our slippers are on, our feet spread out towards the blaze and our drinks at our elbows; when the whole world, and something beyond the world, opens itself to our minds as we talk; and no one has any claim on or any responsibility for another, but all are freemen and equals as if we had first met an hour ago, while at the same time the Affection mellowed by the years enfolds us. Life—natural life—has no better gift to give.[29]

Though Lewis goes on in this chapter to discuss such matters as group dynamics, misplaced goals, corporate pride, and negative influences, it remains clear that Lewis considers friendship among the most satisfying of loves.

Concerning *eros* Lewis has much to say that is surprising and even amusing, but there is remarkable depth here as well. At the onset he delineates between a man's desire for pleasure and a man's desire for a woman. The former is definitely not eros. Concerning the latter, Lewis writes:

> We use a most unfortunate idiom when we say, of a lustful man prowling the streets, that he "wants a woman." Strictly speaking, a woman is just what he does not want. He wants a pleasure for which a woman happens to be the necessary apparatus. . . . Now Eros makes a man really want, not a woman, but one particular woman. In some mysterious but quite indisputable fashion the lover desires the Beloved herself, not the pleasure she can give.[30]

In this way eros transforms a natural need into the most appreciative of the natural loves.

Among the many fascinating peripheral discussions to be found in *The Four Loves*, Lewis's comments on sex and laughter are worth repeating. Lewis feels that we are always being encouraged to take sex too seriously, and he decries this modern "solemnisation" of sex ". . . as if a long face were a sort of moral disinfectant."[31] He is speaking, of course, of the whole enterprise of sexology—the books and pamphlets with their awkward terminology, and the films with their stone-faced narrators assuring us that we are being very scientific in all of our talk about sex. "We have reached the stage," Lewis argues, "at which nothing is more needed than a roar of old-fashioned laughter."[32]

Here Lewis is making a point that is far more important than we at first might think. Using the word "Venus" where we would use the word "sex," Lewis explains his point:

> We must not be totally serious about Venus. . . . We must not
> attempt to find an absolute in the flesh. Banish play and
> laughter from the bed of love and you may let in a false god-
> dess.[33]

So here again is the familiar warning. While eros is indeed a great
love to be experienced with full joy and even laughter, it can also
lead to a form of idolatry. To Lewis the greatest danger does not lie
in the lovers coming to idolize one another, but in their idolizing love
itself. In our society the inducements to do so are legion.

As in the natural loves already discussed, the question again
comes as to whether eros in itself is enough. Consistent with his earlier logic, Lewis again points out the dark side, the perversions of
eros that demonstrate the need for a guiding force—that in time eros
requires a rather continuous program of common-sense guidance to
see it through. In this regard Lewis writes:

> This all good lovers know, though those who are not reflec-
> tive or articulate will be able to express it only in a few con-
> ventional phrases about "taking the rough along with the
> smooth," not "expecting too much," having "a little com-
> mon sense," and the like. And all good Christian lovers
> know that this programme, modest as it sounds, will not
> be carried out except by humility, charity and divine
> grace. . . .[34]

And thus the stage is set for Lewis's discussion of that guiding principle, that greater force that is necessary to complete the first three
natural loves.

Lewis writes that the natural loves in themselves are like a garden. They are each unique and beautiful in their own way, though
they are not self-sufficient. He explains:

> To say this is not to belittle the natural loves but to indicate
> where their real glory lies. It is no disparagement to a garden

to say that it will not fence and weed itself, nor prune its own fruit trees, nor roll and cut its own lawns.[35]

Likewise does Lewis take great care not to disparage the three natural loves—affection, friendship, and eros—on the grounds that they too need a special kind of care. Indeed he celebrates the natural loves and then adds that the special care they need is called charity.

Here Lewis makes one of his most insightful claims, making the relationship between love and pain perfectly clear. He writes:

> There is no safe investment. To love at all is to be vulnerable. Love anything, and your heart will certainly be wrung and possibly be broken. If you want to make sure of keeping it intact, you must give your heart to no one, not even to an animal. Wrap it carefully round with hobbies and little luxuries; avoid all entanglements; lock it up safe in the casket or coffin of your selfishness. But in that casket—safe, dark, motionless, airless—it will change. It will not be broken; it will become unbreakable, impenetrable, irredeemable. The alternative to tragedy . . . is damnation. The only place outside heaven where you can be perfectly safe from all the dangers and perturbations of love is Hell.[36]

Finally, Lewis discusses the Gift-love of God, saying that "God, who needs nothing, loves into existence wholly superfluous creatures in order that He may love and perfect them."[37] In doing so, God gives a measure of that Gift-love to human beings, enabling people to have a Gift-love toward God and toward other people. This Gift-love, bestowed by God's grace, is called charity. And as this charity enters into the natural loves it transforms them, in a sense glorifies them, and makes them instruments of God. As Lewis puts it:

> Charity does not dwindle into merely natural love but natural love is taken up into, made the tuned and obedient instrument of, Love Himself.[38]

Lewis's picture of love is now complete. He has shown the good and the bad in the three natural loves—affection, friendship, and eros. He has argued that each needs something else to keep it from taking a bad turn. He has explored the Gift-love of God, the source of all charity. And finally he has shown how charity can transform the natural loves into better, higher, more God-like loves.

In reading *The Four Loves* look for Lewis's insights into the bright side and the dark side of the natural loves. Pay close attention to the ways that human "loves" can camouflage many less noble motives. Follow the author's logic leading to the need for charity as the guiding principle for all the loves. Enjoy C.S. Lewis's illustrations, and notice how much they add to the writer's credibility. Finally, look for Lewis's remarkable analogies of the loves as a garden, and seek to understand the workings of the hand of the gardener. In reading *The Four Loves* expect to end with a greater appreciation of the loves in your life and the truth that "the greatest of these is charity."

Miracles: A Preliminary Study

Another important nonfiction work by C.S. Lewis is *Miracles*, his analysis of the miraculous in general and particularly the miracles recorded in the New Testament. It is a book in which the scholar Lewis applies his formidable logic to an examination of those biblical events that the modern materialist imagination is compelled to deny altogether and that modern liberal theologians are wont to explain away with various natural causes. It is an occasion for Lewis to spell out more completely some of his logic mentioned only in passing in his other nonfiction works.

The argument of *Miracles* begins, characteristic for C.S. Lewis, with a great amount of foundation work—a kind of setting the stage for the logic to follow. Indeed, the validity of rational thought itself becomes one of the first cornerstones, as Lewis asks the reader to agree at the onset that reason is valid or else to abandon the discussion altogether. This first of Lewis's assertions will come as somewhat of a surprise to those who might imagine an affinity between miracle and unreason, but Lewis is vehement in his insistence that the New Testament miracles are the rational acts of the rational God.

The popular point of view that Lewis does take issue with, however, is what he calls "naturalism." He explains:

> What the Naturalist believes is that the ultimate Fact, the thing you can't go behind, is a vast process in space and time which is going on of its own accord. . . . All the things and events are so completely interlocked that no one of them can claim the slightest independence from the whole show.[39]

By this definition it is obvious that the naturalist cannot believe in anything like a free human will. And in fact, the very phenomenon that we call rational thought must be seen as the result of the movement of atoms. In other words, to the naturalist the human mind is the effect of irrational causes. If one is to believe that his own thoughts are determined by mechanistic and irrational forces, then there is surely no purpose in arguing about miracles—or about anything else, for that matter.

So Lewis sets his arguments on the foundation that reason comes from God. Using the analogy of water lilies in a pond, he writes:

> In a pond whose surface was completely covered with scum and floating vegetation, there might be a few water lilies . . . from their structure you could deduce that they had stalks underneath which went down to roots in the bottom. The Naturalist thinks that the pond (Nature—the great event in space and time) is of an infinite depth—that there is nothing but water however far you go down. My claim is that some of the things on the surface (i.e. in our experience) show the contrary. These things (rational minds) reveal, on inspection,

that they are not floating but attached by stalks to the bottom. Therefore the pond has a bottom.[40]

Lewis explains his analogy by stating that human reason ". . . is the little telltale rift in Nature which shows that there is something beyond or behind her."[41]

In other words, we could well think of nature and its laws as being "the whole show" except for one persistent, problematic fact: human reason. In his pond analogy Lewis is telling us that the water lilies of human reason indicate that nature is indeed not "the whole show."

The next issue that Lewis takes up is the modern boast of taking nothing on mere tradition or authority—the idea that we scientific moderns must find out everything for ourselves. While it is clear that Lewis himself has nothing against facing a question squarely and following its conclusions wherever they may go, he nevertheless decries the situation wherein we are duty-bound to disbelieve all traditional knowledge. He writes:

> It might be that humanity, in rebelling against tradition and authority, have made a ghastly mistake; a mistake which will not be the less fatal because the corruptions of those in authority rendered it very excusable. . . . *A society where the simple many obey the few seers can live: a society where all were seers could live even more fully.* But a society where the mass is still simple and *the seers are no longer attended to can* achieve only superficiality, baseness, ugliness, and in the end extinction. On or back we must go; to stay here is death.[42]

Here and elsewhere Lewis attacks the widespread modern assumptions—those "givens" that few ever stop to reconsider—about the nature of truth. So thoroughly have the views of H.G. Wells and the scientific materialists become the exclusive acceptable doctrine that Lewis must take great pains to remind his readers of exactly what is being taken for granted. Like G.K. Chesterton before him, Lewis takes to task the narrow, materialist, skeptic point of view for failing to admit the evidences of tradition into its logic.

In *Miracles* Lewis examines the evidences for the New Testament miracles. In his inimitable way he exposes—particularly in his Chapter VIII—the illogic and folly of those who deny unilaterally that miracles are possible. Lewis grants that most of what we hear about miracles is probably false. In fact, he says that most of what we hear and read about anything is false. "Lies, exaggerations, misunderstandings and hearsay make up perhaps more than half of all that is said and written in the world," he writes.[43] But there is particularly great irony when an ostensibly "natural explanation" of a miracle turns out to be even more far-fetched than the miracle itself. Lewis writes of the modern skeptic:

> That is, he will accept the most improbable 'natural' explanations rather than say that a miracle occurred. Collective hallucination, hypnotism of unconsenting spectators, widespread instantaneous conspiracy in lying by persons not otherwise known to be liars and not likely to gain by the lie— all these are known to be very improbable events: so improbable that, except for the special purpose of excluding a miracle, they are never suggested. But they are preferred to the admission of a miracle.[44]

Lewis is particularly distressed by the liberal theologians who go to great pains to "explain" the New Testament miracles in scientific terms.

But the major theme of *Miracles* is that the miracles of the New Testament are not the unnatural actions of an alien power; they are rather the reasonable acts of the author of nature. Lewis explains:

> I contend that in all these miracles alike the incarnate God does suddenly and locally something that God has done or will do in general. Each miracle writes for us in small letters something that God has already written, or will write, in let-

ters almost too large to be noticed, across the whole canvas of Nature. . . . Not one of them is isolated or anomalous: each carries the signature of the God whom we know through conscience and from Nature. Their authenticity is attested by the style.[45]

Here we come to see the miracles of the New Testament not as opposed to nature, nor even as interrupting nature, but as an instance of the reasonable God doing before our eyes what God does all of the time in nature. Therefore we speak not of reason versus the miraculous, but of reason in the miraculous.

In reading *Miracles: A Preliminary Study*, look for Lewis's foundational work in the area of ontological assumptions. Appreciate as well Lewis's logic with regard to the validity of reason and the limitations of materialism. Notice what he says about the supposed "values-free" and "objective" cast of the modern skeptical mind. Think about the role of tradition and authority in knowledge and the quest for truth.

Look as well for Lewis's classifications of miracles, and notice how these categories help us to understand the integral nature of God's miracles. Particularly fascinating are Lewis's comments on the miracles of resurrection and their implications for the future. Finally, as always, enjoy that marvelous C.S. Lewis style of logic and argumentation as Lewis the scholar tackles a subject that very few others dared to address.

8

SCHOLARLY
WORKS

Because of the great success of his children's stories and his apologetics, many overlook the fact that C.S. Lewis was a university scholar by profession. Indeed, after a distinguished tenure of thirty years as a Fellow at Oxford University, Lewis finished his career as Professor of Medieval and Renaissance Literature at Cambridge University. Academically Lewis was widely known and highly respected for his studies in sixteenth-century English literature and particularly his works on Edmund Spenser and John Milton.

It should be mentioned here that even C.S. Lewis experienced his share of widespread prejudices in higher education, which historian Page Smith has given the name "academic fundamentalism." In his fascinating book *Killing the Spirit*, Smith explains with regard to higher education:

> There is a mad reductionism at work. God is not a proper topic for discussion, but "lesbian politics" is. . . . Academic fundamentalism is the issue, the stubborn refusal of the academy to acknowledge any truth that does not conform to professorial dogmas. In the famous "market place of ideas," where all ideas are equal and where there must be no "value judgements" and therefore no values, certain ideas are simply excluded, and woe to those who espouse them.

Such individuals are terminated lest their corruption spread to others.[1]

This "academic fundamentalism" is certainly not indigenous to America, nor even to the twentieth century. Its roots reach back to the New Enlightenment and the subsequent wave of scientific orthodoxy that swept through the universities of Europe and America in the nineteenth century.

At Oxford University C.S. Lewis suffered on two counts. The first and probably most important was his aggressive and outspoken Christianity. The second was that he wrote popular fantasies and science fiction stories. As Page Smith so poignantly illustrates, there are certain things that university scholars are simply not allowed to do. At Oxford University these included both Christian apologetics and science fiction. As a result, Lewis served brilliantly those many years at Oxford and yet was never promoted to a professorship.

But again we have a window into the character of the man C.S. Lewis. The forces for conformity on the college campus are formidable, as Lewis has illustrated in his fictional *That Hideous Strength*. Lewis was fully aware of the costs to be paid for his nonconformity, and I would venture to say that he experienced a considerable amount of personal pain over his lack of affirmation at Oxford. Yet he held his ground. He wrote from his heart, he defended what he considered truly important, and he paid the price! Of the many reasons I find for admiring the man C.S. Lewis, it is this moral courage that I respect the most.

In this chapter we examine five of C.S. Lewis's scholarly works in medieval and Renaissance literature. *The Allegory of Love* is widely known as Lewis's academic masterpiece. In it he traces an essential theme from the writings of antiquity down to modern English literature. His book *English Literature in the Sixteenth Century—Excluding Drama* is a much more detailed survey of the authors of the Renaissance period. In both *The Discarded Image* and *Studies in Medieval and Renaissance Literature* Lewis presents some of his most illuminating perspectives on the medieval world-view and its implications for modern philosophy and scientific thought. Finally, in *A Preface to Paradise Lost* Lewis provides an excellent preparation not only for readers of Milton's famous poem, but for readers of narrative and epic poetry from any age. All of these works ought to be essential reading for students of English literature, and I recommend them to all readers who seek a greater depth and appreciation of literature in general.

The Allegory of Love

The masterpiece of C.S. Lewis's scholarly work is his famous *The Allegory of Love*. In this remarkable study Lewis discusses the development of allegorical poetry and the theme of romantic love from antiquity to sixteenth-century English literature. Here we find a fascinating story of literary history focusing primarily on the legacy of Guillaume de Lorris's "The Romance of the Rose" as culminated in Edmund Spenser's "The Faerie Queene." But perhaps more importantly we find a fresh perspective on an intellectual period and a literary genre that is often neglected, misunderstood, and even derogated in modern criticism.

   The Allegory of Love can be as valuable to the social historian as to the historian of literature. For Lewis's discussions reach far beyond the simple-minded equation of literary depiction and social practice, and into an informed analysis of the relationships between literature and society. For example, concerning the early medieval notion that romantic love and adultery are synonymous, Lewis explains:

> Thus if the Church tells them that the ardent lover even of his own wife is in mortal sin, they presently reply with the rule that true love is impossible in marriage.[2]

Lewis goes on to explain how the medievals developed a sort of double standard—on the one hand raising courtly adultery to the status of a noble institution, yet on the other hand continuing to insist on the validity of the church.

In fact, it is this very problem, this historic tension between the mores of the court and the teachings of the church, that comprises the thematic thread running through *The Allegory of Love*. As we follow C.S. Lewis's analyses of the allegorical love poetry on the continent of Europe and then more specifically into English poetry, we watch the subsequent poets deal—each in his own way—with this same basic conflict. Thus Lewis follows two lines of allegorical poetry—the "courtly" and the "homiletic." The courtly stream builds from the romance-as-adultery ethos of medieval high society in the royal courts. The homiletic stream seeks to place love within the ethos inherent in Christian theology. Lewis traces the history of "the allegory of love" along both streams until they are finally synthesized in Spenser's "The Faerie Queene."

In his second chapter Lewis gives a thorough definition and discussion of allegory. To use allegory, he explains, is "to represent what is immaterial in picturable terms."[3] The difference between allegory and symbolism is very important, he says, because symbolism relegates the people and events of the story to a lesser importance than that of the things symbolized. The allegorist writes of what is less real in order to illustrate and vivify what is real inside him. Indeed, it is this medieval discovery of the "inner self" that Lewis calls the "threshold of allegory." Thus Lewis traces the roots of allegory back to the new introspective state of mind, whose evidence first appears in the writings of Seneca, Saint Paul, Epictetus, Marcus Aurelius, and Tertullian. Lewis writes:

> Whatever the causal order may be, it is plain that to fight against 'Temptation' is also to explore the inner world; and it is scarcely less plain that to do so is to be already on the verge of allegory. We cannot speak, perhaps we can hardly think, of an 'inner conflict' without a metaphor; and every metaphor is an allegory in little.[4]

For Lewis, the origin of allegory is to be found in the very structure of our introspective thinking. Further, the evidences of that introspective thinking do not appear until the early centuries of the Christian era.

The first major allegorical poem that Lewis discusses in detail is Guillaume de Lorris's "The Romance of the Rose." The particulars of this discussion I leave to the reader's discovery in the original. But it is here that Lewis grounds his fascinating voyage through the centuries of allegorical love poetry, visiting not only famous poets such as Chaucer, Dante, Lydgate, and Spenser, but also less-known names such as Jean de Muen, Gower, Usk, Dunbar, Skelton, Nevill, Googe, Deguileville, Hawes, Douglas, and Rolland. It is important to recognize that C.S. Lewis the scholar is not one to conform uncritically to literary fads, but he is compelled to follow the scent of his prey wherever it leads him. Thus, he is as willing to analyze the work of a minor poet such as Hawes as he is to join the chorus of praises for a major poet such as Chaucer.

Speaking of Chaucer, incidentally, there is another point that I think illustrates the character of C.S. Lewis as a scholar. Quite often today we hear the works of Geoffrey Chaucer discussed as if Chaucer represents a refreshing liberation from the prison of an earlier, moralistic age. I can still recall my college literature professor touting Chaucer as a sort of sixteenth-century H.L. Mencken flying in the face of literary mores controlled by a repressive church. Lewis exposes the folly in this idea. In fact, he objects to the hackneyed textbook emphasis on "The Canterbury Tales" as entirely unrepresentative of Chaucer's best and most important work. "We have heard," Lewis writes, "a little too much of this 'mocking' Chaucer."[5] As a remedy Lewis offers the "Parlement of Foules" as by far the more essential work of Chaucer, and he argues that Chaucer is in fact a much greater poet than many of his modern admirers even realize.

We have seen that Lewis is always quick to question the intellectual fad and to object to the predictable sneering that is so widespread among scholars. Lewis is often highly critical of literary criticism. As but one example, he mentions how literary criticism tends to create its own illusions:

> If there is any safe generalization in literary history it is this: that the desire for a certain kind of product does not necessarily beget the power to produce it, while it does tend to beget the illusion that it has been produced.[6]

Such a perspective contains important and radical implications for our modern critical technique that so easily plays among "antecedents" and "influences" and "causes."

But what is the essential thesis of *The Allegory of Love*? The principal point is that even today many aspects of these traditional allegories of romantic love still supply the dominant motive force of our popular fiction. Lewis says as much in the very beginning of his treatise:

> We are tempted to treat 'courtly love' as a mere episode in literary history—an episode that we have finished with. . . . In fact, however, an unmistakable continuity connects the Provencal love song with the love poetry of the Middle Ages, and thence . . . with that of the present day. If the thing at first escapes our notice, this is because we are so familiar with the erotic tradition of modern Europe that we mistake it for something natural and universal and therefore do not inquire into its origins. It seems to us natural that love should be the commonest theme of serious imaginative literature. . . .[7]

Throughout *The Allegory of Love* Lewis brings his reader repeatedly to this central thesis. Later he refers to

> . . . those elements in the medieval consciousness which survive in our own. Astrology has died, and so have the court scandals of the fourteenth century; but that new conception

of love which the eleventh century inaugurated has been a mainspring of imaginative literature ever since.[8]

This consistent and persistent mainspring is what C.S. Lewis calls "the allegory of love," and tracing its journey from the eleventh century to the sixteenth century is the purpose of Lewis's study.

In another sense *The Allegory of Love* can be seen as a preface par excellence for Edmund Spenser's "The Faerie Queene." For in the end Lewis presents Spenser's masterpiece as the culmination, the historical synthesis, of the themes he has followed through his work. Lewis observes concerning Spenser:

> The story he tells is therefore part of my story: the final struggle between the romance of marriage and the romance of adultery.[9]

In the end, then, Lewis finds a resolution of the conflict between the two major streams of the allegory of love. He writes of

> The last phase of that story—the final defeat of courtly love by the romantic conception of marriage. . . .[10]

It is this romantic conception of marriage—albeit with the lingering forays into the adultery of the courtly tradition—that has served as the mainspring of imaginative English-language literature to this day.

In reading *The Allegory of Love* look for the depth of C.S. Lewis's scholarship on the ancient and medieval writers. Most modern scholars should find it humbling to discover Lewis reading and conversing not only in Greek and Latin, but in Old French and Old English as well. Look for Lewis's thesis on the historical development of allegory as a literary genre and his ideas regarding the "courtly" and "homiletic" streams of poetry. Watch carefully for Lewis's insights on how literature does—and does not—influence subsequent literature as he takes the question far beyond the popular but simple-minded notions of cause-effect diffusion. Finally, be sure to notice the points at which C.S. Lewis opposes the most widely accepted literary fads and viewpoints—particularly in his comments on Chaucer and Spenser—and enjoy the logic of his unorthodox arguments. In *The Allegory of Love* there is much to learn and much to ponder, and the serious student of English literature should never pass up such an intellectual feast as this one.

English Literature in the Sixteenth Century—Excluding Drama

A critic recently commented that C.S. Lewis did not believe the Renaissance really happened. While this claim is surely an overstatement, there is a sense in which Lewis certainly did not "believe in" the Renaissance as the legion of modern scholars do. For today references to the Renaissance invariably carry much more value-laden baggage than the statements themselves at first reveal. The very word has come to mean an entire complex of assumptions and evaluations regarding the historical events, but more importantly it has come to represent an ideology that casts a definite tint into one's entire conception of history.

Lewis's book *English Literature in the Sixteenth Century—Excluding Drama* begins with a detailed discussion of this very issue. Pointing out that most discussions of the Renaissance make ample use of the words *humanism* and *puritanism*, Lewis characteristically begins with some definitions. Originally, he explains, a humanist was "one who taught, or learned, or at least strongly favoured, Greek and the new kind of Latin."[11] Humanism, then, was a form of classicism emphasizing a specific critical approach to literature. On the other hand, a puritan was technically "one who wished to abolish episcopy and remodel the Church of England on the lines which Calvin had laid down for Geneva."[12] At this juncture Lewis makes the very significant point that a person could be—as many in fact were—a humanist and a puritan at the same time.

But Lewis laments the blurring of definitions and the oversimplifying of ideas that led to the modern situation wherein we often hear of the Renaissance as the triumph of humanism over puritanism. He writes:

> Both words have so changed their sense that puritan now means little more than 'rigorist' or 'ascetic' and humanist little more than 'the opposite of puritan.'[13]

The significance of this change in definitions is that it echoes the modern humanistic telling of the events of the Renaissance. It is this highly biased and arguable recasting of the events of the fourteenth through seventeenth centuries that Lewis refuses to endorse.

The modern humanist rendition of the Renaissance goes something like the following: In the Middle Ages, all of Europe groaned under the weight of church authority. The advancement of knowledge was arrested, the arts were stultified, and the human spirit was imprisoned in tradition. Then suddenly there came the Renaissance, a rebirth of learning and a liberation of the human mind and spirit from its medieval bonds. In England the Renaissance took the form of humanism triumphing over puritanism. This new age was characterized by a rediscovery of the classics, a repudiation of religion, and the amazing opening of new horizons in science and world exploration.

This highly popular bit of historiography makes indeed a delightful story, says Lewis, but it has the unfortunate disadvantage that very little of it is true. Yes, there was, Lewis concedes, a marvelous revival of the classics, but the classicists became so extremely dogmatic in their methods that their effect was anything but liberating. To say that humanism routed religion in England is simply ludicrous in view of the historical facts. The Copernican conception of a tiny earth in a vast universe was hardly new; Ptolemy had said as much centuries earlier. And the discovery of America was not at the time so much a wonder as an economic nuisance; the great hope had been to find another trade route to Cathay.

Probably Lewis's chief objection to the humanist tint on history has as much to do with style of argumentation and criticism as with substance. For issues of substance can be argued; sneering and innuendo cannot. "They jeer and do not refute," Lewis once complained. Decrying the humanists' unreasonable hatred of everything medieval, as well as their doctrinaire rejection of everything that is not purely classical, Lewis writes:

> In the field of philosophy humanism must be regarded, quite frankly, as a Philistine movement: even an obscuritanist movement. In this sense the New Learning created the New Ignorance.[14]

These are very strong words, particularly when directed toward a movement that considers itself the liberator of the human intellect. But on this point Lewis is passionate, for he considers the most popular conception of the Renaissance to be among the most serious misconceptions in the study of history.

By far, the greater part of *English Literature in the Sixteenth Century—Excluding Drama* is devoted to a survey of the many writers of prose and verse during that period of time. As such, the book's contents are far too wide-reaching for a discussion—or even a listing—of the authors and works presented in the limited space we have here. In the book we revisit many of the names we saw in Lewis's earlier *The Allegory of Love*, but here we find many more and much greater detail given to each.

What is unique to Lewis's survey of sixteenth-century English literature is his perspective on the Renaissance and his consequent remarks on the significance of these works. Eschewing the standard cause-effect "rebirth of learning" model, Lewis categorizes the century's literature into three periods. He writes:

> But though 'periods' are a mischievous conception they are a methodological necessity. . . . I have accordingly divided it up into what I call the Late Medieval, the Drab Age, and the 'Golden' Age.[15]

The Late Medieval literature is characterized by simple, straight-forward prose, but poetry that is highly allegorical and metrically irregular. The Drab Age is shown to have produced more clumsy and artificial prose, as well as poetry that is still badly flawed but has lost its allegorical interest as well. Finally, the Golden Age brings in "the great Elizabethans"; names like Spenser, Donne, and Shakespeare appear. Of the Golden Age Lewis writes:

> Men have at last learned how to write; for a few years nothing more is needed than to play out again and again the strong, simple music of the uncontrolled line and to load one's poem with all that is naturally delightful—with flowers and swans, with ladies' hair, hands, lips, breasts and eyes, with silver and gold, woods and waters, the stars, the moon and the sun.[16]

The significance of this development in English literature must not be overlooked, as it constitutes the very thesis of Lewis's book. The liberation of English literature from its past was definitely not brought about by a triumph of humanism. In fact, the triumph of the Golden Age lay to a great extent in its repudiation of the sterile classicism of the humanists in favor of a style more consistent with the Middle Ages. In his introduction Lewis had already alluded to this fact:

> The humanists could not really bring themselves to believe that the poet cared about the shepherds, lovers, warriors, voyages, and battles. They must be only a disguise for something more 'adult.' Medieval readers had been equally ready to believe in a poet's hidden wisdom: but then, perhaps because they had been taught that the multiple meanings of Scripture never abrogated the literal sense, they did not allow the hidden wisdom to obscure the fact that the text before them was 'a noble and joyous history.' They pressed the siege, wept with the heroines, and shuddered at the monsters.[17]

While reading Lewis's *English Literature in the Sixteenth Century—Excluding Drama*, look for the basic thesis regarding the humanist assumptions in the Renaissance model of history and literature. Watch for Lewis's illustrations of how those assumptions not only bias our critiques of literature, but also bias the very questions considered important enough to ask. Notice how Lewis demonstrates the power of an alternative model to cast the various authors and their works in a very different light from that of the standard model. Look as well for Lewis's thoughts on critical humanism, and ponder their implications for literary criticism as it is commonly practiced today. This question, incidentally, is pursued in greater depth in Lewis's later book, *An Experiment in Criticism*.

The student of medieval and Renaissance literature in England, of course, should pay great attention to each of Lewis's many reviews of the authors covered. Students of theology and church history will find here a rich resource on the history of English Bibles and on the Tyndale versus More controversies. Students of European history should not miss Lewis's challenge to what has now become the standard historical perspective, as Lewis's alternative thesis is both credible and far-reaching in its implications. Finally, the casual reader will find here a wealth of history, poetry, biography, and insights well worth the reading of this hefty volume on a little-remembered century of England's past.

The Discarded Image: An Introduction to Medieval and Renaissance Literature

Shortly before his death in 1963, Lewis put into book form a series of his lectures delivered over the years at Oxford and Cambridge Universities. In this his last book Professor Lewis again demonstrates the breadth of his knowledge in classical philosophy and the remarkable depth of his scholarship in medieval and Renaissance literature.

This book is not recommended for the casual reader, as it is a truly scholarly investigation of the worldview that was taken for granted by the medieval and Renaissance European writers. For the serious student of the literature of these periods, however, *The Discarded Image* is essential. If one is to delve below the most superficial understanding of authors such as Chaucer, Spenser, Donne, or Shakespeare, one needs Lewis's kind of familiarity with the medieval mind.

Professor Lewis's book takes its title from the fact that the medieval image—the all-encompassing view of the cosmos and existence itself—has long been discarded in favor of more modern views. This image, or "the Model" as Lewis calls it, consisted of the vast body of knowledge and assumptions held in common by most people in medieval times. As Lewis demonstrates with ample specific citations, many aspects of this medieval Model actually date back to antiquity, particularly to the thoughts of Plato and his interpreters.

Consequently, the body of *The Discarded Image* is filled with discussions of the contributions to medieval ideas by such classical writers as Cicero, Lucan, and Apuleius, and by such "seminal" writers as Chalcidius, Macrobius, and Pseudo-Dionysius. The topics of these discussions include such matters as cosmology, geography, God, demons, angels, and even fairies. In these discussions Lewis exposes some of the popular misconceptions regarding medieval thought—for example, the erroneous notion that medieval knowledge was merely passed down from unquestioned ecclesiastical authority—and traces the development of those ideas that were genuinely a part of the accepted Model.

In the concluding chapters of *The Discarded Image* Professor Lewis offers some interesting thoughts on the processes by which popular and scientific thought shifts from one model to another. With conclusions similar to Thomas Kuhn's work on "paradigm shifts" in science, Lewis points out that the major models of thought do not change so much through the newer somehow disproving the older, but more often as a response to a subjectively perceived need for something new. Lewis writes:

> The most spectacular differences between the Medieval Model and our own concern astronomy and biology. In both

fields the new Model is supported by a wealth of empirical evidence. But we should misrepresent the historical process if we said that the irruption of new facts was the sole cause of the alteration.[18]

And later Professor Lewis explains:

Sufficient disrelish of the old Model and a sufficient hankering for some new one, phenomena to support that new one will obediently turn up.[19]

The broader significance of this idea becomes obvious when Lewis discusses the popular modern attitudes toward medieval thought. Throughout *The Discarded Image* Lewis makes occasional reference to the many distortions and misconceptions widely held today on the subject of the medieval mind. Pointing out that even the modern conceptions of "knowing" and "truth" are in a state of flux, Lewis concludes:

It would therefore be subtly misleading to say "The medievals thought the universe to be like that, but we know it to be like this." Part of what we now know is that we cannot, in the old sense, "know what the universe is like" and that no model we can build will be, in that old sense, "like" it.[20]

To put Lewis's conclusion perhaps more simply, it is time to wake up from the spell of modern popular thought that assumes the superiority of what most of us happen to think and believe at this moment. Such an assumption is consistent with evolutionary thinking but not, in fact, with the most recent developments even in our natural sciences.

In the end Lewis's is an argument not unilaterally against the established, positivist, rational-empirical methods of science per se, but against the modern habit of setting them up as something more than they have any right to claim to be. In conclusion he writes:

I am only suggesting considerations that may induce us to
regard all Models in the right way, respecting each and idol-
ising none. . . . We can no longer dismiss the change of
Models as a simple progress from error to truth.[21]

While *The Discarded Image* is an entirely academic work, the
implications of its conclusions reach into the areas of theology and
church doctrine as well. Briefly, Lewis's call to respect and consider
the truths in the "older" models is relevant to the widespread *a priori* rejection of Christian orthodoxy by most of the modern intelligentsia. Christian doctrine has most definitely not been somehow
disproven by newer facts; it is more a matter of having become
unfashionable. We are reminded here of G.K. Chesterton's statement, "The Christian ideal has not been tried and found wanting.
It has been found difficult; and left untried."[22]

The first thing for the reader to look for in an academic book
such as this one is the author's overall purpose in this particular piece
of scholarship. In this case we would want to ask what are the
widespread misconceptions that Professor Lewis wishes to dispel
with regard to the medieval mind. One need not be a Christian
believer to benefit from Lewis's painstaking researches of the roots
of the medieval and Renaissance worldview. Indeed, an adequate
understanding of the early British writers would call for a working
knowledge of these antecedents.

The Christian reader should look as well for the implied underpinnings of Christian apologetics in our modern, anti-religious
milieu. The important questions here revolve around what has and
has not really been established as truth. Professor Lewis is ready to
grant that medieval thought contained many errors of fact, and yet
he is far from ready to grant that our newer popular and scientific
thought simply represents a progression from error to truth. The situation is much more complicated than that, as the best among modern scientists would point out.

Look for a larger view of knowledge, one in which the models
of truth stand or fall on their own internal merits rather than on tem-

poral popularity or intellectual imprimatur. In Lewis's *The Discarded Image* the reader finds an example of scholarship looking toward that larger view. This book is another case of Professor Lewis's swimming against the intellectual stream and insisting that unpopular ideas be heard and considered seriously.

Studies in Medieval and Renaissance Literature

Three years after C.S. Lewis's death, many of his shorter writings on various literary topics were brought into one collection. Though most of the materials in these essays and addresses are of a highly technical nature concerning primarily the use of imagery and metaphor by such authors as Dante, Malory, Tasso, and Spenser, there is nevertheless much to be gained by the less literary reader in pursuing Lewis's literary ideas.

Here Lewis's work continues to demonstrate the professor's scholarship aside from the apologetics and fantasies for which he had become famous. Indeed, in *Studies in Medieval and Renaissance Literature* one sees clearly the astounding depth and breadth of the author's knowledge of his subjects—a degree of exhaustive scholarship that has become increasingly rare among the professors at our modern universities.

A reading of Lewis's scholarly work merely increases my wonder at this man's ability to communicate so simply and clearly in his apologetics and stories for children. I find myself respecting him all the more for thus choosing to come out and show himself rather than to hide in a great, wordy cloud of obfuscations and sophistry—"claptrap," Lewis would call it—so typical of lesser men of intellect. Judging by his life and work, Lewis was clear in his belief that the intellectual's highest calling is to communicate so that even the uneducated can understand.

But the writings in this collection were not intended for popular reading. These works of technical scholarship represent that other side of C.S. Lewis that his popular readers seldom seek out. These essays are bits of arguments, delineations of finer points in controversies carried on over decades by scholars in a highly specialized field. Thus, for example, the reader will find rather long and detailed discussions on why a certain French poet's works are preferred in England over another's, or the finer points of the interpretation of a particular word in Malory's *Morte D'Arthur* by various scholars, or perhaps why Spenser's sensual passages in "The Faerie Queene" serve an entirely different purpose than those of Tasso in his earlier work. These are not topics that typically seize the imagination of the reading public.

So what, then, can the casual reader look for in this collection of essays? For one thing, a reader can gain a greater sense of the depth of Lewis's literary knowledge and thus a greater degree of trust in the underpinnings of his work in fantasy and myth. For another, the reader can certainly look for Lewis's insights and opinions on art and literature as found scattered incidentally throughout his discussions. For example:

> All old works of art show the same contrast to modern works, and the history of all art tells the same miserable story of progressive specialization and impoverishment.[23]

Lewis develops this theme of impoverishment through specialization fully in his book *An Experiment in Criticism*. There he particularly laments the fate of modern poetry, which has become so very specialized that only an extremely esoteric few can understand it.

It is difficult to review a book of writings on so many different subjects, and again in this case I shall take a closer look at only one essay, perhaps representative of the work as a whole. The third chapter in *Studies in Medieval and Renaissance Literature* is called "Imagination and Thought in the Middle Ages." This chapter actually consists of two lectures delivered by C.S. Lewis to an audience of scientists at Cambridge University in 1956, thus once again demonstrating Lewis's commitment to making the attempt to communicate with those who might be indifferent or even hostile to his ideas.

The importance of these lectures cannot be overstated because they address in clear and simple form the structure of the medieval cosmology—not as the irrational obscurantism that modern scientific triumphalists would pretend it, but as an entirely rational and sensible system given the information available at the time. With regard to the widespread misconception that the medieval mind was occupied with romantic fables of knights and dragons and the like, Lewis points out:

> But the paradox is that the note is one which the real Middle Ages struck only in a minority of Ballads and Romances and hardly at all in any other form. That boundlessness, indefiniteness, suggestiveness are not the common or characteristic medieval mood. The real temper of those ages was not romantic.[24]

Lewis goes on to remind his audience that the more characteristic product of the medieval mind would be Thomas Aquinas's *Summa* or Dante's *Divine Comedy*, neither of which represents the work of a romantic dreamer so much as of a painstakingly methodical systematizer. Lewis concludes:

> Characteristically, medieval man was not a dreamer nor a spiritual adventurer; he was an organizer, a codifier, a man of system. His ideal could be not unfairly summed up in the old housewifely maxim 'A place for everything, and everything in its (right) place.'[25]

The point that Lewis was trying to stress to his scientific listeners is that a true historical perspective on the medieval cosmology precludes any condescending remarks about ignorance and superstition. Given the data available in their time, the medievals developed a remarkably coherent and rational view of the universe and their place in it.

Students of medieval history and literature will find in this chapter perhaps the finest explication of the medieval cosmology to be found anywhere. In but one example of Lewis's concise summary, he says of the medievals:

> They will distinguish animate and inanimate as clearly as we do; will say that stones, for example, have only being; vegetables being and life; animals, being, life and sense; man, being, life, sense and reason.[26]

A working knowledge of this cosmology should be prerequisite to any examination in the history of science, as well as to studies of Chaucer, Spenser, and even Shakespeare; and Lewis's "Imagination and Thought" lectures stand as a highly recommended summary for that necessary background.

Finally, in reading C.S. Lewis's *Studies in Medieval and Renaissance Literature*, one can look for the insights of a medievalist working at his trade. Due to its abundance of technical scholarship in literary critique, this collection is not recommended for the casual reader. On the other hand, it is highly recommended for the serious student of early English and other literature—particularly to those interested in Chaucer, Dante, and Spenser. Additionally, the chapter on the medieval cosmology is essential for students of literature and of the history of science as well.

A Preface to Paradise Lost

Every student or potential reader of John Milton's *Paradise Lost* should certainly read C.S. Lewis's preface first. The reason is that Lewis's commentary serves as a necessary counterpoint to many of the notions and opinions about the poem that have become traditional fare in modern literary criticism. If one were to judge Milton's works solely on the basis of the most popular critiques, one would most likely come to conclusions that are quite biased in rather predictable directions.

In this regard C.S. Lewis reiterates—as he has in other contexts—the importance of making a great effort to understand the perspective of an author subjectively, as if from inside the author's mind in that particular time and place. Lewis writes:

> To enjoy our full humanity we ought, so far as possible, to contain within us at all times . . . all the modes of thinking and feeling through which man has passed. You must, so far as in you lies, become an Achaean chief while reading Homer, a medieval knight while reading Malory, and an eighteenth century Londoner while reading Johnson. Only thus will you be able to judge the work 'in the same spirit that its author writ' and to avoid chimerical criticism.[27]

Here we have the reason why Lewis in his *A Preface to Paradise Lost* devotes an entire chapter to Saint Augustine's theology, as well as another chapter to an explanation of the hierarchical perspective of Milton's time. For without a solid understanding of these issues, the modern reader is bound to misunderstand what Milton is about in *Paradise Lost*.

Consequently, Lewis's *Preface* begins by establishing Milton's intention in writing the poem. What Milton meant *Paradise Lost* to be is a special kind of narrative poem called the epic poem. Epic poetry is, of course, about great and meaningful events, but it also requires a certain kind of style and structure. As an inheritance from the earliest epic poems, which were not written but were delivered orally, a certain amount of repetition of stock words and phrases is used to build a feeling over many lines in the poem. Thus in epic poetry one does not look for short sentences to serve as quotable gems in themselves; instead, the reader is called upon to ride the waves of the poet's language over the long expanse of the poem.

Milton's *Paradise Lost* is often criticized for being formal and ritualistic, with many repetitions like an incantation. Lewis argues:

> The Virgilian and Miltonic style is there to compensate for—to counteract—the privacy and informality of silent reading

in a man's own study. Every judgement on it which does not realize this will be inept. To blame it for being ritualistic and incantatory, for lacking intimacy or the speaking voice, is to blame it for being just what it intends to be and ought to be. It is like damning an opera or an oratorio because the personages sing instead of speaking.[28]

Later Lewis develops this thought further:

As far as style of the poem, I have already noted this peculiar difficulty in meeting the adverse critics, that they blame it for the very qualities which Milton and his lovers regard as virtues. Milton institutes solemn games, funeral games, and triumphal games in which we mourn the fall and celebrate the redemption of our species; they complain that his poetry is 'like a solemn game'. He sets out to enchant us and they complain that the result sounds like an incantation. . . . If a man blames port wine for being strong and sweet . . . or the sun for shining, or sleep because it puts thought away, how can we answer him?[29]

There is no good, says Lewis, in complaining about Milton's style, for it is the very style that the poet went to great lengths to accomplish. If one is to enjoy *Paradise Lost*—or even to understand it—one must enter into the world and the language and the style of epic poetry and experience the poem from within.

This idea brings us to another important point in Lewis's *A Preface to Paradise Lost*, and that is the relationship between the poet and his reader. Milton's poetry has been popularly referred to as being like organ music—the effect coming in full, broad waves of sound, one upon the other. Lewis alters this view a bit:

It is common to speak of Milton's style as organ music. It might be more helpful to regard the reader as the organ and Milton as the organist. It is on us he plays, if we will let him.[30]

As an illustration, Lewis shows how Milton uses this effect in intro-
ducing the reader to Paradise in the poem. The poet does not give
stark description; he draws the picture out of our own imaginations.
Lewis explains:

> Yet Milton must seem to describe—you cannot just say noth-
> ing about Paradise in *Paradise Lost*. While seeming to
> describe his own imagination he must actually arouse ours,
> and arouse it not to make definite pictures, but to find again
> in our own depth the Paradisal light of which all explicit
> images are only the momentary reflection. We are his organ:
> when he appears to be describing Paradise he is in fact draw-
> ing out the Paradise Stop in us.[31]

We, the readers, have become the organ, and Milton's artistry is to
bring the music out of us.

There are many in the academic world who will inevitably stumble over Milton's Christianity. There is always the attempt to interpret *Paradise Lost* in terms more consistent with materialist
philosophy and humanist assumptions. Lewis quotes a Professor
Saurat as having invited the reader of Milton ". . . to disentangle
from theological rubbish the permanent and human interest. . . ."[32]
Lewis's reply to the professor is instructive:

> This is like asking us to study *Hamlet* after the 'rubbish' of
> the revenge code has been removed, or centipedes when free
> of their irrelevant legs, or Gothic architecture without the
> pointed arches. Milton's thought, when purged of its theol-
> ogy, does not exist.[33]

Milton's theology is the essence of Milton's mind. Surely it is folly
to seek an understanding of Milton apart from his theology.

Later in his *A Preface to Paradise Lost* Lewis concedes that one
need not be a Christian believer to appreciate *Paradise Lost*. There
is indeed a meaning—if even a deep mythological meaning—in the

poem for the agnostic seeker. But it is a meaning that not too many modern scholars would care to face. Lewis explains:

> But *Paradise Lost* records a real, irreversible, unrepeatable process in the history of the universe; and even for those who do not believe this, it embodies (in what for them is mythical form) the great change in every individual soul from happy dependence to miserable self-assertion and thence either, as in Satan, to final isolation, or, as in Adam, to reconcilement and a different happiness. The truth and passion of the presentation are unassailable. They were never, in essence, assailed until rebellion and pride came, in the romantic age, to be admired for their own sake.[34]

It was the Romantics, says Lewis, who taught us to admire rebellion and pride for their own sake. Though Lewis himself can in some ways be considered a Romanticist, here we see one of the points at which Christian thought differs sharply from the Romantic tradition. Here is the great stumbling-block that compels so many modern scholars to avoid Milton. In the end, the poet simply cannot be separated from his theology.

Addison is said to have stated: "The great moral which reigns in Milton . . . is the most universal and most useful that can be imagined, that Obedience to the will of God makes men happy and that Disobedience makes them miserable."[35] To this statement C.S. Lewis adds:

> . . . there can be no serious doubt that Milton meant just what Addison said: neither more, nor less, nor other than that. If you can't be interested in that, you can't be interested in *Paradise Lost*.[36]

This state of the matter puts the modern materialist-relativist scholar in a bind with regard to *Paradise Lost*. On the one pole is the idea of accepting Milton's Christian theology and enjoying the poem as it was intended by the author. On the other pole is Professor Saurat calling Milton's theology mere "rubbish" and trying to wring a semblance of meaning from what is left. But the result of the latter will always be unsatisfactory. For *Paradise Lost* is a poem born of a perspective that leaves no comfortable middle ground. Lewis comments:

> Where *Paradise Lost* is not loved, it is deeply hated. . . . We have all skirted the Satanic island enough to have motives for wishing to evade the full impact of the poem. . . . Satan wants to go on being Satan. This is the real meaning of his choice 'Better to reign in Hell, than serve in Heav'n.' Some, to the very end, will think this a fine thing to say. . . .[37]

But, then, thinking this "a fine thing to say" comes back to the very point of *Paradise Lost*. Lewis adds:

> But that is just the point. Satan's monomaniac concern with himself and his supposed rights and wrongs is a necessity of the Satanic predicament.[38]

We begin to see here the foundation for Lewis's diabolical fantasies in *The Great Divorce* and especially in *The Screwtape Letters*. The issue is clearly one of demanding one's rights versus grateful obedience; the middle ground does not hold up.

The question of influences in literature was one that deeply interested the scholar C.S. Lewis, as we can see clearly in his *An Experiment in Criticism*. Lewis often laments the modern critical practice of making simple-minded assumptions regarding the "influence" of an earlier author upon a later one. Thus we must be very careful in drawing possible influences of Milton upon Lewis. It is obvious that Lewis was profoundly influenced by Milton, and yet probably less profoundly than both were influenced by Saint Paul, Saint Augustine, and the corpus of Christian doctrine. In the end we find these influences all blended together in this statement by the scholar C.S. Lewis about the poet John Milton:

For this is perhaps the central paradox in his vision. Discipline, while the world is yet unfallen, exists for the sake of what seems its very opposite—for freedom, almost for extravagance. The pattern deep hidden in the dance, hidden so deep that shallow spectators cannot see it, alone gives beauty to the wild, free gestures that fill it. . . .[39]

The discipline that leads to freedom is, indeed, a key to the Christian faith, and it is likewise a central theme in Milton's *Paradise Lost*.

In reading Lewis's *A Preface to Paradise Lost* look for Professor Lewis's instruction on the elements of primary and secondary epic poetry. Pay close attention to the epic poet's purpose and the book's implications for modern criticisms of *Paradise Lost*. Consider Lewis's advice on entering into the times and perspectives of an author in order to understand truly what the author has written. Notice throughout the preface the several ways in which *Paradise Lost* can be appreciated.

C.S. Lewis aficionados can find particular gratification here in discovering the foundations for many of the ideas developed in Lewis's other works—particularly in the fantasies, the science fiction books, and the Narnia stories. Look especially for the diabolical characteristics—the aggrandizement of the self, the exaggerated concern for one's rights, and the spirit of rebellion. And finally, ponder Lewis's opposition to the standard critiques of Milton in view of the larger context of an intellectual milieu that is hostile to Christian doctrine.

9

THE COMPLETE SCHOLAR

In an earlier chapter we encountered the book *The Abolition of Man*, wherein C.S. Lewis wrote of "men without chests," meaning those modern materialist skeptics with great intellect but with atrophied hearts. In the last chapter we briefly visited Page Smith's *Killing the Spirit*, wherein "academic fundamentalism" is shown to be channeling modern scholarship into increasingly narrower passages. There are, in fact, a growing number of scholars who are protesting the sterile constrictions of modern academia.

As the academic disciplines become more specialized and sophisticated in their methodologies, they necessarily become more esoteric, more exclusive in their audiences. This "narrowing" that Lewis laments in the field of poetry is really a problem in all fields, as fewer and fewer people understand (or care, for that matter) what scholars are talking and writing about. Even the academicians are finding it increasingly difficult to fathom the work of their colleagues in other disciplines. Are these developments the inevitable result of the knowledge itself becoming "too deep" for the general understanding? Some would say so, but I think not. There are norms within our intellectual subcultures that actively work toward these unnecessary and undesirable ends.

My purpose here is not to develop this thesis—it can be pursued in the works of Page Smith,[1] Allan Bloom,[2] and others—but to point out that C.S. Lewis was more than the mere critic crying in the intellectual wilderness. For even as the academic world was so busy specializing, constricting, "deconstructing," and enforcing its "fundamentalist" norms, Lewis was busy writing books of first-rate scholarship, science fiction, apologetics, spiritual nourishment, and fantasy. We have seen that Lewis paid a price for this rebellion, but we can recognize now that Lewis is something much closer to the complete scholar than are most of his colleagues and critics.

There is yet another sense in which C.S. Lewis is the more complete scholar, and that is in the area that Lewis chose to call "the heart." Again, if Smith and Bloom and others are correct in their assessment that higher learning has banished its own heart and soul, C.S. Lewis stands out as one scholar who chose to retain his. In a widespread context where scholars must pretend to be "value-free," Professor Lewis's values and beliefs and passions are written all over his scholarship; that is why even his scholarship is so fascinating and alive. The selections in the last chapter reveal as much, and those of the present chapter will illustrate my point even further.

In this chapter we continue with Lewis's scholarly works by looking first at his *The Literary Impact of the Authorized Version*. Those who might expect to find partisan propaganda due to Lewis's Christianity will be disappointed, as Lewis's analysis is both balanced and objective. Next we visit Lewis's important little book *An Experiment in Criticism*, which is among other things a plea for a semblance of decency and sensibility in the forum of literary criticism. The third book to be reviewed in this chapter is Lewis's *Studies in Words*, the product of a philologist at work and at play. And finally we broaden our scope again to look at *They Asked for a Paper*, a collection of essays and addresses compiled shortly before Lewis's death in 1963.

The Literary Impact of the Authorized Version

A short book, or more like a pamphlet, from the pen of C.S. Lewis is the record of his Ethel M. Wood Lecture delivered at the

University of London in 1950. In this fascinating address, Lewis the scholar takes an intellectual look at the Authorized Version of the Bible considered as a book among books, and he discusses its influences on English literature in general. It is indeed a remarkable discussion because here Lewis shows himself to be much more the scholar and much less the Christian propagandist than the Christian reader might have anticipated or perhaps hoped for. But Lewis is about seeking the truth, even if the truth turns out to be problematic to his cherished doctrines.

Characteristically beginning his discussion with some necessary foundation work, Lewis points out that one cannot properly discuss the impact of the Authorized Version without, in fact, discussing that of the Bible itself in its various translations. Consequently there is mention of the Septuagint, the Vulgate, Luther's Bible, those of Tyndale and More, and others—brought to the conclusion that the variations among the versions are quite small and mostly unimportant.

Also in preparation for his argument, Lewis makes an essential distinction between the concepts of source and influence. The presence of quotations from a given work do not necessarily denote a great influence by that work. While the Bible or Shakespeare may serve as a source for ample quotations, they may still exert a negligible influence on the writer who employs them. Lewis uses the writings of Ruskin and Bunyan to illustrate his point. What Lewis is doing here is eliminating the easy answer to the question of the impact of the Authorized Version on English literature in general. It will not do, he reasons, simply to locate and count the quotations from the Authorized Version and then imply influence from that count. The presence of such quotations in no way demonstrates a necessary influence of the source upon the writer's work. If we are to understand the impact of the Authorized Version on the subsequent literature, we shall have to dig deeper into the style, the vocabulary, the imagery, the values, and the meanings of the literature in question.

In the end Lewis concludes that the impact of the Authorized

Version on English literature has been modest at best. According to Lewis, the causes for this relatively limited influence are two. The first is: ". . . until the Romantic taste existed the Authorized Version was not such an attractive model as we might suppose."[3] Recall that the mainstream of modern thought had been in movement away from the poetic and Romantic, toward the more prosaic and literal. Aside from the Romantic reaction discussed earlier, there would be little appreciation in modern literature for the "florid or inflated"[4] style found in the Authorized Version.

Lewis's second reason for the comparatively modest impact of the Authorized Version on English literature is that the Bible itself was so widely known.

> This may sound paradoxical, but it is seriously meant. For three centuries the Bible was so well known that hardly any word or phrase . . . could be borrowed without recognition. If you echoed the Bible everyone knew you were echoing the Bible. . . . It is difficult to conceive conditions less favourable to that unobtrusive process of infiltration by which profound literary influence usually operates.[5]

In other words, Lewis felt that quotations from the Bible would be far too doctrinally obtrusive and thus would lack the subtlety to operate as a literary influence.

A peripheral but important point that Lewis makes has to do with the "Bible as literature" approach. In this connection Lewis makes some rather startling comments, such as:

> There is a certain sense in which 'the Bible as literature' does not exist. It is a collection of books so widely different in period, kind, language, and aesthetic value, that no common criticism can be passed on them.[6]

But even more significant are Lewis's opinions on the Bible's future in the canon of English literature:

It may be asked whether now, when only a minority of Englishmen regard the Bible as a sacred book, we may antic- ipate an increase of its literary influence. I think we might if it continued to be widely read. But this is not very likely. Our age has, indeed, coined the expression 'the Bible as literature'. It is very generally implied that those who have rejected its theological pretensions nevertheless continue to enjoy it as a treasure house of English prose. It may be so. There may be people who, not having been forced upon familiarity with it by believing parents, have yet been drawn to it by its literary charms and remained as constant readers. But I never hap- pen to meet them. . . . I cannot help suspecting . . . that those who read the Bible as literature do not read the Bible.[7]

It is as if Lewis were saying, "Come now, let us be honest about this. Is anybody reading the Bible who does not believe it?"

In conclusion, Lewis states that the Bible will not likely return to public prominence unless it returns as a sacred book. He writes:

It contains good literature and bad literature. But even the good literature is so written that we can seldom disregard its sacred character. . . . It is, if you like to put it that way, not merely a sacred book but a book so remorselessly and con- tinuously sacred that it does not invite, it excludes or repels, the merely aesthetic approach. You can read it as literature only by a tour de force. You are cutting the wood against the grain, using the tool for a purpose it was not intended to serve. . . . I predict that it will in the future be read, as it always has been read, almost exclusively by Christians.[8]

In academic circles one sometimes hears discussions of the issue of intellectual honesty, often including the hidden assumption that those who hold religious beliefs are somehow *ipso facto* among the intellectually dishonest. However, an honest observer would have to acknowledge the existence of an alarming measure of dishonesty dis- tributed pretty evenly among the advocates and practitioners of every point of view under the sun. We live unfortunately in an age in which the very idea of truth is widely ridiculed and wherein the importance of winning the argument takes precedence over finding the truth.

Yet here again we find C.S. Lewis the scholar and C.S. Lewis the Christian shining in the darkness. Here we find the kind of intellectual honesty that will forego the easy approach and the flip answer but is instead willing to probe the question even to the point of finding unfriendly results. Lewis was asked to assess the literary impact of the Authorized Version of the Bible. While the overzealous partisan of Christianity might have hoped for a treatise showing the great influence of the Bible on English literature, Lewis's conclusion is honest and perceptive. "Actually," he says in effect, "its influence has been negligible, and here are my guesses as to why."

In reading Lewis's reasonings we see the man's broad base of knowledge in English literature and the English language. We find as well his clear thinking on the uses of the sacred and the profane. In reading *The Impact of the Authorized Version*, look for Lewis's discussion of the influences of the Renaissance humanists, as well as his points on allegory and literalism. Follow Lewis's arguments as to why the Bible resists the "Bible as literature" movement, and on the Bible's probable impact in the future. And finally, enjoy the verbal banquet by imagining yourself in the audience listening to C.S. Lewis as he masterfully plays with words and ideas in his explorations on this subject.

An Experiment in Criticism

A few years before his death, C.S. Lewis wrote this fascinating call for reform in the field of literary criticism. As a recognized and respected member of the cultured literati himself, Lewis was fully aware of the widespread abuses of criticism in English literature, and his thesis calls for nothing less than a radically altered critical technique, as well as a change of heart among the critics.

To read *An Experiment in Criticism* today is to discover that in the subsequent decades since it was written, the problems of which

Lewis complained have become worse instead of better. Clearly, the specifics of his argument are even more relevant today than when Lewis first wrote them, and the need for change is more acute than ever. Perhaps it is needless to say that Lewis's book has been completely ignored by the pundits of English literature, but it is important to say again that they have done so to the field's own considerable detriment.

Lewis initiates his argument with a frontal attack on the pretensions and snobbery of the critics, particularly for their habit of summarily dismissing entire categories of books—for example, mysteries, westerns, and science fiction—as being too unliterary even to discuss. Protesting the widespread habit of sneering at a given kind of book and its readers, Lewis suggests considering kinds of reading as a starting point. Writing that invites a mature, cultured kind of reading is good writing; that which does not is not. Using this new formula for criticism would certainly yield surprises as to the accepted canon of good literature in the English language.

Lewis's argument is essentially a critique of the academic fields of English and American literature. For many of us who have taken university courses in literature, Lewis's criticisms ring remarkably true. In describing the majority of his honors students he writes:

> On every play, poem, or novel, they produce the view of some eminent critic. An amazing knowledge of Chaucerian or Shakespearean criticism sometimes co-exists with a very inadequate knowledge of Chaucer or Shakespeare.[9]

The learned critiques of literature have come to be more important than the literature itself.

One of the unhappy results of this overemphasis on the critics is that literature has come to be seen primarily as vehicles for various philosophies or points of view, rather than as works of art. Consequently, in the push and shove among competing schools of thought, the critiques of literary works can become so politicized that one by one very good pieces of literature are rejected from the popular canon, while more "correct" pieces of clearly inferior artistic quality are included. Lewis explains:

> The use of the guillotine becomes an addiction. Thus under Vigilant criticism a new head falls nearly every month. The list of approved authors grows absurdly small.[10]

In another context Lewis writes that his new critical method would

> . . . silence the type of critic for whom all the great names in English literature—except for the half dozen protected by the momentary critical 'establishment'—are as so many lamp posts for a dog.[11]

Thus Lewis anticipates the widespread situation in academia today wherein ideologues feel free to define good and bad literature in terms of their own favorite social causes.

But Lewis's book goes beyond protest and presents his plea for a more humane, more artistically centered method of criticism. He writes:

> The proposed system . . . admits from the outset that there can be no question of totally and finally 'debunking' or 'exposing' any author. . . . We start from the assumption that whatever has been found good by those who really and truly read probably is good. All probability is against those who attack.[12]

The popular critical habit of attacking and debunking the authors of great literature, says Lewis, is worthless to the art of literature. He continues:

> These dethronements are a great waste of energy. Their acrimony produces heat at the expense of light. They do not improve anyone's capacity for good reading. The real way of

mending a man's taste is not to denigrate his present favourites but to teach him how to enjoy something better.[13]

Concerning the onslaught of negative evaluative criticism, Lewis concludes, "I suggest that a ten or twenty years' abstinence both from the reading and from the writing of evaluative criticism might do us all a great deal of good."[14]

But one of the most noteworthy aspects of Lewis's *An Experiment in Criticism* is that it seeks to practice what it preaches. Having pointed out that the bulk of negative evaluative critical commentary does little or nothing to improve the writing or reading of literature, Lewis then provides instruction with a view to just such improvement.

The foundation of his thesis is the important distinction between using the arts and receiving the arts. He writes:

> A work of (whatever) art can be either 'received' or 'used.' When we 'receive' it we exert our senses and imagination and various other powers according to a pattern invented by the artist. When we 'use' it we treat it as assistance for our own activities.[15]

With regard to literature, this receiving is ". . . to get ourselves out of the way"[16] and to let the words do their work without interference.

The unfortunate situation is that the English literature departments in the universities have been producing generations of critics who are unable to receive the art of literature. Lewis concludes:

> [S]ince a text is 'but a cheveral glove' to a determined critic— since everything can be a symbol, or an irony, or an ambiguity—we shall easily find what we want. . . . We are so busy doing things with the work that we give it too little chance to work on us.[17]

Lewis's call for a new approach to literary critique is nothing less than a call for a new attitude toward the art of literature.

And the model for the receiving attitude turns out to be the child. Lewis points out that such terms as "childish" and "infantile" are often used in literary circles as terms of derision. Yet, Lewis argues, some of the childlike qualities are those most conducive to good reading. With regard, for instance, to imaginative stories Lewis writes:

> If few but children now read such stories, that is not because children, as such, have a special predilection for them, but because children are indifferent to literary fashions. What we see in them is not a specifically childish taste, but simply a normal and perennial human taste, temporarily atrophied in their elders by a fashion. It is we, not they, whose taste needs explanation.[18]

On the one hand Lewis has no trouble admitting the less desirable qualities of childhood, but on the other he argues strongly for retaining the imaginative qualities. He writes:

> The sooner we cease to be as fickle, as boastful, as jealous, as cruel, as ignorant, and as easily frightened as most children are, the better for us and for our neighbors. But who in his senses would not keep, if he could, that tireless curiosity, that intensity of imagination, that facility of suspending disbelief, that unspoiled appetite, that readiness to wonder, to pity, and to admire? . . . To have lost the taste for marvels and adventures is no more a matter for congratulation than losing our teeth, our hair, our palate, and finally, our hopes.[19]

Lewis's argument is clearly against the type of critical snobbery that refuses to appreciate the imaginative literature of children, but it goes much deeper than that. Lewis is saying that the negative critical technique that now dominates the field of English literature has the effect of a stranglehold on artistic imagination in both readers and writers. *An Experiment in Criticism* is an important and timely call to release literature from the grip of philosophically and politically motivated negative criticism and to free the imagination once again to appreciate the fine art of writing.

In reading this book, look for Lewis's analogies on music, painting, and literature as art. Pay special attention to his thoughts on "using" versus "receiving" art. Look for his interesting distinctions between good reading and bad reading. Ask yourself whether you agree with Lewis's assessment of the effects of literary criticism as practiced in scholarly circles. Be sure to read the epilogue, for it contains one of the finest discussions I have seen on the topic of why it benefits us to read good literature.

Studies in Words

C.S. Lewis once mentioned in passing that a philologist is a person who loves words and who therefore enjoys studying them. Though the technical definition of the word in academic settings may be quite different today, by his own definition we can certainly say that Lewis himself was a philologist. Lewis explored the origins and development of words not only as an incidental tool in his studies of literature, but also simply because he loved words and found them interesting in their own right.

In his book *Studies in Words* Lewis passes along to his students the fruit of his explorations regarding certain key words found often in English literature. He writes:

> One of my aims is to facilitate, as regards certain words, a more accurate reading of old books; and therefore to encourage everyone to similar exploration of many other words.[20]

To read the older books—even those written as recently as the nineteenth century—one must keep in mind the often greatly altered meanings that certain words may have. Simply to assume that a key word meant then what it means today is to invite misunderstanding and error.

One of Lewis's first pieces of advice is that we study words carefully in their context. He explains:

> And all the while one seems to be learning not only about words. In the end the habit becomes second nature; the slightest semantic discomfort in one's reading arouses one, like a terrier, to the game. . . . One understands a word much better if one has met it alive, in its native habitat.[21]

In this way the reading of old books becomes somewhat like hunting, where the game is the meaning of a given word or passage in the context of its time and place. Lewis adds that in this matter it is the highly intelligent who are most apt to err, because it is they who can most easily imagine several possible meanings, all of which might incidentally be untrue.

Early in his *Studies in Words* Lewis introduces the term *verbicide* to denote the murder of words. He then discusses several common methods of verbicide. The most common method is inflation—for example, the use of "awfully" for "very." Another popular method is called verbiage—illustrated by the use of "significant" with no explanation of what the thing is significant of. Yet another method is the tendency to use words less descriptive and more evaluative—as when words like "adolescent" and "modern" become mere synonyms for "bad" and "good."

The body of Lewis's *Studies in Words* concentrates on thorough semantic studies of these several key words: "nature," "sad," "wit," "free," "sense," "simple," "conscience" and "conscious," "world," "life," and the phrase "I dare say." In these studies Lewis imparts not only a great amount of knowledge and insight on the historical meanings of each word and its semantic relatives, but he also uses this study as a forum for discussing his ideas on why words change as they do.

Thus, for one example among many possible, he writes of the "methodological idiom," wherein we find confusion as to the referent of a given word. Lewis gives an example:

The methodological idiom, applied to history, has produced some confusion. It is often hard to be sure whether the word means the past events themselves as they really were or the study that tries to discover and understand them.[22]

We have all heard someone say, "History tells us . . ." and perhaps we have each stopped to wonder who or what is doing the telling— the events themselves or the people who study history?

Lewis's typical treatment of the chosen key words can be illustrated by a look at his explorations on the word "nature." After tracing several early variations in meaning, he discusses the development of the concept of Nature, in the New Enlightenment sense of Mother Nature. Here he analyzes three developments: (1) the Platonic, (2) the Aristotelian, and (3) the Christian; leading into the relatively modern idea of a deified Mother Nature. Lewis explains:

> But once you can talk about nature . . . you can deify it—or 'her'. Hence the sense which I shall call Great Mother Nature; nature used to mean not simply all the things there are, as an aggregate or even a system, but rather some force or mind or elan supposed to be immanent in them.[23]

We find here the meaning of nature as used in much of the evolutionary writing of the nineteenth and twentieth centuries.

But then there is also the Christian perspective, wherein the word "nature" often appears in opposition to grace. Lewis quotes *The Imitation of Christ* as saying, "Diligently watch the motions of nature and grace . . . nature is subtle and always has self for end . . . grace walks in sincerity and does all for God." Here we discover yet another semantic variation on the word "nature," and again the reader must discern what is meant by the word through careful study of its context.

There are many other fascinating issues addressed by Lewis, but we shall have to be content here with one last piece of advice for students and writers of literature. Lewis says that while it is indeed the poet's challenge to arouse emotions in the reader, the better writer will not do so through the use of emotional words. The trick is to use non-emotional words to elicit the desired emotions from the reader. Lewis advises:

> Poetry most often communicates emotions, not directly, but by creating imaginatively the grounds for those emotions. . . . This, which is eminently true of poetry, is true of all imaginative writing. . . . Avoid all epithets which are merely emotional. It is no use telling us that something was "mysterious" or "loathsome" or "awe-inspiring" or "voluptuous." Do you think your readers will believe you just because you say so? You must go quite a different way to work. By direct description, by metaphor and simile, by secretly evoking powerful associations, by offering the right stimuli to our nerves . . . you must bring it out that we, we readers, not you, exclaim, "how mysterious!" or "loathsome" or whatever it is. Let me taste for myself, and you'll have no need to tell me how I should reach to the same flavour.[24]

Lewis's advice to writers is to use the language to arouse the readers' imaginations and to lead them to the emotional conclusions desired by the author.

In reading *Studies in Words* look for Lewis's example in how to study the key words found in the writings of centuries past. It was Lewis's explicit intention to model this method of investigation for his students of literature. Also look for the substance of Lewis's scholarship on the various words in this study. One cannot help but be greatly enriched by this broader understanding of the semantic nuances discussed.

Pay careful attention to the various kinds of verbicide presented by Lewis, as well as the "moralisation of status words," the "semantic halo," and the many other forces and habits that transform the meanings of words. Finally, be sure to notice Professor Lewis's sense of responsibility to the English language. He writes:

It is well we should become aware of what we are doing when we speak, of the ancient, fragile, and (well used) immensely potent instruments that words are. . . . I should be glad if I sent any reader away with a new sense of responsibility to the language.[25]

In *Studies in Words* explore the many ways in which C.S. Lewis models this "sense of responsibility to the language" for his students and readers.

They Asked for a Paper

Of the many available collections of essays and lectures by C.S. Lewis, *They Asked for a Paper* is the one I choose for my final review, and for good reasons. It seems fitting to end with this volume because it is one of the last of Lewis's books before his death. As such, we know that he had a hand in its editing and structure. Furthermore, this collection is somewhat unique in the breadth of its topics as it contains brief representatives from a wide array of Lewis's nonfiction writings—from apologetics to literary criticism.

The first two addresses, "De Descriptione Temporum" and "The Literary Impact of the Authorized Version," are mentioned or discussed in some detail elsewhere in this book, so I will not belabor them here. But the third, called "Hamlet: The Prince or the Poem?," is an interesting address. Here Lewis the critic laments the modern habit of critiquing everything except the work of art itself. Recall that in *An Experiment in Criticism* Lewis deplored the popular critical forays into the politics and personal lives of authors. Here Lewis condemns the widespread overemphasis on character in dramatic criticism.

With regard to Shakespeare's *Hamlet* there is a school of criticism that considers the play an artistic failure on the grounds that the character of Hamlet is problematic. In response to this notion, Lewis tells his audience, "I confess myself a member of that school which has lately been withdrawing our attention from the characters to fix it on the plays."[26] In the end, Lewis concludes that—regardless of what anyone says about the character of Prince Hamlet—the play *Hamlet* has been an artistic delight for generations, and it has been so because of its enduring artistic merit.

As he has done in other contexts, Lewis calls for an end to the complicated sophistries of the literary establishment and a revival of the capacity for taking sheer delight in a well-written story. Lewis writes:

> I am trying to recall attention from the things an intellectual adult notices to the things a child or a peasant notices—night, ghosts, a castle, a lobby where a man can walk four hours together, a willow-fringed brook where a sad lady drowned, a graveyard and a terrible cliff above the sea, and amidst all these a pale man in black clothes . . . a dishevelled man whose words make us at once think of loneliness and doubt and dread, of waste and dust and emptiness, and from whose hands, or from our own, we feel the richness of heaven and earth and the comfort of human affection slipping away.[27]

Here is Lewis's familiar call to recapture the joy of appreciating the arts, as opposed to the somber business of dissecting and analyzing them.

The collection called *They Asked for a Paper* continues with short pieces on Rudyard Kipling and Walter Scott and an essay titled "Lilies That Fester," wherein Lewis discusses the pursuit of "culture" in education. There follows a fascinating look at Freud and Jung, where Lewis confronts the widespread use of psychoanalytic theory in literary criticism, and an address called "The Inner Ring," a delightful speech telling a group of young men the best way to avoid becoming scoundrels. The book is well worth reading if even for this one address.

Also included are two papers presented by Lewis to the Socratic Club at Oxford University—one called "Is Theology Poetry?" and the other "Obstinacy in Belief." As the Socratic Club was a forum deliberately set up for argument between atheists and Christians, the Socratic Club papers tend to contain a clarity of explanation that may be absent from some of Lewis's papers intended for Christian audiences. The result is often useful, because in speaking to atheists Lewis took great care to explicate all assumptions, to clarify all definitions, to follow his logic meticulously, and to defend all claims with experience.

For example, in "Is Theology Poetry?" Lewis replies to the opposition's claim that there is nothing in Christianity that had not already appeared in previous pagan myths—thus, that Christianity must be false. Here Lewis replies:

> The Divine Light, we are told, "lighteth every man." We should therefore expect to find in the imagination of great Pagan teachers and myth-makers some glimpse of that theme which we believe to be the very plot of the whole cosmic story—the theme of incarnation, death and re-birth. And the difference between the Pagan Christs (Balder, Osiris, etc.) and the Christ Himself is much that we would expect to find. The Pagan stories are all about someone dying and rising, either every year, or nobody knows where and nobody knows when. The Christian story is about a historical personage, whose execution can be dated pretty accurately, under a named Roman magistrate, and with whom the society that He founded is in continuous relation down to the present day. It is not the difference between falsehood and truth. It is the difference between a real event on the one hand and dim dreams or premonitions of that same event on the other. It is like watching something come gradually into focus: first it hangs in the clouds of myth and ritual, vast and vague, then it condenses, grows hard and in a sense small, as a historical event in first century Palestine.[28]

In this sense, says Lewis, at the Incarnation not only did God become Man, but "Myth became Fact."[29] This argument is found in others of Lewis's writings, but nowhere else have I seen it laid out so methodically and concisely as for the Socratic Club.

Another essential piece in *They Asked for a Paper* is a sermon called "Transposition." This sermon is certainly worth the Christian reader's attention, because here Lewis replies to the important problem "... that in what claims to be our spiritual life all the elements of our natural life recur."[30] The popular statement of this problem is that since Christians must appeal to natural images and metaphors to speak of spiritual things, their "spiritual" things must really be mere projections or imaginings from the natural world. This argument was advanced by the witch in *The Silver Chair* and has been used by materialists for many years.

In reply, however, Lewis appeals to the concept of transposition, explaining the matter in this way:

> And the sceptic's conclusion that the so-called spiritual is really derived from the natural, that it is a mirage or imaginary extension of the natural, is also exactly what we should expect; for, as we have seen, this is the mistake which an observor who knew only the lower medium would be bound to make in every case of Transposition. The brutal man never can by analysis find anything but lust in love; the Flatlander never can find anything but flat shapes in a picture; physiology never can find anything in thought except twitchings of the grey matter.[31]

But viewed from above, a transposition is seen as a complicated phenomenon expressed through simplified signs. For example, a dry mouth can signify simple thirst, but it can also signify much more complicated emotional states such as extreme fear. Viewed from "below," a dry mouth is a dry mouth. Viewed from "above," the observer can discern the complicated emotions that may have produced the dry mouth. "Spiritual things are spiritually discerned," writes Lewis.[32]

Of the skeptic who attempts to debunk spiritual matters by use of the words "merely" or "nothing but," Lewis draws the analogy of a dog:

> He sees all the facts but not the meaning. . . . He is therefore, as regards the matter in hand, in the position of an animal. You will have noticed that most dogs cannot understand pointing. You point to a bit of food on the floor: the dog, instead of looking at the floor, sniffs at your finger. A finger is a finger to him, and that is all. His world is all fact and no meaning. And in a period when factual realism is dominant we shall find people deliberately inducing upon themselves this dog-like mind.[33]

The final installment in *They Asked for a Paper* is a sermon called "The Weight of Glory," which is in my opinion one of the finest and most beautiful of Lewis's nonfiction works. Here we find the source of some of the rich imagery in *The Great Divorce* and *Perelandra*. Here we find in concise form some of the foundations of Lewis's apologetics. Here we see Lewis the scholar, Lewis the poet, and Lewis the Christian bring it all together in a sermon that somehow manages to be weighty and uplifting simultaneously.

Lewis writes about the two meanings of glory that he finds in the Bible: that of being appreciated by God, and that of shining like a light. Concerning the former, Lewis discusses the unspeakable grace by which we can be not only noticed, but actually singled out for approval by the omniscient God. He explains:

> The promise of glory is the promise, almost incredible and only possible by the work of Christ, that some of us, that any of us who really chooses, shall actually survive that examination, shall find approval, shall please God. To please God . . . to be a real ingredient in the divine happiness . . . to be loved by God, not merely pitied, but delighted in as an artist delights in his work or a father delights in his son—it seems impossible, a weight or burden of glory which our thoughts can hardly sustain. But so it is.[34]

But the weight of glory does not consist in this alone. There is even more weight in the fact of our neighbor's glory. Lewis continues:

> The load, or weight, or burden of my neighbor's glory should be laid daily on my back, a load so heavy that only humility can carry it, and the backs of the proud will be broken. . . . There are no ordinary people. You have never talked to a mere mortal . . . it is immortals whom we joke with, work with, marry, snub, or exploit—immortal horrors or everlasting splendours.[35]

Next to the sacraments themselves, says Lewis, our neighbors are the holiest objects we shall encounter. The weight of glory is the challenge present in the people we meet in our daily lives.

I cannot bear to close this discussion without one last sampling of Lewis's vision as found in this sermon. Here Lewis speaks of heaven in terms that I find as moving as they are memorable:

> The faint, far-off results of those energies which God's creative rapture implanted in matter when He made the worlds are what we call physical pleasures; and even thus filtered, they are too much for our present management. What would it be to taste at the fountain-head that stream of which even these lower reaches prove so intoxicating? Yet that, I believe, is what lies before us. The whole man is to drink joy from the fountain of joy.[36]

In reading *They Asked for a Paper* look for a great sampler of Lewis's many kinds of nonfiction work. Enjoy the addresses and sermons as if you are hearing each in its context, and you will experience the depth, the wit, and the humor that defined C.S. Lewis. Notice especially Lewis's clear argumentation when addressing the Socratic Club, his grandfatherly humor when addressing his students, his brotherly nurture of his fellow Christians. Use this collection as an introduction, and be alert to which areas of Lewis's nonfiction you might want to pursue further. Finally, be sure to explore the many other fine collections of essays and addresses that are not reviewed here, for in them lies the great pleasure of knowing this remarkable man, C.S. Lewis.

C.S. Lewis and the Third Millennium

There is a sense in which the advent of the third Christian millennium holds no importance other than what we symbolically give it. There is nothing intrinsically meaningful about a decade or a century or a millennium, and we certainly do not expect some great and radical change to take place as we turn our calendars from the year 1999 to 2000. No doubt the course of our daily lives and of history will move along smoothly without taking undue notice of this arbitrary milestone.

On the other hand, there are great and important changes coming, many of which are already on their way. Few are unaware of the burgeoning communications revolution that promises to use electronic technology to transform the way we live. Books are being written on the changing conditions of the global economy and their probable implications for generations to come. The world watches and wonders about future political trends in the wake of the decline of the Soviet Empire. And some are asking whether the free western societies are disintegrating from within as they drift away from their ideological and moral foundations.

Symbolic as the coming of the new millennium may be, there is something about the moment that compels us to stand back and take stock of where we are, what we are doing, and what we ought to be doing. If such an exercise in corporate introspection is a relatively rare thing, it is nonetheless a wise thing to do. For if our history teaches us anything, it teaches us that we are as prone to misdirection and folly collectively as we are individually. Evolutionary optimism aside, it seems we never outgrow our need for critical self-examination.

The coincidence of the C.S. Lewis centennial and the advent of the third millennium invites us to look carefully at these two events in relation to each other. It seems a perfect time to review the works of this remarkable scholar and Christian with an eye toward the next century and beyond. Due to the importance of C.S. Lewis's thought in the twentieth century, there is wisdom in asking ourselves what he is saying of significance for our future.

Now that we have read and loved C.S. Lewis, we have discovered that he speaks not only to our minds, but to our hearts as well. This is due at least in part to his style—his masterful storytelling, his use of symbol and metaphor and allegory, his marvelous imagery, and his disarming simplicity and clarity. But it is due no less to his substance—his unflinching habit of taking the bull by the horns and addressing the subjects that matter to us most: God, love, pain, joy, miracles, and death, to name a few. We are indeed creatures not only with minds, but with hearts and souls as well. The great appeal of C.S. Lewis is that he speaks not only to that one cognitive part of us, but to the whole of us, including heart and soul.

Here in conclusion we revisit the three major modern streams of thought—the New Enlightenment, the Romantic, and the Christian—recalling C.S. Lewis's responses to each. We know now that Lewis was a Romanticist and a Christian, and we can explore the guidance and temperance that his perspective can offer to the juggernaut of the New Enlightenment. In the end we will ponder Lewis's thoughts about the future and consider his ideas as to where we might go from here.

The New Enlightenment Stream Revisited

I would never want my earlier comments to leave the reader with the erroneous impression that the ideas of the New Enlightenment have retreated to unimportance as the twentieth century comes to its conclusion. The truth is very much the opposite, and therein lies the continuing relevance and urgency in C.S. Lewis's writings today. Materialist philosophy and a vague sense of evolutionary progressivism are by far the dominant perspective, particularly in America and western Europe. The cult-like belief in empirical science and technology—and even in positivism—still dominates the field, especially among American intellectuals. Make no mistake, in the western world the New Enlightenment remains by far the most popular creed of all.

However, as we have seen, there have been cracks in the edifice from the beginning. Not only has there been the ongoing Romantic reaction especially in the arts and literature, but there have been controversies within the halls of science as well. Early in the twentieth century many scientifically-minded people were troubled by Freud's speculations on the role of subconscious sexual urges in determining human behavior. In time, disturbing ideas began to emerge in the social sciences as well—such as the "idiographic" views of Dilthey and Windelband, and later the relativist perspectives of the "phenomenologists." The popular theories of evolution had always known their detractors, especially among the physical scientists. And now post-Einstein physics has adopted a much less "positive" attitude, culminating in some fascinating discoveries of "chaos" at the subatomic level.

To follow C.S. Lewis's thoughts on the various New Enlightenment issues is to see more clearly how Christian doctrine responds to each point in question. To begin, it can be said that while Christian doctrine contained no basic quarrel with the Old Enlightenment's high regard for human reason, there developed a very basic antipathy as the advocates of the New Enlightenment moved further into materialist philosophy and especially into the positivist notions of empirical science. The positivists' aggressive rejection of all things metaphysical was answered by Lewis the Romanticist as their rejection of all things religious was answered by Lewis the Christian. Recall the incident in *The Silver Chair* where the queen equates the prince's non-material thoughts with mental illness, and the unforgettable scenes in *Prince Caspian* where everything metaphysical is called "nonsense for babies" and "eggs in moonshine." To the materialist, nothing exists that cannot be perceived with the senses; to the naturalist, nature is "the whole show." These are Lewis's fictional illustrations of the kind of naturalism he controverts at length in *The Abolition of Man* and in *Miracles*.

However, Lewis asserts in his fiction and nonfiction works that both our logic and our experience tell us there is much more to human life than meets the eye. Lewis's argument is that our very consciousness indicates more than a merely quantitative superiority to the other animals. He argues further that our deepest human needs reveal a lost glory for which each of us yearns in the depths of our souls—a yearning that is explained in the Christian doctrines of our special creation, our fall, and our consequent alienation from our Creator.

Regarding the positivist assertion that the methods of the natural sciences are the only legitimate road to truth, Lewis's objections are based in both his Romanticism and his Christianity. As a poet Lewis is far from willing to concede that such things as beauty, imagination, mystery, rhyme, rhythm, music, and joy are merely the necessary effects of natural causes. As a Christian, Lewis is far too familiar with the realities of sin, prayer, spirit, miracles, and the soul to concede that human beings can be best understood by studying them as one would study rocks, trees, or chimpanzees.

An essential pillar in New Enlightenment thinking is the evolutionary paradigm, wherein all things are involved in a natural and inexorable process of development from simpler to more complex and efficient forms. This evolutionary development is said to follow the principle of "survival of the fittest" under the benevolent and watchful eye of Mother Nature or Life. Given the fact that the evolutionists so readily ridicule the idea of Providence or the hand of God as a causal agent, Lewis cannot resist an occasional sarcastic tweak in the face of the evolutionists' alleged "Life force." In *Out of the Silent Planet* Lewis portrays the evolutionist Professor Weston lecturing on how the Life force will carry humankind to conquer distant planets:

> 'She——' began Weston.
> 'I'm sorry,' interrupted Ransom, 'but I've forgotten who She is.'
> 'Life, of course," snapped Weston.[1]

Here Lewis portrays his Ransom questioning the evolutionist in the same way that Lewis himself did in his debates and nonfiction writings. For in both *The Abolition of Man* and *Mere Christianity* we find Lewis questioning the personification of Nature and asking if that is not, in fact, appealing to a metaphysical concept after all. In the latter book Lewis points out as well the absurdly immense probabilities against a series of accidental mutations resulting in the development of creatures as marvelous as human beings.

A part of the ideology of the New Enlightenment that was borrowed from Old Enlightenment thinking is a residing optimism that humanity will take its destiny into its own hands and eventually come to perfect itself. However, a very strong theme in Lewis's space trilogy is exactly the opposite view: when humans aspire to be their own gods, they end by becoming the slaves of forces far beyond their powers to control. Also, in *The Abolition of Man* Lewis develops the thesis that when people talk of "Man's power over Nature," the reality comes down to some men's power over some other men. When it comes to the question of humanity perfecting itself, he asserts that humans are indeed capable of being perfected, but only by the opposite road—humility, trust, and obedience to their Creator.

Finally, a discussion of Lewis's responses to New Enlightenment ideas is incomplete without paying attention to the concept of progress. Recall that a rather vague notion of progress as an inevitable tendency in history was one of the standard foundations of New Enlightenment thought, and notice that such thinking is still quite popular in our day. Despite the growing alarm over various ills in our society, there remains a widespread belief and hope that things in general will continue to improve by means of science and technology. There is still a widely unquestioned habit of assuming the superiority of the new product, the new method, and the new idea.

On the subject of progressivism as a creed, C.S. Lewis had much to say in a short essay called "Is Progress Possible?"[2] Here Lewis begins by pointing out the obvious: "Progress means movement in a desired direction, and we do not all desire the same thing for our species."[3] Immediately the essential differences between the scientific imperialist and the Romanticist come to the surface. In response to Professor Haldane, H.G. Wells, and others who advocate inter-planetary colonialism to ensure the survival of the human species, Lewis casts his own definition of progress in rather different terms. He writes:

> The desire here is for mere survival. Now I care far more for how humanity lives than how long. Progress, for me, means increasing goodness and happiness of individual lives. For the species, as for each man, mere longevity seems to me a con-temptible ideal.[4]

There are several important points packed into Lewis's statement.

The main point of difference is that of quantitative versus qual-itative value. While we surely cannot claim a complete correlation here, we can nevertheless point to the scientific materialist's propen-sity to quantify, and then to the Romanticist's propensity toward more qualitative concerns. In general, such things as goodness and joy remain among the more elusive data for the scientist but are among the most central themes for the poet.

But the concept of progress concerns the larger picture of human history as a whole. Lewis's rather offhand comment, "As a Christian I take it for granted that human history will some day end. . . ."[5] may have surprised some readers. Yet, it is true. Traditional Christian doctrine holds that as there was a definite beginning to human history, there will be a definite ending to it. Furthermore, while no one can know when the end will come, there are some pretty specific descriptions in the biblical books of Daniel and Revelation as to how it will come. The important point here, though, is the Christian belief that history will come to an end, and that the end for the Christian will mean glory instead of disaster.

In this sense the Christian's attitude toward the future of humankind can be seen as a kind of paradox—though not as a true contradiction. On the one hand, it would seem that one's own time, one's own place, one's own life will be swallowed up in the great cosmic events of the births and deaths of galaxies, stars, and worlds—perhaps as portrayed in Lewis's *The Last Battle*. Yet, we see in *Perelandra* that the actions of a single, mortal individual can have effects of the greatest spiritual and cosmic importance.

So, then, does human life and human action ultimately matter or does it not? Anyone who is tempted to interpret Lewis's Christianity as a kind of fatalism wherein human actions make no difference finds a clear enough reply in the pages of *Perelandra*. Here Ransom is wrestling with the terrible temptation to give up the fight on the grounds that God would never leave such weighty matters to depend on the piteously weak efforts of a mere mortal. Lewis writes:

> And at that moment, far away on Earth, as he now could not help remembering, men were at war, and white-faced subalterns and freckled corporals who had but lately begun to shave, stood in horrible gaps or crawled forward in deadly darkness, awaking, like him, to the preposterous truth that all really depended on their actions; and far away in time Horatius stood on the bridge, and Constantine settled in his mind whether he would or would not embrace the new religion, and Eve herself stood looking upon the forbidden fruit and the heaven of heavens awaited her decision. He writhed and ground his teeth, but could not help seeing. Thus, and not otherwise, the world was made. Either something or nothing must depend on individual choices. And if some-

thing, who could set bounds to it? A stone may determine the course of a river. He was that stone at this horrible moment which had become the centre of the whole universe.[6]

In our earlier discussion of Lewis's sacramental mysticism, we saw how the actions "behind the scenes" contain an even greater substance and meaning than those visible to us, as portrayed by Lewis in *The Great Divorce*. For the Christian, every decision and every act has consequences of spiritual, cosmic, and even eternal importance.

So how, then, can Lewis so blithely "take it for granted that human history will some day end . . ."?[7] The answer is that human history per se is not what is important. This point is argued at length in Lewis's space trilogy. It is the flash point of conflict between modern humanism and Christianity. In New Enlightenment reckoning the important things are the big things, such as the survival of the species, the future of the nation, or the progress of the movement. In Christian doctrine the important thing is the will of God, and the will of God is the goodness, well-being, and happiness of the individual. In this sense, Christianity is the most individualistic of all the creeds.

Returning, however, to the question of progress, what are C.S. Lewis's thoughts on scientific progress? In this regard Lewis writes:

> We shall grow able to cure, and to produce, more diseases— bacterial war, not bombs, might ring down the curtain—to alleviate, to inflict, more pains, to husband, or to waste, the resources of the planet more extensively. We can become either more beneficent or more mischievous. My guess is we shall do both; mending one thing and marring another, removing old miseries and producing new ones, safeguarding ourselves here and endangering ourselves there.[8]

In other words, science is an extremely effective method for finding certain kinds of knowledge and doing certain things, but experience tells us that the things we choose to do with science can be for good or ill.

Another point of concern in Lewis's comments on progress is the changing relationship between government and the people. We are moving, he says, in western societies away from a conception of government as arbiter among responsible individuals and toward one of government as a force "to do us good and make us good."[9] The most obvious example is found in the treatment of criminals, as we see a rejection of the idea of bringing justice to one who has chosen to do wrong, and a growing acceptance of the idea of rehabilitating the unwitting victim of social pathology. Modern criminology tends to deemphasize individual choice and personal responsibility. In Lewis's view, this trend is merely symptomatic of the New Enlightenment's valuing of the collective rather than the individual.

In Lewis's view, all of this collectivism runs against the grain of men and women as they were created. In this vein he writes:

> To live his life in his own way, to call his house his castle, to enjoy the fruits of his own labour, to educate his children as his conscience directs, to save for their prosperity after his death—these are wishes deeply ingrained. . . .[10]

In Christian doctrine, a human being is not "the naked ape," nor a *tabula rasa*, nor an anonymous cog in a great machine called progress; each human being is a unique creature with an important purpose. Each is created in a given time and place, subject to given environmental influences, exposed to given circumstances, called upon to make given specific decisions, and held personally responsible for actions taken. In this sense the importance of the big picture of human history fades into the background, becoming something much closer to an effect than a cause of human behavior.

Does C.S. Lewis believe in progress? No. He believes in the Christian God. Is Lewis, then, anti-progressive? No. He is something closer to a-progressive. In other words, progress per se is not an important value—certainly not something to be believed in like a creed. The important question is, of course, "Progress toward what?" Scientific and technological progress can forge results that are either wonderful or terrible. Material progress toward more wealth and belongings can bring either greater convenience or a subtler form of bondage. Intellectual progress can lead either to greater knowledge or to a crippling skepticism and egocentric pride. In whatever realm we may choose, mere progress without a guiding moral principle can lead to spiritual poverty and personal disaster.

What, then, is the Christian conception of progress? The answer is found in the old catechisms that begin with the question and answer, "What is the chief purpose of man? To love God and to enjoy Him forever." C.S. Lewis spoke of the Christian conception of progress in both quantitative and qualitative terms. Progress would mean movement toward the greatest number of people coming to know and love God. But it would also mean the movement of individual Christian believers "further up and further in" to the love and joy of God for the remainder of human history and beyond.

The Romantic Stream Revisited

There is less to be said here regarding C.S. Lewis's differences with the Romantic stream of thought. Even before his conversion to Christianity, Lewis's life and work were very much those of a Romanticist. Thus, there are not many points at which Lewis takes issue with Romanticism, as he does continually with the materialism and scientific positivism of the New Enlightenment. We can say with confidence that Lewis was a Romanticist through and through, and furthermore that his Romantic philosophy served as a necessary *via media* on his journey into Christian belief. This very thesis, in fact, dominates Lewis's autobiographical works in *Surprised by Joy* and *The Pilgrim's Regress*.

Recall that even before Lewis's time, the Romanticists rejected the narrow materialism and positivism that came to dominate the creeds of the industrial societies, insisting instead that there was more to the human being than the scientific view would allow.

Romantic thought asserted that humans are much more than exceptionally intelligent animals, that they are feeling beings as much as thinking beings. Consequently, the Romanticists tended to emphasize the wild and unpredictable in human life and to embrace the transcendent and the metaphysical.

As Lewis explains in his *Surprised by Joy*, even without parental influence he found himself drawn toward the Romanticism of W.B. Yeats, William Blake, and Wagner's "twilight of the gods." The young Lewis experienced that perpetual longing for something faraway, something beyond the horizon, something like the distant island in *The Pilgrim's Regress* or like the Joy described in *Surprised by Joy*. Until he became a Christian, he did not recognize the source of this longing for what it is: the intrinsic yearning of the creature to be reconciled with his Creator. He could not then have understood the longings of the Romanticist as shadowy and unfocused gropings toward the brightness and clarity of the real Light.

It is important, however, to recognize the points of difference between generic Romanticism and the Christian faith. For in Lewis's case, it is as if he discovered Christianity after a finer tuning or focusing of selected Romantic ideals. I think that Lewis would have called his Romanticism a flawed lens that perceived the truth only partially and inaccurately. Thus, with correction the human uniqueness sharpens into a special creation "in the image of God." The emotions and instincts focus into an immortal soul. The transcendent cravings and yearnings become the spirit and the desire for God. In this sense we can see Lewis's Romanticism as a preliminary approximation of the clearer truth of Christian doctrine.

Consequently, we see occasionally in Lewis's writing those points of departure of the Christian from the Romanticist. In *The Pilgrim's Regress* we see the "southern" qualities as roughly those of the Romanticists, and the protagonist, John, soon discovers the dangers therein. At the beginning of the story, John is still in his undefined, undisciplined, and irresponsible Romantic state when he fornicates with the brown girl and then runs away. Indeed, one of the major themes in Lewis's allegory *The Pilgrim's Regress* is John's (and Lewis's) growth from mere Romanticism into Christianity.

A most important departure of Christianity from the Romanticist view concerns the human ego. One of the few ideas that many Romanticists share with New Enlightenment thinkers is a high expectation of human self-determination. Thus, we find writers as disparate as H.G. Wells, Percy Bysshe Shelley, George Bernard Shaw, and even Friedrich Nietzsche looking for humanity's perfection through human efforts. Here we see a type of egoism that easily crosses many philosophical boundaries but must stop at the frontiers of the Christian faith. For in Christian doctrine, pride is among the most egregious of sins, and rebellion of the human ego against God is the prototype of all self-destructive behavior.

Like many before him in the Romantic tradition—notably Robert Browning, William Blake, G.K. Chesterton, and others—C.S. Lewis came to find in orthodox Christian doctrine the clarifying and perfecting of many of his Romantic ideas. In following the movement of Lewis's thinking from popular materialism, through vague metaphysics, through pantheism, through theism, to specific Christian belief, we are reminded of Lewis's comments in another context of how "myth became fact" in the advent of Jesus in history. In this case it appears that Lewis's Romanticism served as the rather vague precursor or approximation of truth that would be brought fully into focus at his conversion to Christianity.

THE CHRISTIAN STREAM REVISITED

Almost immediately after C.S. Lewis became a Christian in 1931, he began writing what would become a great body of apologetic and inspirational works spanning the remaining thirty years of his life. His first book as a Christian was *The Pilgrim's Regress*, in which Lewis traced his own progression from "popular realism" to Christianity. But already in *The Pilgrim's Regress* we see in allegorical form the specific kind of Christian that Lewis would become.

First, we see the positive roles of both reason and virtue throughout Lewis's story. In his apologetics Lewis never concedes that Christianity is an irrational or unreasonable belief, asserting instead that God is the God of reason and that humans are made in God's image. Also, in Lewis's allegory we cannot miss the necessity of the church. John finds that if he had listened to Mother Kirk in the first place, his journey would have been much shorter and easier. Lewis always insisted that every Christian needs to belong to the church.

As to his own preferred communion within the church, Lewis's opinions were rather obvious as well. At one point in his story we find a character named Neo-Angular, who claims that John has no business trying to talk to Mother Kirk except through a qualified priest. This is Lewis's portrayal of the Roman Catholic Church, and he makes no secret of the fact that he rejects this position entirely. While Lewis was fully aware of the earlier "Oxford Movement" and the defection of John Henry Newman and others from the Anglican to the Roman church, Lewis maintained his Anglican loyalty throughout his life. Sadly, this disagreement between Lewis and his Roman Catholic friend J.R.R. Tolkien would later become the cause of a cooling and then an ending of their long and fruitful friendship.

On the basics of orthodox Christian doctrine Lewis was very clear. It was, in fact, his remarkable clarity that rendered his broadcast talks and the subsequent *Mere Christianity* so very successful. Here we find cogent discussions of the Triune God, the creation, the Fall, original sin, the Incarnation, Jesus' death and resurrection, atonement, and many other basic issues of Christian theology. And much of what Lewis covers in his nonfiction apologetics, he vivifies and illustrates in his fiction and fantasy, particularly in the Narnia stories.

Recall our discussion of the liberal trends in Protestant theology during the nineteenth and twentieth centuries—the "higher criticism" of the Bible, the "explaining away" of the miracles, the subjecting of Christian theology to the claims of the social and behavioral sciences. The early names here were Woolston, Tindal, Wollaston, and Lessing. Later we saw the mythologizing of the Gospel by Strauss, the de-mystifying efforts of Ritschl, Herrmann, and von Harnack, and the "history of religions" approach of Ernst Troeltsch. What this rather mixed bag of theologians appeared to hold in common was a certain degree of embarrassment over the supernatural aspect of orthodox Christian doctrine and an exaggerated sense of validity in the social and behavioral sciences.

In this regard Lewis makes his position very clear as well, perhaps most cogently in his study called *Miracles*. It will not do, says Lewis, to take the supernatural out of Christian doctrine, because the incarnation of God is the very point of the Christian story. Without the metaphysical, the spiritual, the supernatural, there is nothing left that can really be called Christianity. Lewis points out that most of this liberal theologizing is based on the false assumption that God is a mere construct of human reason—that the attributes of the Creator depend upon the outcome of theological debate.

We see a similarity between the liberal theologians' relativizing and shifting of ground and Lewis's fictional depiction of Shift the ape in *The Last Battle*. The whole business about all religions being equal, culminating in the combining of Aslan and Tash to form Tashlan, is Lewis's way of illustrating the folly that results from human redefinitions of God. But even more powerful is Lewis's rendition in *The Great Divorce* of the liberal clergyman who is heard saying to his old friend who has retained his orthodox beliefs:

> "Ah, Dick, I shall never forget some of our talks. I expect you've changed your views a bit since then. You became rather narrow-minded towards the end of your life: but no doubt you've broadened out again."
>
> "How do you mean?"
>
> "Well, it's obvious by now, isn't it, that you weren't quite right. Why, my dear boy, you were coming to believe in a literal Heaven and Hell!"
>
> "But wasn't I right?"
>
> "Oh, in a spiritual sense, to be sure. I still believe in them in that way. I am still, my dear boy, looking for the Kingdom. But nothing superstitious or mythological. . . . Ah, but we

must all interpret those beautiful words in our own way! For me there is no such thing as a final answer."[11]

Here we have the sophisticated, intellectual clergyman who feels he has outgrown literal interpretations of the Bible and has purged his religion of the supernatural. In Lewis's view, this relativizing of the Gospel involves a certain amount of dishonesty.

In a speech called "Christian Apologetics," delivered to Anglican priests and youth leaders in 1945, Lewis makes perhaps his most candid statements on the matter of theological liberalism among the clergy. Here he complains that from a layman's point of view the teaching of many Anglican priests ". . . may be so 'broad' or 'liberal' or 'modern' that it in fact excludes any real Supernaturalism and thus ceases to be Christian at all."[12] It is one thing, says Lewis, to make room for differing opinions among people, but it is quite another thing to occupy the position of priest in an Anglican church while holding beliefs that lie outside those of the church. Lewis writes:

> But I insist that wherever you draw the lines, bounding lines must exist, beyond which your doctrine will cease either to be Anglican or to be Christian: and I suggest also that the lines come a great deal sooner than many modern priests think. I think it is your duty to fix the lines clearly in your own minds: and if you wish to go beyond them you must change your profession. . . . We never doubted that the unorthodox opinions were honestly held: what we complain of is your continuing your ministry after you have come to hold them.[13]

These are hard words, but they are the honest words of a layman to a professional clergyman. Lewis adds, "This is your duty not specially as Christians or as priests but as honest men."[14] To continue to serve and to be employed by a communion with whose doctrines one disagrees is not an honest course of action.

The writings of C.S. Lewis are so rich in materials relevant to Christian doctrine that it would be impossible even to summarize them here. We shall have to settle for a few important examples and then go about our business of C.S. Lewis and the third millennium. For example, an essential element in Lewis's style of Christianity is his keen sense of the importance and meaning of repentance and renewal. Here is the pivotal turning-point of the Christian faith—founded in the death and resurrection of Jesus the Christ—calling for the repudiation of the old life and the embracing of the new.

Indeed, we find the theme of repentance and renewal throughout Lewis's fiction and nonfiction works. We see it in *The Horse and His Boy* when the once-proud Aravis realizes that she would rather humble herself than go back to the life she had lived before. We see it even more clearly in Eustace Scrubb's painful metamorphosis in *The Voyage of the "Dawn Treader"*. We see it as well in the fortunes of Mark and Jane Studdock in *That Hideous Strength*. Lewis states the issue pragmatically in his preface to *The Great Divorce*:

> I do not think that all who choose wrong roads perish; but their rescue consists in being put back on the right road. . . . Evil can be undone, but it cannot "develop" into good. . . . It is still "either-or."[15]

Lewis reminds us again that Christian doctrine presents hard choices. One cannot have it both ways; one must choose to take the one road and forsake the other. Again, Lewis's definite picture is a far cry from the vague talk of myth and metaphor found among the liberal Protestant theologians.

Looking back through the pages of C.S. Lewis's works, we find that Lewis has even more to say about repentance and renewal and the future. In a chapter called "We Have Cause to Be Uneasy" in his book *Mere Christianity*, Lewis speaks with his usual candor about our present and future:

There is nothing progressive about being pigheaded and refusing to admit a mistake. And I think if you look at the present state of the world, it is pretty plain that humanity has been making some big mistakes. We are on the wrong road. And if that is so, we must go back. Going back is the quickest way on.[16]

There are many who will agree with Lewis that humanity has made a mess of things; there are fewer who will agree that going back may be the quickest way onward.

TIME, ETERNITY, AND THE QUICKEST WAY ONWARD

We know that C.S. Lewis was not one to venture specific predictions as to what lay immediately in store for his homeland (England) or the United States or even the world. He did, however, share with all Christians the biblical outline of human history, wherein there was a definite beginning and there will be a definite ending. In addition, there is the rather clear perspective of the Old Testament regarding God's people—their safety and prosperity depends ultimately upon their obedience to God. But as we look ahead into the third millennium, what is in store for us? Shall we prosper? Shall we struggle? Shall we even survive? What would C.S. Lewis say about these things?

The first thing, I think, that C.S. Lewis would say is, "I haven't the foggiest idea." The second thing he would likely say, though, is that our futures depend very much upon what we choose to believe and how we choose to act. For while the Christian believes that God is the author of history, the Christian also knows that God regularly uses the acts of individuals to forge momentous changes and to achieve great purposes. This theme is illustrated repeatedly in Lewis's Narnia stories.

For the most part, what C.S. Lewis sees in the history of humanity is a continuing struggle to achieve greatness—if not immortality—punctuated by the regular and periodic downfalls that the respective civilizations have brought upon themselves. In *Mere Christianity* he writes:

> That is the key to history. Terrific energy is expended—civilisations are built up—excellent institutions devised; but each time something goes wrong. Some fatal flaw always brings the selfish and cruel people to the top and it all slides back into misery and ruin.[17]

So in reply to our questions, Lewis would at the very least say that if we don't find a way to forge a radical change in the hearts of human beings, we are most likely to see a mere continuation of the old pattern.

According to Lewis, the root of the problem lies not in the large picture of history, but in the small picture of the human heart. The source of the mischief is not found in the social order, nor the type of government, nor the basis of the economy, but in the nature of individual men and women. The ultimate solutions, therefore, lie neither in social movements, nor political revolutions, nor economic reforms, but in individual people choosing to do what is right, what is good, what is just, and what is merciful. In modern discourse this idea has the ring of heresy, but it is not therefore untrue. If our history provides our data, then our data indicate that every human system can be and has been corrupted by human pride, greed, lust, and hatred.

C.S. Lewis tells us, then, that what we really need for the future is a new kind of human being. Those who might at first find this idea laughable need to recall that such a prescription is far from novel. It seems that every social thinker—from Plato to Comte to More to Huxley to Marx to Nietzsche to Shaw to Skinner—is looking for the Superman. So we should not find it so terribly quaint or surprising when C.S. Lewis writes that the "Next Step" is a new, qualitatively different kind of person. But what many will no doubt find shocking is Lewis's assertion that the "Next Step" has already been taken. He explains:

Now, if you care to talk in these terms, the Christian view is precisely that the Next Step has already appeared. And it is really new. It is not a change from brainy men to brainier men: it is a change that goes off in a totally different direction—a change from being creatures of God to being sons of God.[18]

This "Next Step" was inaugurated with the incarnation of the Christ; Jesus of Nazareth was in this sense the first "new person." Lewis goes on to explain:

I have called Christ the "first instance" of the new man. But of course He is something much more than that. He is not merely a new man, one specimen of the species, but *the* new man. He is the origin and centre and life of all new men. He came into the created universe, of His own will, bringing with Him the . . . new life. . . . Everyone who gets it gets it by contact with Him. Other men become "new" by being "in Him."[19]

So the new kind of men and women that humanity needs is already being produced and perfected among us. They are a qualitatively different kind, who have the laws of humility and charity written in their hearts in place of the pride, greed, lust, and hatred that came so naturally to them. They are those whose motto is "Love one another" and whose ideals are love, joy, peace, patience, kindness, goodness, faithfulness, gentleness, and self-control.

Where are these people? Lewis says they are here and there, if we know what to look for. He writes:

On this view the thing has happened: the new step has been taken and is being taken. Already the new men are dotted here and there all over the earth. Some, as I have admitted, are still hardly recognisable: but others can be recognised.[20]

And so the Christian picture of history that at first seemed so very pessimistic now comes alive with newness and possibility. Who can imagine it? The seats of power and influence would come to be occupied by people with the heart of the Good Samaritan, and those who now seek to aggrandize themselves would instead look to their neighbor's well-being. We are truly talking about a new kind of men and women who would surely forge a new kind of world in the future.

But remember, Jack Lewis was never one to let friend or foe rest comfortably in a featherbed of vague wishes or utopian dreams. We would not be the first to wish that C.S. Lewis would refrain from being C.S. Lewis, but I am certain that he would nevertheless ask the very uncomfortable question, "What about you?"

For to C.S. Lewis, that is in fact the whole point. It is the point in the Narnia stories, in the space trilogy, in the allegories and fantasies, and in most of his apologetics. Lewis is not interested in passing so much "idealistic gas" (his phrase), nor in intellectual speculation for its own sake. The radical individualism of his Christianity always demands a personal response to this personal challenge.

Thus, Lewis focuses history and eternity on the present moment, and he asserts that the shape of the future depends very much upon our individual choices. He concludes:

> For now the critical moment has arrived. Century by century God has guided nature up to the point of producing creatures which can (if they will) be taken right out of nature. . . . Will they allow themselves to be taken? In a way, it is like the crisis of birth. Until we rise and follow Christ we are still parts of Nature, still in the womb of our great mother. Her pregnancy has been long and painful and anxious, but it has reached its climax. The great moment has come.[21]

So, in the end C.S. Lewis would say that the future is now—this in the sense that our discussions and speculations about the big pictures merely obfuscate the truly important question of the present. Even in the context of a social and intellectual milieu that denies the human soul and rejects the very concept of personal responsibility for one's actions, the work of C.S. Lewis still stands strong and beautiful, like the stones of those grand old cathedrals— giving visible testimony to the rational and experiential foundations of Christian doctrine, calling reasonable men and women everywhere to make that most important personal choice of all.

APPENDIX

OTHER BOOKS BY C.S. LEWIS

1919   *Spirits in Bondage* (pseudonym: Clive Hamilton).

1926   *Dymer* (pseudonym: Clive Hamilton).

1939   *Rehabilitations and Other Essays.*

1939   *The Personal Heresy: A Controversy* (with E. Tillyard).

1948   *Arthurian Torso: Containing the Posthumous Fragments of the Figure of Arthur by Charles Williams and A Commentary on the Arthurian Poems of Charles Williams by C.S. Lewis.*

1949   *Transposition and Other Addresses.*

1958   *Reflections on the Psalms.*

1960   *The World's Last Night and Other Essays.*

1964   *Letters to Malcolm: Chiefly on Prayer.*

1964   *Poems* (edited by W. Hooper).

1966   *Of Other Worlds: Essays and Stories* (edited by W. Hooper).

1966   *Letters of C.S. Lewis* (edited by W.H. Lewis).

1967   *Christian Reflections* (edited by W. Hooper). *Spencer's Images of Life.*

1968   *A Mind Awake: An Anthology of C.S. Lewis* (edited by Clyde Kilby).

1969   *Narrative Poems* (edited by W. Hooper).

1969   *Selected Literary Essays* (edited by W. Hooper).

1969   *Letters to an American Lady* (edited by Clyde Kilby).

1970   *God in the Dock: Essays on Theology and Ethics* (edited by W. Hooper).

1975   *Fern-Seed and Elephants and Other Essays on Christianity* (edited by W. Hooper).

1975   *The Dark Tower and Other Stories* (edited by W. Hooper).

1977   *The Joyful Christian: Readings from C.S. Lewis.*

1979   *They Stand Together: The Letters of C.S. Lewis to Arthur Greeves 1914-1963* (edited by W. Hooper).

1982   *On Stories, and Other Essays in Literature* (edited by W. Hooper).

1984   *First and Second Things* (edited by W. Hooper).

1985   *The Business of Heaven* (edited by W. Hooper).

1985   *Letters to Children* (edited by Lyle Dorsett and Marjorie Lamp Mead).

1985   *Boxen: The Imaginary World of the Young C.S. Lewis* (edited by W. Hooper).

NOTES

CHAPTER 1: A SNEAK PREVIEW

1. C.S. Lewis, *Prince Caspian* (New York: Macmillan, 1974), 192.
2. C.S. Lewis, *English Literature in the Sixteenth Century—Excluding Drama* (Oxford: The Clarendon Press, 1954), 327-328.
3. C.S. Lewis, *Surprised by Joy* (New York: Harcourt, Brace, Jovanovich, 1955), vii.
4. C.S. Lewis, *The Literary Impact of the Authorized Version* (London: The Athlone Press, 1950), 16-17.
5. C.S. Lewis, *The Last Battle* (New York: Macmillan, 1974), 3-4.
6. C.S. Lewis, *The Screwtape Letters* (New York: Macmillan, 1982), 128-129.
7. C.S. Lewis, "Scraps," pp. 216-217 in *God in the Dock* (Grand Rapids, MI: Eerdmans, 1970), 216.
8. "Work and Prayer," pp.104-107 in *God in the Dock*, 105.
9. C.S. Lewis, *The Four Loves* (London: Harcourt, Brace, Jovanovich, 1960), 73-74.
10. "Horrid Red Things," pp. 68-71 in *God in the Dock*, 71.
11. C.S. Lewis, *Perelandra* (New York: Macmillan, 1974), 41.
12. C.S. Lewis, *The Allegory of Love* (London: Oxford University Press, 1948), 79.
13. C.S. Lewis, *The Great Divorce* (New York: Macmillan, 1946), 106-107.
14. "Myth Became Fact," pp. 63-67 in *God in the Dock*, 67.
15. *The Four Loves*, 64-65.
16. "Miracles," pp. 25-37 in *God in the Dock*, 25.
17. C.S. Lewis, *The Voyage of the "Dawn Treader"* (New York: Macmillan, 1974), 24-25.
18. "The Laws of Nature," pp. 76-79 in *God in the Dock*, 78.
19. *The Great Divorce*, 72-73.
20. C.S. Lewis, *A Preface to Paradise Lost* (London: Oxford University Press, 1960), 11.
21. *The Last Battle*, 151.

CHAPTER 2: THE STAGE IS SET

1. Franklin L. Baumer, *Modern European Thought* (New York: Macmillan, 1977), 306.
2. Walter Wallbank, A.M. Taylor, and G.B. Carson, *Civilization: Past and Present*, Volume II, 5th edition (Palo Alto, Calif.: Scott, Foresman and Company, 1965), 132.

3. *Modern European Thought*, 184.
4. Ibid., 275-276.
5. *The Allegory of Love*, 112.

CHAPTER 3: ENTER C.S. LEWIS

1. *Surprised by Joy*, 5.
2. Ibid., 18.
3. Ibid., 19.
4. Ibid.
5. Ibid., 63.
6. Ibid., 67.
7. Ibid., 68.
8. Ibid., 73.
9. Ibid.
10. C.S. Lewis, *The Pilgrim's Regress* (New York: Bantam Books, 1981), vii.
11. *Surprised by Joy*, 174.
12. Ibid., 175.
13. Ibid., 179.
14. Ibid., 181.
15. Ibid., 191.
16. Ibid., 198.
17. Ibid., 203.
18. Ibid., 288.
19. Ibid., 211.
20. Ibid., 227.
21. Ibid., 228.
22. Ibid., 235.
23. Ibid., 236.
24. Ibid., 237.

CHAPTER 4: THE CHRONICLES OF NARNIA

1. Page Smith, *Killing the Spirit* (New York: Penguin Books, 1990), 1.
2. Paul Ford, *Companion to Narnia* (San Francisco: Harper and Row, 1980).
3. The alternative sequence places the stories chronologically in relation to Narnian time, rather than in the order in which they were written.
4. C.S. Lewis, *The Lion, the Witch and the Wardrobe* (New York: Macmillan, 1974), 16.
5. Ibid., 38.
6. Ibid., 78.
7. Ibid., 45.
8. Ibid., 44, 47.
9. Ibid., 159-160.
10. *Prince Caspian*, 39.
11. Ibid., 90.
12. Ibid., 117.
13. Ibid., 24.

14. Ibid., 58.
15. Ibid., 170.
16. Ibid., 195.
17. *The Voyage of the "Dawn Treader,"* 60.
18. Ibid., 75.
19. Ibid., 90.
20. Ibid., 93
21. Ibid., 135-136.
22. Matthew 6:33 in the *King James Version.*
23. C.S. Lewis, *The Silver Chair* (New York: Macmillan, 1974), 17.
24. Ibid., 19.
25. Ibid., 59.
26. Ibid., 151-152.
27. Ibid., 155-156.
28. Ibid., 159.
29. C.S. Lewis, *The Horse and His Boy* (New York: Macmillan, 1974), 14.
30. Ibid., 69-70.
31. Ibid., 10.
32. Ibid., 20.
33. Ibid., 40.
34. Ibid., 31.
35. Ibid., 146.
36. Ibid., 145-146.
37. See Matthew 20:16 and Luke 9:48.
38. *The Horse and His Boy*, 146.
39. C.S. Lewis, *The Magician's Nephew* (New York: Macmillan, 1974), 104.
40. Ibid., 111.
41. Ibid., 116.
42. Ibid., 119.
43. Ibid., 157.
44. Ibid., 174.
45. Ibid., 150.
46. *The Last Battle*, 28.
47. Ibid., 81-82.
48. Ibid., 83.
49. Ibid., 145-146.
50. Ibid., 50.

Chapter 5: Science Fiction and Fantasy

1. C.S. Lewis, *Out of the Silent Planet* (New York: Macmillan, 1965), 142.
2. Brian Murphy, *C.S. Lewis* (Mercer Island, Wash.: Starmont House, 1983), 15.
3. *Out of the Silent Planet*, 146.
4. Ibid., 102.
5. Ibid., 136.
6. Ibid., 127.
7. Ibid., 127-128.
8. *Perelandra*, 47.

9. Ibid., 90-91.
10. Ibid., 141.
11. Ibid., 141-142.
12. Ibid., 133.
13. C.S. Lewis, *That Hideous Strength* (New York: Macmillan, 1965), 23.
14. Ibid., 38.
15. Ibid., 41.
16. Ibid., 133.
17. Ibid., 42.
18. Ibid., 178.
19. Ibid., 203.
20. Ibid., 185.
21. Ibid., 87.
22. Ibid., 40.
23. Ibid., 371.
24. Ibid., 351.
25. *The Screwtape Letters*, 151.
26. Ibid., v.
27. Ibid., ix.
28. Ibid., 20.
29. Ibid., 54.
30. Ibid., 165.
31. Ibid., xiv.
32. *The Great Divorce*, 39.
33. Ibid., 40-41.
34. Ibid., 5.
35. Ibid., 6.
36. Ibid., 27.
37. Thomas C. Peters, *Battling for the Modern Mind: A Beginner's Chesterton* (Saint Louis: Concordia Publishing House, 1994), 133-146.
38. Ian Boyd, "Chesterton and C.S. Lewis," pp. 303-311 in *The Chesterton Review*, Volume XVII, Numbers 3/4, August/November 1991.
39. *The Great Divorce*, 49.
40. C.S. Lewis, *Till We Have Faces* (New York: Harcourt Brace and Company, 1956), 73.
41. Ibid., 41.
42. Ibid., 148.
43. Ibid., 152.
44. Ibid., 305.
45. Ibid., 295.
46. Ibid., 294.

CHAPTER 6: BASIC APOLOGETICS

1. *The Pilgrim's Regress*, vii.
2. Ibid., 5.
3. Ibid., x.
4. Ibid., 194.
5. C.S. Lewis, *The Abolition of Man* (New York: Macmillan, 1977), 28-29.

6. Ibid., 34-35.
7. Ibid., 35.
8. Ibid., 41-42.
9. Ibid., 68.
10. B.F. Skinner, *Beyond Freedom and Dignity* (New York: Bantam Books, 1972).
11. George A. Lundberg, *Can Science Save Us?* (New York: David McKay Company, 1967).
12. *The Abolition of Man*, 77.
13. Ibid., 72.
14. Ibid., 81.
15. Ibid., 83.
16. C.S. Lewis, *Mere Christianity* (New York: Macmillan, 1960), 12.
17. Ibid., 21.
18. Ibid., 18.
19. Ibid., 31.
20. Ibid., 38.
21. Ibid.
22. Ibid., 52.
23. Ibid., 95.
24. Ibid., 99.
25. Ibid., 106.
26. Ibid., 116.
27. Ibid.
28. Ibid., 117.
29. Ibid., 123-124.
30. Ibid., 136.
31. Ibid.
32. Ibid., 141.
33. Ibid., 188-189.
34. Ibid., 189.

CHAPTER 7: ON PAIN, LOVE, AND MIRACLES

1. C.S. Lewis, *The Problem of Pain* (New York: Macmillan, 1962), 26.
2. Ibid., 23-24.
3. Ibid., 32.
4. Ibid., 34.
5. Ibid., 40.
6. Ibid.
7. Ibid., 46-47.
8. Ibid., 48.
9. Ibid., 107.
10. C.S. Lewis, *A Grief Observed* (New York: Bantam Books, 1979), 4-5.
11. Ibid., 16.
12. Ibid., 28.
13. Ibid., 38.
14. Ibid., 42.
15. Ibid., 49.

16. Ibid., 53-54.
17. *The Four Loves*, 83-84.
18. Ibid., 11.
19. Ibid., 19.
20. Ibid., 12.
21. Ibid., 14.
22. Ibid., 20.
23. Ibid., 61.
24. Ibid., 55.
25. Ibid., 62.
26. Ibid., 82.
27. Ibid., 97.
28. Ibid., 98.
28. Ibid., 104-105.
30. Ibid., 135.
31. Ibid., 139.
32. Ibid.
33. Ibid., 140.
34. Ibid., 160.
35. Ibid., 163.
36. Ibid., 169.
37. Ibid., 176.
38. Ibid., 184.
39. C.S. Lewis, *Miracles: A Preliminary Study* (New York: Macmillan, 1953), 16-17.
40. Ibid., 38.
41. Ibid.
42. Ibid., 53.
43. Ibid., 121.
44. Ibid., 122.
45. Ibid., 162.

Chapter 8: Scholarly Works

1. Smith, *Killing the Spirit*, 5.
2. *The Allegory of Love*, 17-18.
3. Ibid., 44.
4. Ibid., 60.
5. Ibid., 163.
6. Ibid., 67.
7. Ibid., 3.
8. Ibid., 177.
9. Ibid., 340.
10. Ibid., 298.
11. *English Literature in the Sixteenth Century—Excluding Drama*, 18.
12. Ibid., 17.
13. Ibid.
14. Ibid., 31.
15. Ibid., 64.

16. Ibid., 65.
17. Ibid., 28.
18. C.S. Lewis, *The Discarded Image: An Introduction to Medieval and Renaissance Literature* (London: Cambridge University Press, 1964), 219.
19. Ibid., 221.
20. Ibid., 218.
21. Ibid., 223.
22. G.K. Chesterton, *What's Wrong with the World* (London: Cassell and Company, 1913), 39.
23. C.S. Lewis, *Studies in Medieval and Renaissance Literature* (London: Cambridge University Press, 1966), 68.
24. Ibid., 44.
25. Ibid.
26. Ibid., 49-50.
27. *A Preface to Paradise Lost*, 64.
28. Ibid., 40.
29. Ibid., 134.
30. Ibid., 41.
31. Ibid., 49.
32. Ibid., 65.
33. Ibid.
34. Ibid., 133.
35. Ibid., 71.
36. Ibid.
37. Ibid., 103.
38. Ibid., 102.
39. Ibid., 81.

CHAPTER 9: THE COMPLETE SCHOLAR

1. Smith, *Killing the Spirit*.
2. Allan Bloom, *The Closing of the American Mind* (New York: Simon and Schuster, 1987).
3. *The Literary Impact of the Authorized Version*, 21.
4. Ibid., 20.
5. Ibid., 21-22.
6. Ibid., 4.
7. Ibid., 22-23.
8. Ibid., 25.
9. C.S. Lewis, *An Experiment in Criticism* (London: Cambridge University Press, 1961), 128.
10. Ibid., 127.
11. Ibid., 112.
12. Ibid.
13. Ibid.
14. Ibid., 129.
15. Ibid., 88.
16. Ibid., 93.

17. Ibid., 85.
18. Ibid., 70-71.
19. Ibid., 72.
20. C.S Lewis, *Studies in Words* (Cambridge: Cambridge University Press, 1960), 3.
21. Ibid., 1-2.
22. Ibid., 20-21.
23. Ibid., 41.
24. Ibid., 317-318.
25. Ibid., 6-7.
26. C.S. Lewis, *They Asked for a Paper* (London: Geoffrey Bles, 1962), 57.
27. Ibid., 70.
28. Ibid., 158.
29. Ibid.
30. Ibid., 174.
31. Ibid.
32. Ibid., 175.
33. Ibid., 181.
34. Ibid., 205-206.
35. Ibid., 210.
36. Ibid., 209.

Chapter 10: C.S. Lewis and the Third Millennium

1. *Out of the Silent Planet*, 136.
2. *God in the Dock*, 311-316.
3. Ibid., 311.
4. Ibid.
5. Ibid., 312.
6. *Perelandra*, 142.
7. *God in the Dock*, 312.
8. Ibid.
9. Ibid., 314.
10. Ibid., 316.
11. *The Great Divorce*, 38, 43.
12. *God in the Dock*, 89.
13. Ibid., 89-90.
14. Ibid., 90.
15. *The Great Divorce*, 6.
16. *Mere Christianity*, 36.
17. Ibid., 54.
18. Ibid., 185.
19. Ibid., 186.
20. Ibid., 187.
21. Ibid.

BIBLIOGRAPHY

Baumer, Franklin L. *Modern European Thought*. New York: Macmillan, 1977.

Bloom, Allan. *The Closing of the American Mind*. New York: Simon and Schuster, 1988.

Boyd, Ian. "Chesterton and C.S. Lewis," pp.133-146 in *The Chesterton Review*, Volume XVII, Numbers 3/4, August/November 1991.

Chesterton, G.K. *What's Wrong with the World*. London: Cassell and Company, Ltd., 1913.

Ford, Paul F. *Companion to Narnia*. San Francisco: Harper and Row, 1980.

Harrison, G.B. (ed.). *Major British Writers*, enlarged edition. New York: Harcourt, Brace and World, 1959.

Lewis, C.S. *The Abolition of Man*. New York: Macmillan, 1977 (1947).

——*The Allegory of Love*. London: Oxford University Press, 1948 (1936).

——"Beyond Personality" (see *Mere Christianity*).

——"Christian Behaviour" (see *Mere Christianity*).

——*The Discarded Image: An Introduction to Medieval and Renaissance Literature*. London: Cambridge University Press, 1964.

——*English Literature in the Sixteenth Century—Excluding Drama*. Oxford: The Clarendon Press, 1954.

——*An Experiment in Criticism*. London: Cambridge University Press, 1961.

——*The Four Loves*. London: Harcourt, Brace, Jovanovich, 1960.

——*The Great Divorce*. New York: Macmillan, 1946.

——*The Horse and His Boy*. New York: Macmillan, 1974 (1954).

——*The Last Battle*. New York: Macmillan, 1974 (1956).

——*The Lion, the Witch and the Wardrobe*, New York: Macmillan, 1974 (1950).

——*The Literary Impact of the Authorized Version*. London: The Athlone Press, University of London, 1950.

——*The Magician's Nephew*. New York: Macmillan, 1974 (1955).

——*Mere Christianity*. New York: Macmillan, 1960 (1943).

——*Miracles: A Preliminary Study*. New York: Macmillan, 1953 (1947).

——*Out of the Silent Planet*. New York: Macmillan, 1965 (1938).

——*Perelandra*. New York: Macmillan, 1974 (1944).

——*The Pilgrim's Regress*. New York: Bantam Books, 1981 (1933).

——*A Preface to Paradise Lost*. London: Oxford University Press, 1960 (1942).

——*Prince Caspian*. New York: Macmillan, 1974 (1951).

——*The Problem of Pain*. New York: Macmillan, 1962 (1940).

——*The Screwtape Letters*, revised edition including *Screwtape Proposes a Toast*. New York: Macmillan, 1982 (1942).

——*The Silver Chair*. New York: Macmillan, 1974 (1953).

——*Spirits in Bondage* (under the pseudonym Clive Hamilton). London: William Heinemann, 1919.

——*Studies in Medieval and Renaissance Literature*. London: Cambridge at the University Press, 1966.

——*Studies in Words*. Cambridge: Cambridge University Press, 1960.

——*Surprised by Joy*. New York: Harcourt Brace Jovanovich, 1955.

——*That Hideous Strength*. New York: Macmillan, 1965 (1946).

——*They Asked for a Paper*. London: Geoffrey Bles, 1962.

——*Till We Have Faces*. New York: Harcourt, Brace, and Company, 1956.

——*The Voyage of the "Dawn Treader."* New York: Macmillan, 1974 (1952).

Lundberg, George A. *Can Science Save Us?* New York: David McKay Company, 1967 (1947).

Murphy, Brian. *C.S. Lewis*. Mercer Island, Wash.: Starmont House, 1983.

Peters, Thomas. *Battling for the Modern Mind: A Beginner's Chesterton*. Saint Louis: Concordia Publishing House, 1994.

Skinner, B.F. *Beyond Freedom and Dignity*. New York: Bantam Books, 1972.

Smith, Page. *Killing the Spirit*. New York: Penguin Books, 1990.

Wallbank, Walter, A.M. Taylor, and G.B. Carson. *Civilization: Past and Present*, Volume II, 5th edition. Palo Alto, Calif.: Scott, Foresman and Company, 1965.

INDEX